AF412672

The Global Crash

The Global Crash

Towards a New Global Financial Regime?

Edited by

Leila Simona Talani

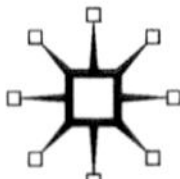

First published 2010 by
PALGRAVE MACMILLAN

Palgrave Macmillan in the UK is an imprint of Macmillan Publishers Limited,
registered in England, company number 785998, of Houndmills, Basingstoke,
Hampshire RG21 6XS.

Palgrave Macmillan in the US is a division of St Martin's Press LLC,
175 Fifth Avenue, New York, NY 10010.

Palgrave Macmillan is the global academic imprint of the above companies
and has companies and representatives throughout the world.

Palgrave® and Macmillan® are registered trademarks in the United States,
the United Kingdom, Europe and other countries.

ISBN-13: 978–0–230–24341–5 hardback

This book is printed on paper suitable for recycling and made from fully
managed and sustained forest sources. Logging, pulping and manufacturing
processes are expected to conform to the environmental regulations of the
country of origin.

A catalogue record for this book is available from the British Library.

Library of Congress Cataloging-in-Publication Data
The global crash : towards a new global financial regime? / edited by
    Leila Simona Talani.
        p.   cm.
    ISBN 978–0–230–24341–5 (hardback)
    1. Global Financial Crisis, 2008–2009.   2. Banks and banking.
    3. Capitalism.   4. International economic relations.   I. Talani, Leila
    Simona.
    HB37172008.G55 2010
    332′.042—dc22   2010010923

10   9   8   7   6   5   4   3   2   1
19   18   17   16   15   14   13   12   11   10

Printed and bound in Great Britain by
CPI Antony Rowe, Chippenham and Eastbourne

Al piccolo Gabriellino

Contents

List of Figures and Tables

Figures

Tables

List of Contributors

Alan W. Cafruny is Henry Bristol Professor of International Affairs in the Department of Government, Hamilton College, USA.

Stefan Collignon is Professor of Political Economy at Sant'Anna School of Advanced Studies, Pisa and Chairman of the Scientific Committee of the Centro Europa Ricerche (CER), Rome.

Paul De Grauwe is Professor of International Monetary Economics at the Katholieke Universiteit Leuven, Faculty of Economics and Applied Economics and Research Fellow at the Centre for Economic Policy Research, London.

Giorgio Fazio is Lecturer in Economics at the DSEAF, University of Palermo.

Erik Jones is Resident Professor of European Studies at the Johns Hopkins Bologna Center.

Henrik Plaschke is Associate Professor and Jean Monnet Professor of European Studies and Political Economy at Aalborg University.

Leila Simona Talani is Lecturer in International Political Economy at King's College, London.

Introduction

Leila Simona Talani

The financial crisis hit the global economy unexpectedly from August 2007, producing consequences comparable to the ones experienced in the course of the 1930s. One of the its most serious characteristics, unlike previous financial crises in the 1990s and early 2000s, is that it originated in the very heart of the global economy, the US, to spread first and foremost to the most developed countries in Europe and Asia. The debate is still very open on what caused these events. It is, however, clear that the crisis, although originating from the US housing and mortgaging markets, found a very fertile terrain in the uncontrolled possibility of the financial markets to develop and sell new financial instruments that allowed the banking sector to expand enormously their capacity to extend loans and provide mortgages to the least solvent clients. Indeed, whether or not customers were able to repay their mortgages was of no interest to mortgage lenders which, in any case, were earning a commission for each mortgage deal sealed and therefore had a vested interest in multiplying the number of loans. Mortgage dealers could sell back to investment banks the home loans they had provided to their clients and they could mix them with other securities and resell them as 'investment-grade' mortgage-backed securities (MBS).[1]

These securities were yielding very high interest rates as they included sub-prime loans made to people with low credit scores, but were often awarded 'triple-A' rating by the major credit-rating agencies, as the latter were paid fees directly by the issuers and therefore had a vested interest in giving the highest ratings to their securities. The combination of high interest rates and high ratings allowed for a rapid and uncontrollable spread of these 'toxic' assets whose returns were so appealing that the banking sector itself, to maximize its profits, set up highly leveraged, off-balance-sheet, structured investment vehicles (SIVs) to buy and hold some of these securities on their own accounts (ILO 2009).

The speculative bubble exploded when the increase in the interest rates made it impossible for sub-prime mortgages to be repaid; with the consequence that many borrowers defaulted. From that moment onwards the crisis snowballed from the housing market to the banking and financial sectors in an unstoppable fashion.

Scholars (Orlowski 2008) identify five different stages in the development of the global financial crisis. The first stage is the collapse of the US subprime mortgage market. This spilled over into the credit market with a credit crunch that led to the third phase represented by the liquidity crisis. The fourth phase was given by the commodity price bubble, and the last one by the demise of investment banking in the US. (Orlowski 2008).

Already in February 2007, there were warnings that the situation of the American sub-prime lender industry was unsustainable. However, only in August 2007 did it become clear that the crisis had moved from the American mortgage sector to the global financial and banking ones (ILO 2009).

As no one knew exactly the share of 'toxic' assets held by anyone else, a drastic decrease of trust amongst financial operators produced an unprecedented reduction of credit which soon took the form of a liquidity crisis. Liquidity in the inter-bank markets disappeared in a few days, to the extent that by September 2007 there was speculation that various financial institutions were receiving most of their funding from the wholesale money markets (ILO 2009).

In the UK, Northern Rock became the first institution to witness a bank run for about 150 years. The situation was solved only thanks to the intervention of the Bank of England, first bailing it out and then nationalizing the organization.

In the meantime the global banking sector started experiencing huge losses; on 5 October 2007 Merrill Lynch reported a loss of US\$5.5 billion and three weeks later came back with a figure over US\$8 (ILO 2009). The losses in mortgage derivative markets also triggered a massive run on Bear Stearns liabilities. On 13 and 14 March 2008 they fell by \$17 billion (Orlowski 2008).

At the beginning of 2008, with the massive loss incurred by financial institutions on MBS and other derivatives, they started investing in commodity futures, especially the crude oil futures markets, giving rise to the fourth stage of the global financial crisis. As a consequence, NYMEX oil futures prices experienced almost a 100 per cent increase: from \$75 per barrel in the beginning of October 2007 to their peak of \$147 on 11 July 2008 (Orlowski 2008).

In the fifth phase, from September 2008, the asset bubble moved from commodity futures to US Treasury bills and gold. Banking liquidity froze and the world suddenly realized the extent of the crisis.

The peak of the crisis is reached on the 29 September, when George Bush takes the podium to urge the House of Representatives to pass the \$700 billion bail-out plan.[2] It seems that the decision to pump enormous amounts of public money into the global financial markets avoided the global catastrophe. But what is the impact of these events on the Global financial stability? Lord Adair Turner, the Financial Service Authority chairman, during this tragic week told the *Guardian* that the days of soft-touch regulation were over, warning the City that higher-paid regulators would ask tougher questions in the wake of the credit crisis. However, up to now the consequences of the crisis have been felt mainly by the workers of the global financial sector and there are hints that the financial elite was able to cash in on the crisis itself.[3]

This book aims at providing a comprehensive interdisciplinary account of the events leading to the financial crisis, its institutional causes and consequences, its economic characteristics and its socio-political implications. The book seeks to identify the underlying factors that made it possible to lose control of the global financial markets, to explain why the crisis occurred within a particular time and institutional frame, and to identify the winners and losers that will result from it with an eye to distributional politics and socio-economic interest groups. Above all the book will try to assess the future of global financial stability. The main question the book seeks to answer is whether the financial crisis can lead to the creation of a new global financial order or whether it will produce its disruption.

The book is the outcome of an extremely productive co-operation between very established experts of the working of financial markets resulting in an array of ideas and proposals that will represent a valuable contribution to the debate on the global financial crisis.

This book represents a unique opportunity to gather the opinions of established experts on financial markets from different academic disciplines and from different academic traditions debating over the future of the global financial order. Leading economists are confronted with leading political scientists in an effort to produce an overarching view of the future of financial globalization and to propose solutions to the problems they envisage. The book therefore provides for an interdisciplinary account of the subject which can hardly be overestimated.

The idea is to produce a book which addresses the future of global financial stability from a policy oriented as well as an interdisciplinary perspective. To this aim the book will try and assess the impact of the global financial crisis on various policy areas, from the integration and disintegration of financial markets to the developments of the global regulatory framework; and from the impact of the crisis on different socio-economic groups to its impact on the Economic and Monetary Union and European financial stability.

The structure of the book, as well as the content of the chapters, reflects this objective, and this serves also a didactic purpose. Indeed, the book, although based on original research, may easily be used as an extremely well informed handbook on the causes and consequences of the global financial crisis from different theoretical perspectives, as well as on the future of the financial globalization process as a whole.

The book is divided into three parts. The first part, The Global financial crisis: Rules and Ideas, is theoretical and presents an interdisciplinary review of the causes and consequences of the global financial crisis.

In the first chapter, Paul De Grauwe notes that the paradigm that financial markets are efficient has provided the intellectual backbone for the deregulation of the banking sector since the 1980s, allowing universal banks to be fully involved in financial markets and investment banks to become involved in traditional banking. However, there is now overwhelming evidence that financial markets are not efficient. Bubbles and crashes are an endemic feature of financial markets in capitalist countries. Thus, as a result of deregulation, the balance sheets of universal banks became fully exposed to these bubbles and crashes, undermining the stability of the banking system. The Basle approach to stabilizing the banking system has an implicit assumption that financial markets are efficient, allowing us to model the risks universal banks take and to compute the required capital ratios that will minimize this risk. De Grauwe argues that this approach is unworkable because the risks that matter for universal banks are tail risks, associated with bubbles and crashes. These cannot be quantified. As a result, there is only one way out, and that is to return to narrow banking, a model that emerged after the previous large-scale banking crisis of the 1930s but that was discarded during the 1980s and 1990s under the influence of the efficient market paradigm.

In Chapter 2, Stefan Collignon discusses the moral economy of money and the future of European capitalism. The financial and economic crisis has raised new questions about the future of the capitalist system. Twenty years after the fall of the Wall in Berlin, the alternative is clearly no longer a planned economy, Soviet style, but the fragility of the capitalist system is again apparent to everyone. Curiously, Marx never fully understood the nature of money, finance and capital. He explained the capitalist crisis by the fall of return on real capital, but the system's systemic instability resides in the financial sphere. Financial crises have occurred frequently in the history of capitalism. Their re-occurrence was slowed down after central banks assumed responsibilities as lenders of last resort, although the inter-war period saw major breakdowns in 1919–1920 (UK), 1924 (France) and 1929 (US, Germany, Austria, Hungary). The period of Bretton Woods was marked by exceptional stability, but after the collapse of the System in 1971, successive waves of crisis have again occurred around the world: the turmoil of 1972–1973 in the exchange markets was followed by Herstatt bank failure in Germany in 1974 and the fringe bank crisis in the UK 1974–1975; the LDC debt crisis threatened the stability of the world financial system in the early 1980s. The 1990s saw the ERM crisis in Europe (1992–1993), the Japanese and Swedish banking crisis, the Mexican peso crisis in 1994, the Asian crisis in 1997, the Russian crash in 1998 followed by the near-bankruptcy of the LTCM hedge fund. It may not be a coincidence that these disturbances started to become more frequent in an era when neo-liberalism was on the ascent. Re-thinking the future of capitalism requires today re-examining the fundamental assumptions underlying the economic model that has dominated policymaking for the last 40 years. In this chapter, Collignon looks at some paradigmatic foundations of economic policy in a modern monetary economy and then draws conclusions for policymaking.

In Chapter 3, Erik Jones re-examines the role of ideas in times of crisis. He argues that while some crises may be determined by political narratives, others are not. The trick is to develop an empirical strategy for distinguishing between the two cases. The global economic and financial crisis is a good example. The problem was not that policymakers chose to narrate the failure of neo-liberal ideas; rather it was the narrative of efficient markets that broke down under the weight of changing material conditions. Now policymakers are struggling to make sense of the situation, to design and implement appropriate policies and to assess their effectiveness as a response. In understanding their behaviour, it is not enough to consider the political forces – ideational entrepreneurs, distributive coalitions – behind policy innovation; it is necessary also to understand how the policy is supposed to work and why. Hence, this re-examination concludes with an appeal for greater inter-disciplinarity in the study of politics.

In the second part, The International Causes and Consequences of the Financial Crisis, the analysis focuses on the international dimension of the financial crisis.

In Chapter 4, Henrik Plaschke addresses the question of the impact of the crisis on the US dollar and its status as the international reserve currency. More specifically, the author investigates whether the crisis places the euro in a better position to substitute the dollar in international monetary relations. As often claimed the European Union (EU) remains a huge economic entity in the global political economy but yet the EU has problems in or is incapable of transforming its economic potentials into political influence or power. In terms of its external policies the EU disposes of several instruments – political as well as economical. Monetary policies – and in particular the euro – in this regard remain an interesting case. Money is intrinsically a social and political as well as an economic device; and with the euro the EU has created a potentially powerful instrument for shaping and influencing the global political economy as well as for strengthening the autonomy of Europe in global political and economical affairs. The domestic and the international side of the euro are interlinked. Yet the focus of Plaschke's contribution is limited to the external role of the euro while the domestic side of the euro is only touched upon when relevant for the external side. In more precise terms the author deals with the question of whether the euro is increasingly becoming an international currency, that is, a currency increasingly used in international transactions not only between Europe and the rest of the world but also in transactions between third-countries. This inevitably also raises the question of whether the euro may challenge the role of the dollar as the present main reserve currency in the international monetary system. The international status of the euro has been on the international agenda since the very creation of the euro a decade ago. It has gained even further attention in the wake of the global financial crisis as the latter could have been expected to imply an increased questioning of the global role of the dollar. While the international role of the dollar *is* currently under scrutiny, the EU and its currency have not played any sort of proactive role in this regard. The financial crisis has – if anything – rather exposed the lacking leadership of the EU with regards to global monetary and financial governance, as well as the lack of credibility of the euro as an alternative to the dollar in the global political economy.

Chapter 5, by Giorgio Fazio, is concerned with the sources and the impact of the crisis on emerging countries. Throughout the 1990s, emerging markets were both at the origin and the receiving end of financial crises. At the end of the 2000s, the world seems to have gone upside down, as the 2008/2009 global financial crisis started in one of the most advanced nations and the largest world economy, the US, to later spread onto other industrial countries and develop into a full blown world crisis and recession. At the outbreak of the crisis, emerging markets, traditionally characterized by poor fundamentals, seemed to be the good news. However, the better fundamentals have not warranted immunity. For once, emerging markets seem to be the victims.

This chapter discusses the global crisis with a special focus on emerging markets. It argues that in order to assess the impact of the crisis on emerging markets, it is important to analyse their role in the development of the crisis. In particular, the causes behind the large global imbalances, which saw emerging market surpluses as the counterpart of large industrial countries deficits, should be considered more carefully in order to better understand the long-term implications of the crisis for both emerging markets and the global economy.

In the third part, Europe in Crisis, the focus moves to Europe. Indeed, as Alan Cafruny notes in Chapter 6, the global financial crisis began in the US, but it has thrown a spotlight on the problems and contradictions of what he calls the second or neoliberal phase of European construction. These contradictions include the inability to 'de-couple' from Atlantic circuits of capital and trade and establish an autonomous growth model; the reluctance of the ECB to transcend its monetarist origins; the paralysis of the Commission; the tendency towards dis-integration and intra-state or capitalist class rivalry in the context of German mercantilism; and, finally, the subordination of central and Eastern European countries to the strategies of Western European banks and multinational corporations.

Chapter 7, by Leila Simona Talani, analyses the impact of the Global financial crisis on the City of London asking whether the UK will finally decide to join the European Monetary Union (EMU). The EMU is already ten years old and the UK still have not decided to join it. Despite some timid attempts to revamp the debate about British entry into the EMU made by the early Labour administration, the issue has been left aside for a long time, to surge again to the attention of the public only with the explosion of the global financial crisis. Is there a link between the renewed interest in the British academic and political quarters towards the EMU and the crisis of the financial sector? What is the relation between the City of London and the EMU? Is this relation rooted in the structure of British capitalism? This chapter answers the above questions starting from the 'exceptional' nature of British capitalism development. The British system is 'exceptional', because of the persistence of aristocratic, pre-industrial elements in British polity (Stanworth and Giddens 1974). In Anderson's conceptualization (Anderson 1964), this 'exceptionalism' is owed to structural considerations about the development of British capitalism: namely the dual nature of British capitalism, that is, the divide between the financial fraction of capital and the industrial one, and the dominance of the former over the latter. The separation between the industrial and the financial fractions of British capital and the prevalence of City's interests over industrial macroeconomic preferences has also been recognized as an important factor of the British decision to keep the UK outside the EMU (Talani 2000). This chapter seeks to understand whether the global financial crisis, and the subsequent, alleged crisis of the City of London is likely to modify the relation between the industrial and the financial components of the British capitalist elite and put an end to British 'exceptionalism'. The final aim is to ascertain whether the preferences of the British capitalist elite with respect to the euro have changed as a consequence of the global financial crisis and whether this will finally convince the UK to join the EMU. To this aim, the chapter is divided into three sections. In the first section the author analyses the case for entry into the EMU recently put forward in the British public debate as a consequence of the impact of the global financial crisis on the City of London. After reviewing the events leading up to the crisis, the chapter identifies the arguments proposed in the public debate by leading academics and public opinion makers in favour of British entry into the euro-area. In the second section the author reviews the reasons why the UK decided not to join the EMU in the first place, with reference to the theoretical debate on British exceptionalism. Conclusions will be drawn on whether the impact of the global financial crisis on the City of London justifies a rethinking of the British decision not to enter the EMU.

In the conclusion Leila Simona Talani assesses the likelihood that a new global financial regime will emerge as a consequence of the crisis in the light of the discussion proposed by the different authors in the book.

Notes

1. Among similar securities there were: RMBSs (Residential Mortgage Backed Securities), CDOs (Collateralized Debt Obligations), SIVs (Structured Investment Vehicles) and CDOs of CDOs.
2. See *The Guardian* on-line, www.guardian.co.uk.
3. See Dispatches, Channel 4, 25th August 2008 and 18th May 2009, http://www.channel4.com/programmes/dispatches/ as accessed on 18 May 2009. Financial Times, October/November 2009, various issues.

References

Anderson, P. (1964), 'The origins of the present crisis', *The New Left Review*, 1(23): 26–55.

Dispatches, Channel 4, 25 August 2008 and 18 May 2009, http://www.channel4.com/programmes/dispatches/ as accessed on 18 May 2009.

International Labour Organization, (2009), 'Impact of the Financial Crisis on Finance Sector Workers', Issues paper for discussion at the Global Dialogue Forum on the Impact of the Financial Crisis on Finance Sector Workers, Geneva, 24–25 February 2009, International Labour Office: Geneva http://www.ilo.org/wcmsp5/groups/public/---dgreports/---dcomm/documents/meetingdocument/wcms_103263.pdf as accessed on 18 May 2009.

Orlowski, L.T. (2008). Stages of the 2007/2008 Global Financial Crisis: Is There a Wandering Asset-Price Bubble? Economics Discussion Papers, No 2008–43. http://www.economics-ejournal.org/economics/discussionpapers/2008-43 as accessed on 18 May 2009.

Stanworth, P. and Giddens, A. (1974), *Elites and Power in British Society*, Cambridge University Press.

Talani, L.S. (2000), *Betting for and against EMU*, London: Ashgate Publishing.

1
The Banking Crisis: Causes, Consequences and Remedies

Paul De Grauwe

The basics of banking

In order to analyse the causes of the banking crisis it is useful to start from the basics of banking.[1] Banks are in the business of borrowing short and lending long. In doing so they provide an essential service to the rest of us, that is, they create credit that allows the real economy to grow and expand.

This credit creation service, however, is based on an inherent fragility of the banking system. If depositors are gripped by a collective movement of distrust and decide to withdraw their deposits at the same time, banks are unable to satisfy these withdrawals, as their assets are illiquid. A liquidity crisis erupts.

In normal times, when people have confidence in the banks, these crises do not occur. But confidence can quickly disappear, for example, when one or more banks experience a solvency problem due to non-performing loans. Then bank runs are possible. A liquidity crisis erupts that can bring down sound banks also. The latter become innocent bystanders that are hit in the same way as the insolvent banks by the collective movement of distrust.

The problem does not end here. A devilish interaction between liquidity crisis and solvency crisis is set in motion. Sound banks that are hit by deposit withdrawals have to sell assets to confront these withdrawals. The ensuing fire sales lead to declines in asset prices, reducing the value of banks' assets. This in turn erodes the equity base of the banks and leads to a solvency problem. The cycle can start again: the solvency problem of these banks ignites a new liquidity crisis and so on.

The last great banking crisis occurred in the 1930s. Its effects were devastating for the real economy. After that crisis the banking system was reformed fundamentally. These reforms were intended to make such a banking crisis impossible. The reforms had three essential ingredients. First, the central bank took on the responsibility of lender of last resort. Second, deposit insurance mechanisms were instituted. These two reforms aimed at eliminating collective movements of panic. A third reform aimed at preventing commercial banks from taking on too many risks. In the US this took the form of the Glass-Steagall Act which was introduced in 1933 and which separated commercial banking from investment banking.

Most economists thought that these reforms would be sufficient to produce a less fragile banking system and to prevent large-scale banking crises. It was not to be. Why? In order to answer this question it is useful to first discuss 'moral hazard'.

In most general terms, moral hazard means that agents who are insured will tend to take fewer precautions to avoid the risk they are insured against. The insurance provided by central banks and governments in the form of lender of last resort and deposit insurance gives bankers strong incentives to take more risks. To counter this, authorities have to supervise and regulate, very much like any private insurer who wants to avoid moral hazard will do.

And that's what the monetary authorities did during most of the post-war period. They subjected banks to tight regulation aimed at preventing them from taking on too much risk. But then something remarkable happened.

The efficient market paradigm

From the 1970s, economists were all gripped by the intellectual attraction of the efficient market paradigm. This paradigm, which originated in academia, became hugely popular also outside academia. Its main ingredients are the following.

First, financial markets efficiently allocate savings towards the most promising investment projects thereby maximizing welfare. Second, asset prices reflect underlying fundamentals. As a result, bubbles cannot occur, and neither can crashes. History was reinterpreted, and those of us who thought that the tulip bubble in the seventeenth century was the quintessential example of a price development unrelated to underlying fundamentals were told it was all fundamentally driven (see Garber 2000).

The third ingredient of the efficient market paradigm is the capacity of markets for self-regulation. The proponents of this paradigm told us that financial markets can perfectly regulate themselves and that regulation by governments or central banks is unnecessary, even harmful, for as we all know bureaucrats and politicians always screw up things. All this led Greenspan to write the poetic words in his autobiography that 'authorities should not interfere with the pollinating bees of Wall Street' (Greenspan 2007).

The efficient markets paradigm was extremely influential. It was also captured by bankers to lobby for deregulation. If markets work so beautifully there was no need for regulation anymore. And bankers achieved their objective. They were progressively deregulated in the US and in Europe. The culmination was the repeal of the Glass-Steagall Act in 1999 by the Clinton administration. This allowed commercial banks to take on all the activities investment banks had been taking, for example, the underwriting and the holding of securities; the development of new and risky assets like derivatives and complex structured credit products. Thus, banks were allowed to take on all risky activities that the Great Depression had us thinking could lead to problems. The lessons of history were forgotten.

The efficient market paradigm provided the intellectual backing for deregulation of financial markets in general and the banking sector in particular. At about the same time financial markets experienced a burst of innovations. Financial innovations allowed the designing of new financial products. These made it possible to repackage assets into different risk classes and to price these risks differently. It also allowed banks to securitize their loans, that is, to repackage them in the form of asset backed securities (ABSs) and to sell these in the market.

This led to the belief, very much inspired by the optimism of the efficient market paradigm, that securitization and the development of complex financial products would lead to a better spreading of the risk over many more people, thereby reducing systemic risk and reducing the need to supervise and regulate financial markets. A new era of free and unencumbered progress would be set in motion.

An important side effect of securitization was that each time banks sold repackaged loans they obtained liquidity that could be used to extend new loans, which later on would be securitized again. This led to a large increase in the credit multiplier. Thus, even if the central bank tightly controlled the money base, credit expansion could go on unchecked with the same money base. The banking sector was piling up different layers of credit on top of each other allowing agents to speculate in the asset markets. All this undermined the control of central banks on expansion of credit in the economy.

Are financial markets efficient?

Deregulation and financial innovation promised to bring great welfare improvements: better risk spreading; lower costs of credit, benefitting firms who would invest more and benefitting millions of consumers who would have access to cheap mortgages. Who could resist the temptation of allowing these market forces to function freely without interference of governments?

The trouble is that financial markets are not efficient. We illustrate this lack of efficiency in the two dimensions that matter for the stability of the banking sector.[2] First, bubbles and crashes are an endemic feature of financial markets. Second, financial markets are incapable of regulating themselves. Both failures would, in the end, bring down the new banking model that had been allowed to emerge and that was predicated on financial markets being efficient.

Bubbles and crashes are endemic in financial markets

Nobody has written a better book on the capacity of financial markets to generate bubbles and crashes than Kindleberger in his masterful *Manias, Panics, and Crashes*.[3] Kindleberger showed how the history of capitalism is littered with episodes during which asset markets are caught by a speculative fever that pushes prices to levels unrelated to fundamental economic variables. But lessons of history were forgotten.

Let us look at some of the bubbles and crashes that littered financial markets during the last 25 years. Take the US stock market during 2006–2008. We show the Dow Jones and the Standard and Poor's in Figure 1.1.

What happened in the US economy between July 2006 and July 2007 to warrant an increase of 30 per cent in the value of stocks? Or, put differently, in July 2006 US stock market capitalization was $11.5 trillion: one year later it was $15 trillion. What happened to the US economy to make it possible that $3.5 trillion was added to the value of US corporations in just one year? During the same year GDP increased by only 5 per cent ($650 billion).

The answer is: almost nothing. Fundamentals like productivity growth increased at their normal rate. The only reasonable answer is that there was excessive optimism about the future of the US economy. Investors were caught by a wave of optimism that made them believe that the US was on a new and permanent growth path for the indefinite future. Such beliefs of future wonders can be found in almost all bubbles in history, as is made vividly clear in Kindleberger's book.

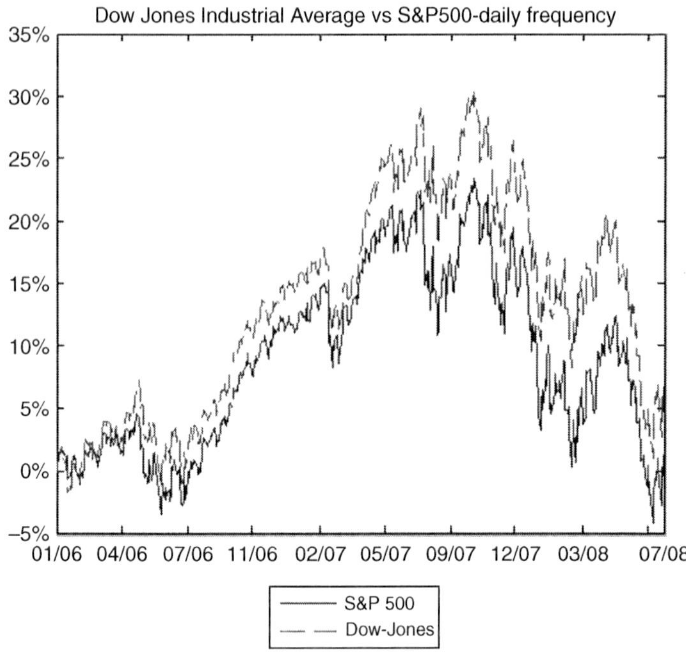

Figure 1.1   The Dow Jones and the S&P 500 2006–2008.
Source: Yahoo Finance.

Then came the downturn with the credit crisis. In a one-year period (July 2007–July 2008) stock prices dropped by 30 per cent, destroying $3.5 trillion of value. The same amount as that created the year before. What happened? Investors finally realized that there had been excessive optimism. The wave turned into one of excessive pessimism.

There were many other episodes of bubbles and crashes in the stock markets in many different countries. The most famous one was probably the IT-bubble at the end of the 1990s that had the same structure of extreme euphoria followed by depression. We show the evolution of the Nasdaq during 1999–2002 that illustrates this phenomenon (see Figure 1.2). In a one-year period the IT-shares tripled in value, and lost it all the next year.

A similar story can be told about the US housing market. Figure 1.3 shows the Case-Shiller house price index for 2000–2008. During 2000–2007 US house prices more than doubled. What happened with economic fundamentals in the US warranting a doubling of house prices over seven years? Very little. Again the driving force was excessive

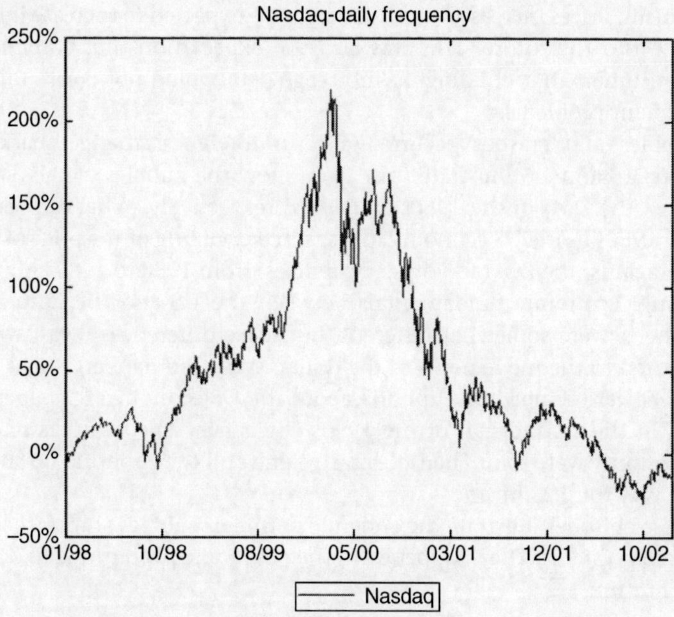

Figure 1.2 Index of share prices, Nasdaq 1999–2002.
Source: Yahoo Finance.

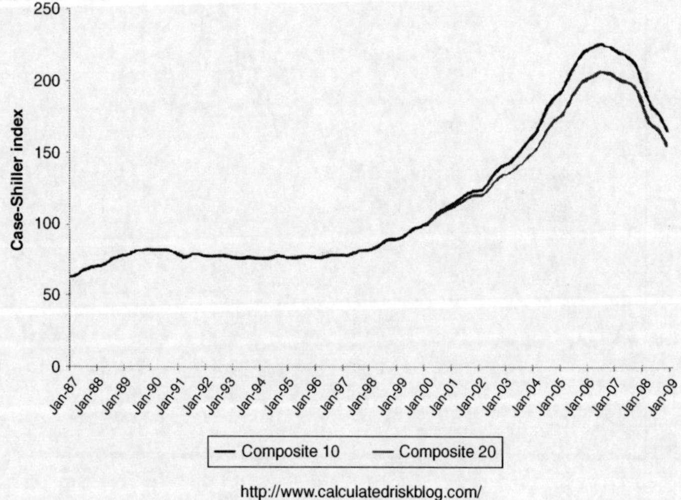

Figure 1.3 Case Shiller composite indices (nominal).
Source: Standard & Poor's.

optimism. Prices increased because they were expected to increase indefinitely into the future. This was also the expectation that convinced US consumers that building up mortgage debt would not create future repayment problems.

Bubbles and crashes occurred also in foreign exchange markets. Figures 1.4 and 1.5 illustrate this. They show the bubbles of the dollar (against the DM) in the 1980s and 1990s respectively. What happened in the 1980s in the US economy to warrant a doubling of the price of the dollar against the DM (and other currencies) from 1980 to 1985? Almost nothing. Economic fundamentals between the US and the European currencies were somewhat different, but these differences dwarf when compared to the movements of the dollar. What did happen is that the markets were gripped by euphoria about the US economy. It happened again in the second half of the 1990s when fairy tale wonders of the US economy were told. Then the crash came and the euphoria instantly made way for pessimism.

These episodes illustrate the endemic nature of bubbles and crashes in capitalist systems. They happened in the past and will continue to occur in the future.

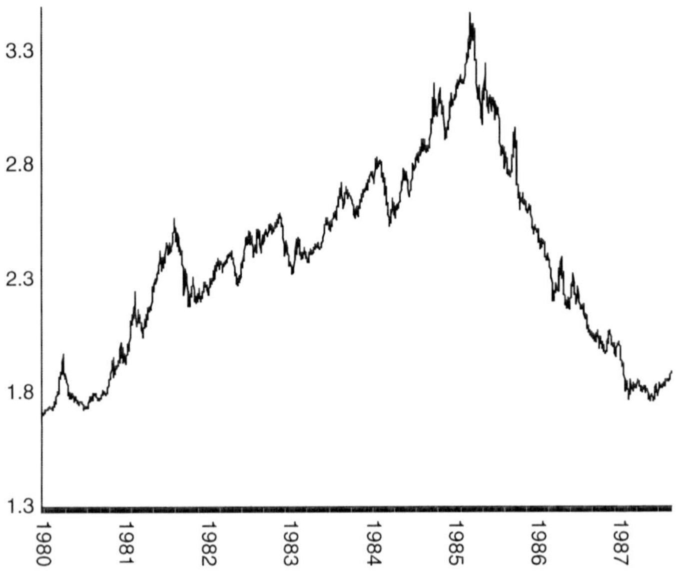

Figure 1.4   DEM–USD 1980–1987.

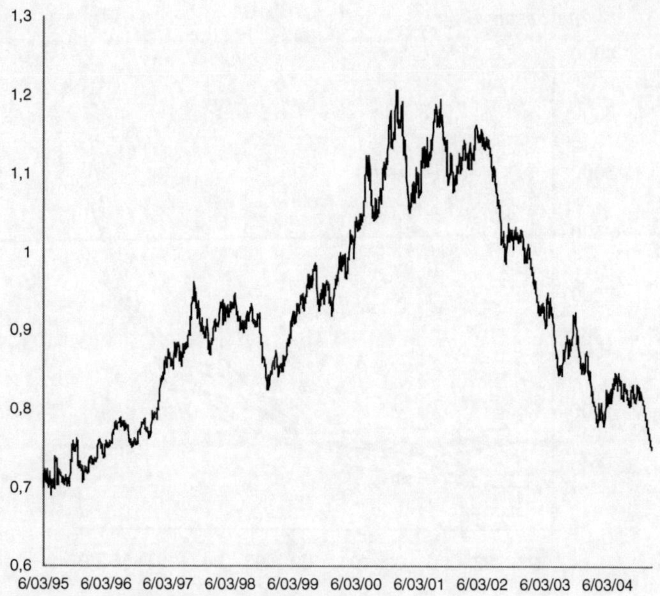

Figure 1.5 Euro–Dollar rate 1995–2004.
Source: De Grauwe and Grimaldi (2006).

The fact that financial markets are continuously gripped by speculative fevers, leading to bubbles and crashes, would not have been a major problem had banks been prevented from involving themselves in financial markets. However, the deregulation of the banking sector that started in the 1980s fully exposed the banks to the endemic occurrence of bubbles and crashes in asset markets. Because banks were allowed to hold the full panoply of financial assets, their balance sheets became extremely sensitive to bubbles and crashes that gripped these assets. Banks' balance sheets became the mirror images of the bubbles and crashes occurring in the financial markets.

This is shown in a spectacular way in Figure 1.6. It illustrates how since the start of the decade the balance sheets of the major European banks exploded, reflecting the various bubbles that occurred at that time (housing bubble, stock market bubbles, commodities bubbles).

While commercial banks were increasingly involving themselves in financial markets, and thus were taking over activities that were reserved to investment banks, the opposite occurred with investment banks. The latter increasingly behaved like banks, that is, they borrowed short and lent long, thereby moving into the business of credit creation. To give

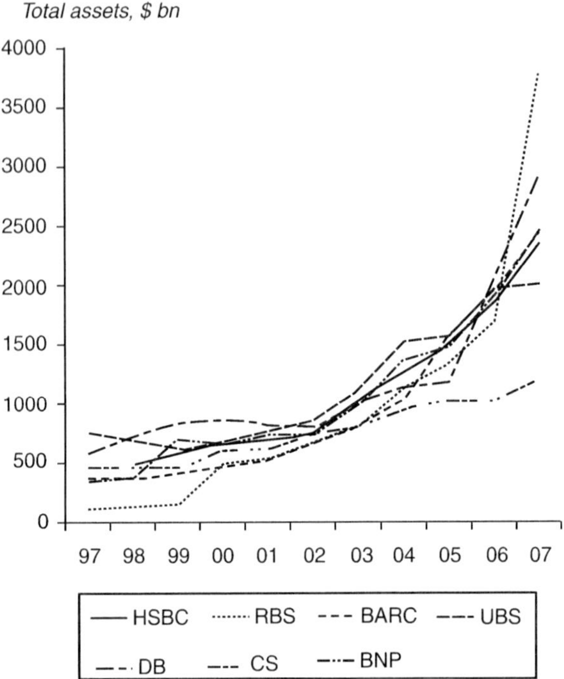

Figure 1.6   European financials' balance sheets.

an example: investment banks (for example, Lehman Brothers) moved into the business of lending money to hedge funds and accepted stocks or other securities as collateral. They then went on and lent that collateral to others so as to make extra money. Thus, investment banks had become banks in that they were creating credit. In the process they created an unbalanced maturity structure of assets and liabilities. Their assets were long term and illiquid while their liabilities had a very short maturity. Note the historical analogy with the gold smiths who accepted gold as collateral for loans and ended up lending out the gold, thereby becoming banks. All this (the gold smiths in the past and the investment banks today) was done in a totally unregulated environment.

Thus, as a result of deregulation a double movement occurred: commercial banks moved into investment bank territory and investment banks moved into commercial bank territory. This led to a situation in which both the commercial banks and the investment banks built up a lethal combination of credit and liquidity risks.

The mirage of self-regulation of financial markets

A centrepiece of the efficient market theory was that financial markets were capable of self-regulation, making government regulation redundant. Also, since bureaucrats lack the expertise and the incentives to regulate, government regulation was seen as harmful.

Two mechanisms were seen as central in making self-regulation work. One was the role of rating agencies; the other was the use of mark-to-market rules.

Rating agencies, so we were told, would guarantee a fair and objective rating of banks and their financial products. This is so because it was in the interest of rating agencies to do so. These agencies were large and had to protect their reputation. Without their reputation the value of their rating would be worthless. So, contrary to government bureaucrats, the rating agents would do the best possible job to ensure that banks created safe financial products because it was in their interest to do so.

It did not happen. The reason was that there was massive conflict of interest in the rating agencies. These both advised financial institutions on how to create new financial products and later on gave a favourable rating to the same products. Their incentives, instead of leading to the creation of sound and safe financial products, were skewed towards producing risky and unsafe products; so far for the superior incentives of rating agencies.

The other aspect to the belief that markets would regulate themselves was the idea of mark-to-market. If financial institutions used mark-to-market rules the discipline of the market would force them to price their products right. Since prices always reflected fundamental values mark-to-market rules would force financial institutions to reveal the truth about the value of their business, allowing investors to be fully informed when making investment decisions.

The trouble here, again, was the efficiency of markets. As we have illustrated abundantly, financial markets are regularly gripped by bubbles and crashes. In such an environment mark-to-market rules, instead of being a disciplining force, worked pro-cyclically. Thus, during the bubble this rule told accountants that the massive asset price increases corresponded to real profits that should be recorded in the books.

These profits, however, did not correspond to something that had happened in the real economy. They were the result of a bubble that led to prices unrelated to underlying fundamentals. As a result mark-to-market rules exacerbated the sense of euphoria and intensified the bubble.

Now the reverse is happening. Mark-to-market rules force massive write-downs, correcting the massive overvaluations introduced the years before, intensifying the sense of gloom and the economic downturn.

Thus, the promise of the efficient market paradigm that financial markets would self-regulate was turned upside down. Unregulated financial markets carried the seeds of their own destruction.

Unintended consequences of regulation

The fact that financial markets do not regulate themselves does not mean that government regulation always works wonderfully. During the 19980s and 1990s attempts were made at imposing capital ratios for banks in all developed countries. This was achieved in the Basle Accords (Basle I and II). It had disastrous consequences because of regulation arbitrage.

Basle I was based on a risk classification of assets and forced banks to set capital aside against these assets based on their risk. For example, Basle I put a low risk weight on loans by banks to other financial institutions. This gave incentives to banks to transfer risky assets (for example, structured products) which were given a high risk weight by the Basle I regulation, off their balance sheets. These assets were transferred in special conduits. The funding of these conduits, however, was often provided by the same or other banks. As a result bank funding of their activities increasingly occurred through the interbank market. Banks were investing in high risk assets, directly or indirectly, and obtained funding from the interbank (wholesale) market. In contrast to the deposits from the public, these interbank deposits were not guaranteed by the authorities. The building blocks of a future liquidity crisis were put into place.

Figure 1.7 illustrates the phenomenon. It shows the ratios of total assets to deposits (from the public) of the five largest banks in a number of countries in 2007. We observe that total assets of banks were more than twice the size of the deposits. Put differently, in all these countries deposits from the public funded less than half of banks' assets. Funding increasingly was done in the (volatile) wholesale market. As a result, banks created large leverage effects, that is, they increased their return on capital by massive borrowing. Unfortunately, they failed to price the large liquidity risks implicit in such leveraging.

Another case of regulatory arbitrage would have equally dangerous consequences. This arbitrage occurred because Basle I made it possible for banks to treat assets that are insured as government securities. As a

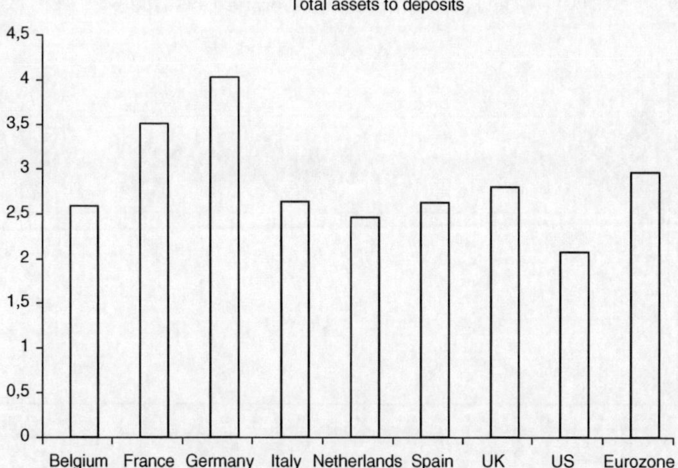

Figure 1.7 Ratio of banks' total assets to deposits (top five banks in each country), in 2007.
Source: Bankscope, Eurostat.

result, Basle I gave these assets a zero risk weight. This feature was fully exploited by banks and led to the explosion of the use of CDSs (credit default swaps), which insured the credit risk of banks' financial assets. In doing so, it created the illusion in the banking system that the assets on their balance sheets carried no or very low risk.

This turned out to be wrong. The reason again has something to do with inefficiencies in financial markets. Financial models used to price CDSs are based on the assumption that returns are normally distributed. There is one general feature in all financial markets, however, and that is that returns are not normally distributed. Returns have fat tails, that is, large changes in the prices occur with a much greater probability than the probability obtained from a normal distribution. This fat tail feature itself is intimately linked to the occurrence of bubbles and crashes. The implication of this is that models based on normal distributions of returns dramatically underestimate the probability of large shocks.

We show an example of this phenomenon in Figure 1.8. This shows the daily changes (returns) of the Dow Jones Industrial since 1928 (upper panel), and we compare these observed returns with hypothetical ones that are generated by a normal distribution with the same standard deviation (lower panel). The contrast is striking.

Dow Jones Industrial Average 1928–2008

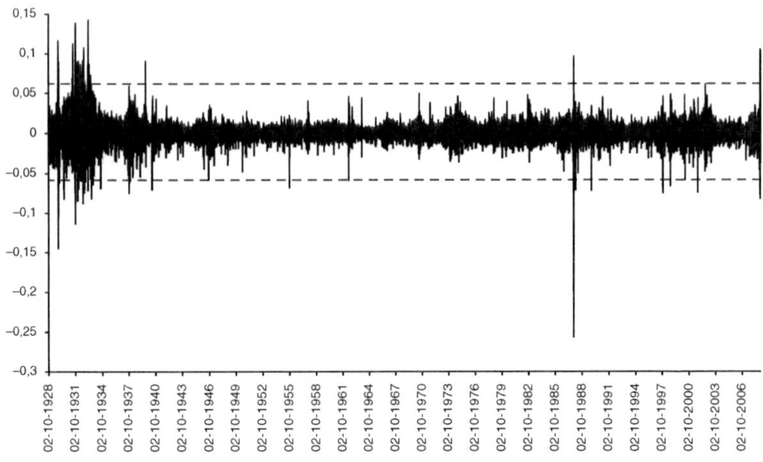

Random normal process

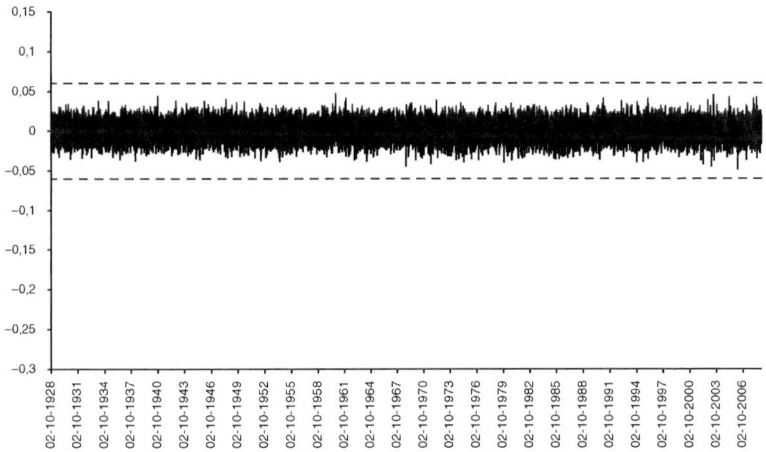

Figure 1.8   Normally distributed returns and observed daily returns in foreign exchange market.

We have added dotted horizontal lines. These represent the returns five standard deviations away from the mean. In a world of normally distributed returns, an observation which deviates from the mean by five times the standard deviation occurs only once every 7000 years (given that the observations are daily). In reality (upper panel), such large changes occurred 74 times during an 80-year period.

The models used to price credit default swaps and many other complex financial products massively underestimated this tail risk. They did not take into account that financial markets are regularly gripped by bubbles and crashes producing large changes in asset prices. Table 1.1 illustrates how spectacularly wrong one can be when one uses standard finance models that routinely assume normally distributed returns. We selected the six largest daily percentage changes in the Dow Jones Industrial Average during October 2008 (which was a month of unusual turbulence in the stock markets), and asked the question of how frequently these changes occur assuming that these events are normally distributed. The results are truly astonishing. There were two daily changes of more than 10 per cent during the month. With a standard deviation of daily changes of 1.032 per cent (computed over the period 1971–2008) movements of such a magnitude can occur only once every 73 to 603 trillion billion years. Yet it happened twice during the same month. A truly miraculous event, for finance theorists living in a world of normally distributed returns. The other four changes during the same month of October have a somewhat higher frequency, but we surely did not expect these to happen in our lifetime.

Table 1.1 Six largest movements of the Dow-Jones Industrial Average in October 2008.

A *non-Normal* October		
Date	**Percentage change**[a]	**Average frequency under Normal Law**[b]
07/10/2008	−5.11	Once in 5,345 Years
09/10/2008	−7.33	Once in 3,373,629,757 Years
13/10/2008	11.08	Once in 603,033,610,921,669, 000,000,000 Years
15/10/2008	−7.87	Once in 171,265,623,633 Years
22/10/2008	−5.86	Once in 117,103 Years
28/10/2008	10.88	Once in 73,357,946,799,753,900, 000,000 Years

[a]Daily returns from 01/01/1971 to 31/10/2008 (Source Datastream).
[b]The mean of the distribution is set to zero and the standard deviation computed over the whole sample (St. Dev. = 1.032 per cent).

Our conclusion should be not that these events are miraculous but that our finance models are wrong. By assuming that changes in stock prices are normally distributed, these models underestimate risk in a spectacular way. As a result, investors have been misled in a very big way, believing that the risks they were taking were small. In fact the risks were very big.

In addition, there were no incentives to price this tail risk because there was implicit expectation that if something very bad were to happen, for example, a liquidity crisis (a typical tail risk), central banks would provide the liquidities. This created the perception in banks that liquidity risk was not something to worry about.

On causes and triggers

The fundamental cause of the banking crisis is a structural one. Deregulation made it possible for commercial banks to also perform activities of investment banks, and for investment banks to also perform activities of commercial banks (that is, to borrow short and to lend long). This had the effect of allowing these institutions to combine liquidity and credit risks in an uncontrolled way. When these risks are mixed too much, they create an explosive cocktail that sooner or later will explode. In this sense the subprime crisis was just a trigger. If the subprime crisis had not erupted, another solvency problem would have done the trick of setting in motion the devilish interaction between solvency and liquidity crises.

A lot has been made of the low interest rate policies pursued for too long by the US Federal Reserve after 2001 as a cause of the credit crisis. There can be no doubt that this policy helped to produce a bubble in the US housing market, and in so doing contributed to the credit crisis. The point we want to stress here is that this policy led to a banking crisis because the banking sector was allowed to create lethal combinations of credit and liquidity risks. Even without the easy money policies pursued by the US, sooner or later a banking crisis would have erupted.

The same can be said of another factor that is often invoked as an important cause of the credit crisis, that is, the international current account imbalances. Asian countries accumulated large current account surpluses during the last decade matched mainly by large current account deficits of the US. This imbalance was the result of large saving surpluses in Asian countries that were channelled (mainly) to the US. Thus the Asian savings surpluses made it possible to finance the dissaving of the US private and government sectors and helped to fuel a consumption boom in the US. Again there is no doubt that these macroeconomic imbalances have created problems: but it is difficult to see how they are responsible for a banking crisis. After all, the essence of banking is to channel saving surpluses from those who want to save to those who want to spend. Banking thrives on these 'imbalances'. Without these imbalances there would be no banking. These imbalances may have contributed to bubbles in the US but these bubbles led to a banking crisis because banks were allowed to fully participate in them.

The reaction of the authorities

The authorities of the major developed countries have reacted to the crisis by using three types of instruments.

First, central banks have performed massive liquidity infusions to prevent a liquidity crisis from bringing down the banking system. Second, governments have introduced state guarantees on interbank deposits aimed at preventing a collapse of the interbank market which would almost certainly have led to large scale liquidity crisis. Third, governments have reacted to bank failures by massive recapitalizations of banks, and in a number of cases by outright nationalizations.

It must be said that these interventions have been successful in that they have prevented a collapse of the banking system. The issue that arises here, however, is whether these interventions will suffice to avert future crises and to bring the banking system back on track so that it can perform its function of credit creation?

The fundamental problem banks face today is that their balance sheets are massively inflated as a result of their participation in consecutive bubbles. As asset prices tumble everywhere, banks face a period during which their balance sheets will shrink substantially. This process is unlikely to be a smooth one, mainly because during the shrinking the devilish interaction of solvency and liquidity crises will occur. This is likely to create a further downward spiral. As a result, there is as yet no floor on the value of the banks' assets.

This mechanism has two negative effects. First, the capitalizations performed by governments are unlikely to be sufficient. With every eruption of the solvency-liquidity downward spiral, governments will be called upon to provide new equity infusions to counter the write-downs banks are forced to do. The government recapitalization programmes will throw money into a black hole. This process is already operating. As Table 1.2 shows, as of 13 October 2008, the amount of state

Table 1.2   Largest Bank Write-downs and Capital raising.

	Write-down	Capital raising
Wachovia	96.7	11.0
Citi	61.0	49.0
Merrill Lynch	52.2	29.9
Washington Mutual	45.6	12.1
UBS	44.2	27.1
HSBC	27.4	5.1
Bank of America	27.4	30.7
JPMorgan Chase	18.8	19.7
Morgan Stanley	15.7	14.6
IKB	14.0	11.5
Lehman	13.8	13.9
RBS	13.3	22.0
Credit Suisse	10.0	3.0
Wells Fargo	10.0	5.8
Deutsche Bank	9.8	5.9
Fortis	8.8	21.5
Credit Agricole	8.2	7.9
Other	158.4	129.0
Total	635.3	419.7

Source: Bloomberg.

capitalizations of the major banks fell fall short of the write-downs performed by the same banks.

A second effect of the massive deleveraging of the banking system is that it will give strong incentives to banks not to extend new loans, thereby dragging down the real economy. How far this will go, and for how long, nobody knows. It is not inconceivable that this leads to a long and protracted downward movement in economic activity.

Short-term solutions

The solutions in the short-term will invariably involve a return of Keynesian economics. First and foremost governments will have to sustain aggregate demand by increased spending in the face of dwindling tax revenues. Large budget deficits will be inevitable and also desirable. Attempts at balancing government budgets would not work, as it would likely lead to Keynes's savings paradox. As private agents attempt to increase savings the decline in production and national income actually prevents them from doing so. This paradox can only be solved by government dissaving.

Second, in the process of recapitalizing banks, governments will substitute private debt for government debt. This also is inevitable and desirable. As agents distrust private debt they turn to government debt, deemed safer. Governments will have to accommodate for this desire. (See Hyman Minsky 1986).

Third, governments and central banks will also have to support asset prices, in particular stock prices. The deleveraging process of the banking system will continue to put downward pressure on asset prices. In order to stop this, governments and central banks may be forced to intervene directly in stock markets and to buy shares. As argued earlier, without a program aiming at stopping the downward spiral involving asset prices, the recapitalization programs that governments have started may in fact imply throwing money into a black hole.

Long-term solutions: a return to narrow banking

Preventing the collapse of the banking system and making it function again are daunting tasks in the short run. Equally important is to start working on the rules for a new banking system. There are two ways to go forward. One can be called the Basle approach, the other the Glass-Steagall approach.

The Basle approach accepts as a *fait accompli* that banks will go on performing both traditional and investment bank activities. This approach then consists in defining and implementing rules governing the risks that these banks can take. Its philosophy is that a suitable analysis of the risk profile of the banks' asset portfolios allows for calculating the required capital to be used as a buffer against future shocks in credit risk. Once these minimum capital ratios are in place, credit risk accidents can be absorbed by the existing equity, preventing banks from going broke and thereby avoiding the devilish spillovers from solvency problems into liquidity problems.

This approach has completely failed. As was argued earlier, it was first implemented in the Basle 1 accord, but was massively circumvented by banks that profited from the loopholes in the system. Basle 2 attempted to remedy this by allowing banks to use internal risk models to compute their minimum capital ratios. The underlying assumption was that scientific advances in risk analysis would make it possible to develop a reliable method of determining minimum capital ratios.

This approach at managing risks of banks does not work and will never do because it assumes efficiency of financial markets; an assumption that must be rejected.[4] Banks that fully participate in the financial markets subject themselves to the endemic occurrence of bubbles and crashes. These lead to large tail risks that with our present knowledge cannot be quantified. In addition, when a liquidity crisis erupts, usually triggered by solvency problems in one or more banks, the interaction between liquidity and solvency crises is set in motion. No minimum capital ratio can stop such a spiral. Perfectly solvent banks capable of showing the best capital ratios can be caught by that spiral eliminating their capital base in a few hours. The Basle approach does not protect the banks from this spiral (a tail risk). In addition, there is no prospect for gaining substantial knowledge about tail risks in the near future. The Basle approach must be abandoned.

This leaves only one workable approach. This is a return to the Glass-Steagall Act approach, or put differently, a return to narrow banking in which the activities banks can engage in are narrowly circumscribed. In this approach banks are excluded from investing in equities, derivatives and complex structured products. Investment in such products can only be performed by financial institutions, investment banks, which are forbidden from funding these investments by deposits (either obtained from the public of from other commercial banks).

In a nutshell a return to narrow banking could be implemented as follows. Financial institutions would be forced to choose between the status of a commercial bank and that of an investment bank. Only the former would be allowed to attract deposits from the public and from other commercial banks and to transform these into a loan portfolio with a longer maturity (duration). Commercial banks would benefit from the lender of last resort facility and deposit insurance, and would be subject to the normal bank supervision and regulation. The other financial institutions that do not opt for a commercial bank status would have to ensure that the duration of their liabilities is on average at least as long as the duration of their assets. This would imply, for example, that they would not be allowed to finance their illiquid assets by short-term credit lines from commercial banks. Thus while commercial banks would be barred from engaging themselves in activities of investment banks, the reverse would also hold, that is, investment banks would not be allowed to borrow short and to lend long thereby taking on liquidity risks.

Thus, we would return to a world where banking activities are tightly regulated and separated from investment banking activities. This also implies that commercial banks would no longer be allowed to sell (securitize) their loan portfolio. The reason is that securitization does not eliminate the risk for the banks, on the contrary. First, when a commercial bank repackages loans it is difficult to eliminate its liability associated with these loans. And as we have seen, when a credit risk materializes, these securitized loans reappear on the balance sheets of the banks, greatly increasing their risks and undermining their capital base. Second, as argued earlier, securitization leads to a build-up of the credit pyramid. When a bank securitizes a loan, it obtains new liquidities that can be used to grant new loans, which in turn can be used to securitize further. As a result, a credit expansion is made possible which occurs outside the supervision and control of the central bank (which, however, will be called upon to buy these assets when it becomes the lender of last resort). Put differently, securitization allows the credit multiplier to increase for any given level the money base provided by the central bank. Credit gets out of control, endangering the whole banking system, including the central bank. It is worth stressing the latter point. The massive credit expansion made possible by securitization also endangers the balance sheet of the central bank. This is so because in times of crisis, the central bank is called upon to function as a lender of last resort. As a result, it will be faced with the need to accept as collateral securitized assets that were created by banks. Allowing banks to securitize thus means that the central bank takes on a substantial part of the risk.

The preceding argument also implies that the 'originate and distribute model' that banks have increasingly used in the recent past must be abandoned. Recent proposals to save it by requiring banks to hold a fraction of the securitized assets on their balance sheets are inappropriate as they do not eliminate the risk arising from the multiplication of credit described in the previous paragraph.

To conclude, banks take extraordinary risks that are implicitly insured by the central bank in the form of lender of last resort. The central banks have the right to impose on banks that they minimize credit risks. These cannot be eliminated completely, but they can certainly be contained by severely restricting the nature of the loans banks can grant.

A return to narrow banking will necessitate a cooperative international approach. When only one or a few countries return to narrow banking, the banks of these countries will face a competitive disadvantage. They will loose market shares to banks less tightly regulated. As a result, they will have forceful arguments to lobby domestically against the tight restrictions they face. In the end, the governments of these countries will yield and the whole process of deregulation will start again.

Conclusion

The paradigm that financial markets are efficient has provided the intellectual backbone for the deregulation of the banking sector since the 1980s. Deregulation has made it possible for banks to be fully involved in financial markets. As a result, these banks combine the activities of traditional banks and investment banks. In addition, the total absence of regulation of investment banks has made it possible for these institutions to move in the direction of commercial banking in the sense that they have become institutions that like traditional banks fund their long-term assets by short term liabilities. This double movement, that is, commercial banks moving into investment bank territory and investment banks moving into commercial bank territory, led to a situation in which both the traditional banks and the investment banks built up a lethal combination of credit and liquidity risks.

There is now overwhelming evidence that the financial markets are not efficient. Bubbles and crashes are an endemic feature of financial markets in capitalist countries. Thus, as a result of deregulation, the balance sheets of banks became fully exposed to these bubbles and crashes. Consequently, banks which by their very nature are subject to liquidity risks added large amounts of credit risks to their balance sheets; an explosive cocktail. Investment banks, that traditionally take on a lot of credit risk (exposed as they are to the vagaries of financial markets), added the liquidity risks typically reserved for traditional banks to their balance sheets.

The Basle approach to stabilize the banking system has the implicit assumption that financial markets are efficient, allowing us to model the risks banks take and to compute the required capital ratios that will minimize this risk. We argue that this approach is unworkable because the risks that matter for banks are tail risks, associated with bubbles and crashes. These cannot be quantified. As a result, there is only one way out, and that is to return to narrow banking, a model that emerged after the previous large-scale banking crisis of the 1930s but that was discarded during the 1980s and 1990s under the influence of the efficient market paradigm. Application of this model will lead to a situation in which activities of commercial and investment banks are strictly separated.

Notes

1. A very useful book is Goodhart and Illing (2002).
2. The empirical evidence against the efficiency of Financial markets has been building up over the last decade. For useful overviews, see Shleifer (2000) and Shiller (2000).
3. See Kindleberger (2005). Chancellor (1999) also provides a vivid account of the many bubbles and crashes in the history of financial markets.
4. There is a second reason why it will not work and that is conflict of interests. Supervisors should not trust complex risk models produced by bankers because the latter have a strong incentive not to reveal their true risk exposures.

References

Chancellor, E. (1999), *Devil Take the Hindmost: A History of Financial Speculation*, New York: Farrar, Straus and Giroux.

De Grauwe, P. and Grimaldi, M. (2006), *The Exchange Rate in a Behavioural Finance Framework*, Princeton: Princeton University Press.

Garber, P. (2000), *Famous First Bubbles: The Fundamentals of Early Manias.* Cambridge, Mass: MIT Press, 2000. xii + 163 pp.

Goodhart, C. and Illing, G. (eds) (2002), *Financial Crises, Contagion, and the Lender of Last Resort, a Reader*, Oxford: Oxford University Press.

Greenspan, A. (2007), *The Age of Turbulence. Adventures in a New World*, London: Penguin Books, 531 p.

Kindleberger, C. (2005), *Manias, Panics, and Crashes*, 5th Ed., New York: Wiley.

Minsky, H. (1986), *Stabilizing an Unstable Economy*, New York: McGraw-Hill.

Shiller, R. (2000), *Irrational Exuberance*, Princeton: Princeton University Press.

Shleifer, A. (2000), *Clarendon Lectures: Inefficient Markets*, Oxford: Oxford University Press.

2
The Moral Economy of Money and the Future of European Capitalism

Stefan Collignon

Karl Marx, was he right – after all?

The financial and economic crisis has raised new questions about the future of the capitalist system. Twenty years after the fall of the Wall in Berlin, the alternative is clearly no longer a planned economy, Soviet style, but the fragility of the capitalist system is again apparent to everyone. Curiously, Marx never fully understood the nature of money, finance and capital. He explained the capitalist crisis by the fall of return on real capital, but the system's systemic instability resides in the financial sphere.

Financial crises have occurred frequently in the history of capitalism. Their re-occurrence was slowed down after central banks assumed responsibilities as lender of last resort, although the inter-war period saw major breakdowns in 1919–1920 (UK), 1924 (France) and 1929 (US, Germany, Austria and Hungary) (see Kindleberger 1984). The period of Bretton Woods was marked by exceptional stability, but, after the collapse of the System in 1971, successive waves of crisis have again occurred around the world: the turmoil of 1972–1973 in the exchange markets was followed by the Herstatt bank failure in Germany in 1974 and the fringe bank crisis in the UK 1974–1975; the LDC debt crisis threatened the stability of the world financial system in the early 1980s. The 1990s saw the ERM crisis in Europe (1992–1993), the Japanese and Swedish banking crisis, the Mexican peso crisis in 1994, the Asian crisis in 1997, the Russian crash in 1998 followed by the near-bankruptcy of the LTCM hedge fund (Goodhart and Illing 2002). It may not be a coincidence that these disturbances started to become more frequent in an era when neoliberalism was on the ascent. Re-thinking the future of capitalism requires today re-examining the fundamental assumptions

32

underlying the economic model that has dominated policymaking for the last 40 years.

In this chapter, we will look at some paradigmatic foundations of economic policy in a modern monetary economy and then draw conclusions for policymaking.

The normativity of money and capital

Are money, banks and finance good or bad? People are angry. Trillions of euros have been spent on bailing out banks, which are thought to be responsible for the economic mess we are in, while no funds are available for schools, hospitals or higher wages. After the excesses of the financial bubble, the conservative reaction is to go back to the fundamentals of the 'real' economy. The French President Nicolas Sarkozy has declared 'Anglo-Saxon' capitalism for dead[1] and called for the 'moralization of capitalism'.[2] But what does it mean? Is it moral if profit is made with ecology, but greed if it is obtained by financial derivatives? Is the source of all misery the economic rationality of the price system of markets that allocates scarce resources to the satisfaction of unlimited wants, or is it the 'irrational exuberance' of financial markets? Should companies adapt a rule book of ethical corporate governance? If the provision of public goods conflicts with private goods, are the first morally right and the second evil? Or is it the other way round? In the confused debate about these issues, one is reminded of the phrase by Coluche, the French satirist: 'Capitalism is the exploitation of man by man, socialism is the opposite'.

Marx (1845) famously wrote: 'Philosophers have only interpreted the world differently; what matters is to change it'. However, he did not see that how we interpret the world, determines how it is. Norms and values give sense and direction to human actions and are the intentional content of institutions (Searle 1995). For this reason, economic doctrines shape the world we live in. Capitalism has its own ethos, a normativity that is functional to the system and that has determined the values of modern society. Some of its elements, notably the issue of balancing liberty against equality are immanent to the modern capitalist economy; others have their roots in traditional hierarchical economic systems and are opposed to a modern democratic society.

Historically, capitalism has emerged together with the financial system. In fact, it was the invention of banking, the de-penalization of usury and the acceptance of interest taking, together with the introduction of double-entry bookkeeping in the Renaissance that ended the repressive culture of the middle ages and liberated individuals: the transformation, which took place between the seventeenth and nineteenth centuries in Europe was the gradual and sometimes violent substitution of the traditional norms of hierarchy by the modern principle of contracts. This principle presupposes and at the same time generates freedom and equality as political norms. Economic agents must be free to conclude (or not) contracts *and they are equal in their freedom*. As a consequence, freedom and equality are the two dimensions which define the modern political space in which individual autonomy and emancipation become possible. The entire political philosophy of modernity is based on this pair of values. Without the contract economy and without financial markets, modernity remains incomprehensible.

These modern values became dominant – Gramsci would have called them hegemonic – after the American and French Revolutions. While the articulation of 'freedom' became the rallying cry of liberalism, 'equality' was trumpeted by social democrats and socialists. However, both these political ideologies and movements are grounded on the same economic principle: contractarian individualism. They stood in stark contrast to conservative hierarchy, which emphasized subordination of individuals to the community and allocation of resources according to the hierarchy of rank and status. John Locke (1988/1689) was the first to design a clear modern counter-programme to the conservative Tory ideology defended by his opponent Robert Filmer (1991/1680). It was based on the private property of free and equal individuals. Karl Popper (1995) has later described the cleavage as the conflict between 'the open society and its enemies'.

The exchange economy

Political values must be consistent with the functional norms on which the reproductive system of a society is based. But the specifics of a moral economy depend on the interpretation of economic paradigms.[3] The dominant paradigm in economic theory is the exchange economy, where people improve their welfare by exchanging goods, of which they produce more than they need. Money is supposed to be at best a neutral *means of exchange*, which facilitates barter transactions, but otherwise can only cause harm and does not contribute to 'real wealth'. If too much of it is put into circulation, inflation distorts the efficient allocation of resources by markets. Thus, monetarists emphasize the control of money supply and price stability as primary objectives for monetary policy. This is the core idea behind Milton Friedman's monetarism, but it has deep roots in the exchange paradigm of classical economic thought, starting with John Locke, Adam Smith and David Hume.

Continuing this line of thought, neoclassical economics has shown that exchanging goods in spot markets in proportion to their marginal utility will maximize individuals' welfare. Subsequently the rational expectations revolution has introduced an inter-temporal dimension to the exchange economy. In these models utility is maximized not only by market transactions today, but also by exchanges into the indefinite future. As a consequence, modern economic theory starts with the assumption of 'complete markets', where there is a system of markets for every good. By carefully defining 'good' to include the date and environment in which a commodity is consumed, economists are able to consider consumption, production and investment choices in a multi-period, risky world. Moreover, they can do so using largely the same utility theory originally developed to analyse timeless certainty (Flood 1991). Complete markets provide consumers, producers and investors with perfect flexibility in allocating payoffs and planning for uncertain contingencies. In this context, markets for futures and options are shown to improve the efficiency of marketplaces and this has far-reaching implications for regulatory policy. Even if it is acknowledged that in the real world markets are not complete, they still often serve as a theoretical benchmark. In practical terms this approach has reduced uncertainty to calculable risk and has set off the dramatic development of financial derivative products and markets, through Hedge Funds, forward contracts, futures options, swaps and similar products. The over-the-counter (OTC) derivatives market has grown rapidly over the years, standing at $596 trillion in December 2007.[4] In foreign exchange and interest related products alone, global daily turnover increased by 74 per cent between April 2001 and April 2004 to $2.4 trillion.[5]

In political terms, the idea that every contingent state of the world could be traded on a market opened the door for the neoliberal distortion of liberalism, according to which distributional issues and the principle of equality have no place in modern economics and politics. When privatization, liberalization, deregulation and monetarism become the dominant political creed, what role is left for politics?[6]

All of the most influential New Classical and New Keynesian theorists have worked with the 'complete markets paradigm'. But, as Buiter (2009) has pointed out, in a world where there are markets for contingent claims, which span all possible states of nature (all possible contingencies and outcomes), and in which inter-temporal budget constraints are always satisfied by assumption, default, bankruptcy and insolvency are impossible. It is then not terribly surprising that critical questions regarding the functioning of a modern market economy were never answered nor even asked.

The contract economy

This is different in the economic paradigm, which is influenced by the 'banking view' of monetary theory. It goes back to Keynes and is owed to Minsky, Riese (2001), Goodhart and Stiglitz. It sees market agents constrained by limited information and explains the need for money by its function of means of payment, caused by the existence of uncertainty (Goodhart 1989). In an uncertain world, where people lack trust in their trading partners' willingness and ability to make promised future payments, sellers of spot goods (goods that are delivered now) require immediate payment by transfer of a reliable asset. This asset is money (Keynes 1930), because money is liquidity and has the 'advantage of immediacy' (Demsetz 1968). Holding money gives security. Giving up this advantage has a price: the interest rate. In an uncertain environment liquidity trumps other assets. The higher the uncertainty in the economy, the higher is the price of safe liquidity. This may lower the demand for credit, but could also create an adverse selection bias, which would constrain the supply of credit (Stiglitz and Greenwald 2003). Thus, trust and stability in the macroeconomic environment will increase the likelihood that people will pay with money, buy things and lend against promises.

In a modern economy liquidity is provided by the central bank. Commercial banks obtain central bank money by 'discounting' debt against cash, debt they have themselves previously issued or acquired. The need of banks and other agents to hold liquid assets as reserves allows the central bank to steer the interest rate for the whole economy. This has two implications: first, there is a structural shortage in the money market, created by the fact that when a loan plus interest are repaid, more money is needed for repayment than initially borrowed. This additional money must come from the central bank itself and commercial banks have an excess demand for central bank reserve assets. The structural shortage in the money market makes money 'the scarce asset' *par excellence*, but it implies also that other markets, notably the labour market, have a structural surplus.[7] Logically, unemployment is therefore an intrinsic feature of capitalism, although this statement says little about how much unemployment is compatible with a functioning credit economy. The structural shortage in the money market allows the central bank to set the conditions under which money is obtained. Hence, if the interest rate reflects the scarcity price of money, at zero interest rate money becomes disfunctional, and in the long run a zero interest rate policy is the euthanasia of capitalism.

Second, in order to be able to service the debt and repay a credit plus interest, a borrower must generate additional income. If money is created by central banks who buy credit contracts issued by the corporate sector, then the real economy must produce a surplus. This is how money has become the engine of growth. Marx has correctly described the mechanism by which this surplus is produced. What he did not understand was the interaction between liquidity, uncertainty and credit contracts with the need to produce a surplus. Contrary to what Marx thought, the prime driving force of economic development has been the stick of honouring debt obligations, rather than the carrot of profit. Profit may be the incentive, but obligation makes performance persistent. Because dynamic equilibrium is attained when the growth rate equals the interest rate, maintaining a positive real interest rate is the best guarantee for long run economic growth.

However, there is a fundamental distinction between private and public sector debt. Borrowing to finance consumption is serviced by reductions in disposable incomes and consumption. But borrowing for investment purposes increases incomes and therefore increases societies' net wealth. Yet, at the level of the macro-economy, savings are equal to investments. There is, therefore, a major distinction between borrowing for investment and current public expenditure: the first is serviced out of profits and future income, the second out of taxes. As David Ricardo and Robert Barro (1974) have shown, given certain informational assumptions, rational consumers should internalize the government's budget constraint, whereby the present value of future tax liabilities is equal to the value of newly issued government debt. Tax payers will then reduce consumption and start saving today to pay future taxes. The government's choice is between taxing today and taxing in the future, so that public borrowing does not add to the net wealth of society. This is different for investment, private and public, because investment does create additional income. Debt, which finances investment, is serviced by wealth increases and not by reduction in spending.

Keynes taught us that the purpose of macroeconomic policy must be the creation of a stable macroeconomic environment which minimizes uncertainty, so that the liquidity premium is minimized. Before anything else, Keynes was a philosopher of probability. He saw the fragility of financial markets and thought that fiscal policy could play a stabilizing role when the economy was trapped in the liquidity trap. But his thought was more subtle than subsequent Keynesianism, which reduced his vision of a monetary production economy to the so-called neoclassical synthesis.[8] When Keynesianism failed in the 1990s, it was precisely because mainstream economics had returned to the exchange paradigm, forgetting the unstable nature of money in an environment of uncertainty. The monetarist Anti-Keynesian revolution by Milton Friedman was the logically consistent reformulation of this move.

The essential difference between the two economic paradigms consists in the treatment of uncertainty: in the classic/neoclassic/monetarist tradition, uncertainty is by definition reduced to *temporary* disturbances (shocks), which disappear automatically. In most econometric models, these shocks are calculable and assumed to follow a normal distribution. This assumption provides the rational for the often highly complex mathematical models underlying financial derivatives. They have ignored 'unforeseeable' shocks with infinitesimally small probability and statistical distributions with fat tails that have become so fatal when the financial markets took a general downturn. In the Keynesian/informational paradigm *uncertainty is inherent to the human condition* and there is no guarantee that the probability characteristics of past observable events will also govern the probability distribution of future events. If that is so, uncertainty requires management. The implications for economic policy are important. If capitalism and markets have a natural tendency to return to a long-run equilibrium, the role for policy and government is limited: keep out of the way and make markets flexible, because utility maximizing economic agents would then do whatever it takes to overcome the shock. But if uncertainty is a natural condition, which may distort and prevent the return to equilibrium, then government has to stabilize the macro-economy.

Political normativity

The two paradigms also have implications for political values and morality. In a neoclassical world, people strive to maximize their utilities, where more is better. The dominant political value that allows the achievement of this is what Isaiah Berlin (1958) called 'negative liberty', that is, the protection against interference by others. In economic terms, negative freedom signifies free markets. There is a consistent theme from Lockian liberty to Adam Smiths's invisible hand, from modern property rights schools to neoliberalism: reduce the sphere of public/government interference. Few questions are asked about the nature of governments, as long as they successfully implement free market policies. Thus, Leuber (1987) could call Pinochet's Chile 'an amazing political miracle'. This reduction of freedom to negative liberty is what defines *neoliberalism*.

With the alternative Keynesian paradigm, governments have a role to play as guarantors of systemic stability. They must minimize uncertainty; this is the role for macroeconomic policy. However, this is not all. The monetary economy imposes its own normativity on society. It opens the gateway to 'positive' liberty, namely the capacity of individuals to determine their lives as free and equal masters. The most important institution in a modern economy is the contract. By understanding money as a means of payment that extinguishes debt contracts, the Keynesian paradigm sees the monetary economy founded in an extensive web of contracts. As we have seen, this implies the normative matrix of freedom *and* equality. Keynesian liberalism is the political liberalism of *equal* individuals, and not by coincidence do American neo-conservatives define political liberalism as being to the left of the political spectrum.

This normative framework of modernity is distinct from the holistic values that dominated traditional societies and nowadays reappear in neoconservative ideology. In the pre-modern paradigm, resources are allocated by hierarchy and power and the holistic society demands the individual to surrender to the authority of the leader, the dogma of belief, the imperatives of community. In the traditional society, the individual exits to serve the whole; for the modern individual, society is there to empower his or her individual self-realization.[9]

Not surprisingly these two views give rise to two very different interpretations of the State and government. In the traditional/holistic perspective, the State is the incarnation of hierarchical authority. It has the monopoly of power and can legitimately interfere with individuals' freedom. The modern view sees the State founded in the social contract by free and equal citizens, who are owners of common public goods as well as owners of private goods and who decide themselves how to use these goods. Hence, the modern state is democratic, the traditional is authoritarian. It is the collective determination of the public good through democratic public deliberation and choice that gives citizens the positive liberty of determining their life plans, of being their own master. This distinction between the authoritarian and the democratic State is prior to and more fundamental than the conflict between freedom and equality, between economic liberalism and social democracy.

The contract economy is the foundation of modern democracy. If free and equal citizens conclude the social contract, they must have equal rights to appoint governments as their agent, and to charge them with the implementation of policies which reflect their collective preferences. They need a government that is accountable. Contrary to the role of government in traditional societies, where legitimacy is derived from collective identity and cultural homogeneity, modern government is functional and preference choice oriented. These normative considerations have important consequences for how one perceives the interaction between governments and markets. The Anti-Keynesian revolution by Friedman and the monetarists in the 1970s has given priority to the exchange paradigm of microeconomics and ignored the need for macroeconomic policy in minimizing uncertainty. The reduction of liberty to the 'negative' concept of non-interference has prevented using the democratic state as an instrument for positively defining the collective preferences of individual citizens. It therefore has also minimized the redistributive function of the State. Neoliberalism became a programme to dismantle the social welfare State. Redefining a new policy agenda for the post-neoliberal era requires a return to the fundamental norms of modernity.

Models of capitalism

The credit economy has been the historic engine of growth, but also of growing social inequality. Owners of securities have a claim on the increase of income and wealth. The accumulation of capital concentrates property in the hands of few, unless some form of redistribution re-establishes the balance. Thus, the freedom of economic liberalism remains purely formal, unless it is counterbalanced by principles of equality and fairness. The modern social democratic approach to redistribution is to use the democratic state, where citizens are free and equal and will establish a fair balance between economic freedom and equality according to their tastes, even if the balance may shift over time. The conservative approach is to use the authority of the state in conjunction with communitarian identity to restrain the unfettered liberty of the market. Thus, if the monetary economy has produced freedom and equality as fundamental norms of modern individualism, they have interacted, sometimes uneasily, with the norms of traditional society. Communism, fascism and now Islamic fundamentalism are attempts to return to authoritarian, hierarchical forms of social relations that suppress the individual. In Western Europe, as in the US, modern individualism has prevailed, although conservatism has often become an ally of either economic liberalism or socialism. Nevertheless, Europe's greatest achievement after the Second World War was to have found a social equilibrium, which has preserved individual freedom and equality in the context of a stable monetary economy. The European monetary union is the pinnacle of this long process.

Models of welfare capitalism

The emergence of modern individualism as the dominant political philosophy does not mean that Europe has to converge to a single model of capitalism. In fact, despite the common normative structure of a modern contract economy, social models in Europe are highly diversified. Some countries have given greater weight to liberal market freedom, others to social equality. These political norms translate into specific institutional forms with respect to the regulation of capitalism. Each country has developed its own mechanism for providing social protection to less privileged groups and classes. Nevertheless, three basic models of welfare capitalism may be distinguished (Esping-Anderson 1990): the liberal Anglo-Saxon model, the social democratic Scandinavian model and the conservative model at the centre of the European continent. In addition there are some variations in Southern and Eastern Europe that are different, but largely dominated by traditional values of patriarchy and political clientelism.

1. The social democratic model dominates Scandinavia. It is a democratic welfare state financed by taxes. The relatively high level of taxes is supported by electoral consensus. All individuals have equal access to social services and are equally entitled to welfare claims. The fact that the welfare system is financed by taxes prevents economic distortions of relative cost. At the same time it contributes to a fairly equal distribution of income.
2. The conservative model dominates Continental Europe. This model is most prominent in Germany, Austria, France, Belgium and Netherlands. Italy is also leaning to this conservative continental model, although traditional clientelism is more pronounced than in the Rhineland States. The conservative model has evolved from a corporatist welfare state, whereby individuals are protected by a benevolent patriarchal authority, although the financing and the nature of claims are not equal across all citizens. Social security is essentially financed by contributions that are added to wage costs, thereby

strongly distorting the economy and establishing classes of different social protection. The conservative model has been strongly influenced by catholic social ethics and morality with a paternalistic interpretation of social relations, rather than by political equality, which marks the social democratic model.

3. Broad social protection in the liberal model, which is predominant in the UK and Ireland as well as in the US and Canada, is subject to private insurance and individual initiative. These insurance models of welfare usually make social claims dependent on accumulated contributions or, more generally, on individual efforts. However, in most of these countries there are also politically decided minimum standards, such as statutory minimum wages, or state welfare programs by the state, such as National Health in the UK or Social Security and Medicare in the US.

The economic performance of social models

How have these models performed? To what degree have they been able to remedy the inequality caused by unfettered markets? Figure 2.1 compares income distribution measured by the Gini-coefficient with

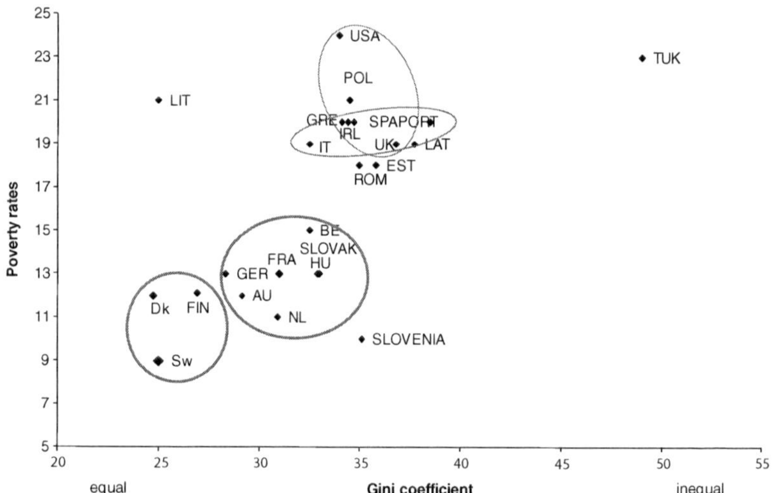

Figure 2.1   Income distribution and poverty.
Source: European Commission, UN and CIA Fact Book.

the relative poverty rate. Not surprisingly, the social democratic model produces the most equal societies with the lowest level of poverty. Also, quite interestingly, the relative income distribution in conservative countries is not very different from liberal economies. Free markets reproduce social hierarchy through unequal distribution of wealth and generate significantly higher levels of poverty than the conservative model. Thus, political discourses in conservative countries like France, Germany or Italy attacking the inequality observed in the liberal model are not credible, because they reconstruct inequality by power and status. By contrast, the social democratic model proves that economic prosperity and equality are compatible with a dynamic monetary economy.

Southern Europe is a group apart, with relatively high levels of poverty, although slightly less than the liberal model. Income inequality varies significantly from one country to the next in the South. Turkey, quite visibly, is not part of any European social model.

To summarize, the social democratic Scandinavian model seems the fairest social model, the conservative model combats poverty but not inequality, while the liberal model is fairer than the performance in some Southern and Eastern European countries, although it accepts high levels of poverty.

Comparing levels of unemployment and economic growth over the last decade and allowing for the catch-up growth in new member states, we find that the social democratic model was at least as efficient as the liberal model in producing economic growth, while economic growth was low and unemployment high in the socially conservative Central Europe.

Is there an optimal social model? What is the 'best-practice' of capitalism in the face of increasing international competition not only for firms, but also for the institutional fitness in the globalization process? A number of different answers have been discussed in the political economy literature.[10] Most prominently, Peter Hall and David Soskice (2001) have argued that the choice of social models is not arbitrary and cannot be 'switched' at will, because each institutional arrangement must be seen in its functional context. For example, the Anglo-Saxon model, which they call *liberal market economy*, is more short-term oriented due to the dominance of financial markets, and therefore also requires highly flexible labour markets; this institutional set-up supports technical innovation. By contrast, the German model of *coordinated market economy* has a long-term bias due to banking regulations and with that goes the long-term orientation in the labour market that produces the German skill machine and a comparative advantage for product development.

Edwards and Fischer (1994) have challenged the consensual view according to which the Anglo-Saxon model is capital market orientated and Germany is dominated by bank-financed structures. Banks are not more involved with running businesses in Germany than in the USA. And the contagion of German banks by the meltdown in the US sub-prime market for mortgages is proof that even in Germany securitization had progressed significantly. Vitols (1998) found that at least until the 1990s the uniqueness of the German banking system lay (1) in its unusually high capacity to provide industrial finance in the form of long-term debt capital, and (2) in its avoidance of the 'speculative boom – credit crunch cycle' experienced by almost every other advanced industrialized country in the 1980s and early 1990s. These two key characteristics are attributable to a regulatory framework, which involves strict prudential regulation, access to long-term refinancing sources and a federalist form of corporatism. However, these features have been gradually eroded in recent years, due to the creation of a single European banking market, the globalization of capital markets and neoliberal economic policies. Nevertheless, these institutional characteristics have made an important contribution to Germany's spectacular economic stability after the introduction of Social Market Economy in 1949. Even if there is no way back to the old days, there may be lessons to be learned from Germany for a future restructuration of Europe's financial system.

Redefining the policy agenda

A new policy agenda for the post-neoliberal era requires preserving the fundamental norms of economic and political modernity, namely freedom and equality. The first, economic, priority must be to stabilize the financial system, so that credit becomes the engine of growth again. This implies rules for financial regulation that restore trust in individual banks, and also macroeconomic policies that stabilize the economy. The second, political, priority must be to prevent conservatism from destroying individual freedom and equality. The narrowing of political discourse to the provincialism of local identities[11] contributes to this as much as the protection of national communities by authoritarian means of the State. They are counterproductive if economic prosperity is to be re-established. In both respects public authorities need to interact with markets. In fact, markets cannot exist without governments because governments guarantee their functionality. This insight is not new, but the two dimensions of government interference need to be acknowledged. For example German ordo-liberals always recognized the need for a strong state as the guardian of market rules, but they were strongly opposed to Keynesian market intervention, where governments become market participants (Tietmayer 1999). On the other side, French interventionism was fond of an active state, but refused to let the government's hands be bound by the functional logic of markets. A proper design of an efficient European market economy must combine prudential supervisory rules with macroeconomic management for the entire euro Area, without inhibiting individuals from becoming market participants.

The state and democracy

The financial crisis does not invalidate the viability of the financial system. Conservatives call for a return to the 'real' economy and the 'good old moral values' of decency and trust. But the problem is that trust depends on systemic stability and this requires government action. There is, today, a real risk that one throws the baby out with the bath water; that the recognition of the excesses of the last decade leads to excessive repression of contractual liberty. The conservative backlash – at the political right and left – blames greedy bankers, fantastic bonuses and financial derivatives for the crisis; it seeks to return to pre-modern forms of regulation, either by imposing authoritarian rules or oppressive morality. In the European context, the backlash takes the form of economic protectionism and the defence of national identities. These ideological reflexes are incompatible with monetary union or a single European market. By definition a single market implies the development of free and equal opportunities to conclude contracts and transactions without the impediments of borders or regulative competition between local authorities. But the democratic will of free and equal citizens must decide a legal framework, within which private contracts may be negotiated without harming others. With the single European market, such legal framework must be European, not national.

When the French president declares 'we cannot be naïve, we must protect our industry',[12] he announces double damage to French and European citizens: he prevents international trade from stimulating demand in the European market, which would support French companies that do not have the privilege of being 'protected'; and he denies French consumers the right to buy goods and services at lower prices and better quality. Similarly, to impose limits on how much a person may earn, as discussed in Germany and even in America, does not remove the growing gap between rich and poor.

Rethinking European policies requires now a further step. The ultimate function of the State is to manage and regulate the externalities, which arise from individual actions. As we have seen, the modern State does so by giving a say to individual citizens, who are affected by policy decisions. It is the citizens who have the ultimate authority (sovereignty) to decide how they want their interests pursued.

In the European Union, an increasing number of policies affect all European citizens, particularly if they use the euro as their currency. But policymaking is dominated not by concerns for collective European interests, but by fractional interests of national governments who often justify their usurpation of power by reference to the defence of national identity. This form of governance is incompatible with the modern idea of free and equal citizens, who are masters of their own destiny. The fundamental break-through of the French Revolution, inspired by the liberalism of the first.

Dutch Republic (Israel 2004) was the principle that people, citizens, are Sovereign, not governments. Citizens conclude the social contract to further their interests, not because they 'belong' to a community with a given identity. Hence, European citizens must have the authority to agree on appointing a European government as the agent of their common concerns and interests.

The economic crisis opens the perspective for re-founding Europe's polity. It is time that European democrats start thinking about delegating policymaking for issues that concern all European citizens to a democratically elected European government. A European government must assume responsibility for macroeconomic policies. Inter-governmental coordination is no longer sufficient to obtain welfare maximizing policy results, because many macroeconomic policy issues require coherent discretionary decisions and that cannot be achieved by non-binding guidelines or open methods of coordination. Most importantly, if the liquidity premium contained in the price of money reflects macroeconomic uncertainty, then it is unthinkable that a policymaking institution is not responsible for the whole of a given currency area. Thus, European monetary union calls for a European government.

French policy élites have proposed to set up a *'gouvernmement économique'*, without ever specifying what it meant. The notion of an economic government is misleading. In order to be coherent with the political-economic norms of modern societies, a modern government must be democratic and accountable to its citizens, who can collectively choose between different policy options. The age of paternalism is gone. Citizens must choose between options elaborated and presented by political parties. The nature of government is political. The problem with the *gouvernement économique* is that it is necessarily bureaucratic and authoritarian, because of its technocratic reduction to the sole economic sphere. A democratic government must be able to propose policy compromises across the entire range of policies, including economics, security and foreign policy. Otherwise citizens' preference-frustration, which emerges when specific issues are rejected without compensating policies in a different domain, will impede the democratic policy consensus that is necessary for a well-functioning democracy. Thus, Europe needs a democratic government. Such a European government does, of course, have a privileged role with respect to economic policies. Here are some of its tasks.

Monetary policy

A European government's overall purpose must be the maintenance of financial and economic stability in the Euro Area in order to minimize the general uncertainty under which investment decisions are made. This is necessary because in a monetary union all financial contracts are written and settled in the same currency, and most economic decisions depend on monetary and interest rate decisions by the ECB. Thus, macroeconomic stability is the precondition for raising the rate of capital accumulation, creating jobs, improving productivity and sustaining equitable standards of living.

Monetarists have argued that an economic crisis is best remedied by providing liquidity to the banking system. They see the cause for the crisis in the collapse of the money stock and seek to restore the flow of money to the economy through open market operations and 'quantitative easing'. They believe that if the central bank 'prints' enough money, economic activity will return. However, a crucial requirement for this strategy to work is that financial markets operate smoothly, so that banks efficiently redistribute the liquidity provided by the central bank. Clearly, this is not the case in the present crisis.

The 'banking view', which understands money as an information tool in an uncertain environment, allows a better interpretation of monetary policy in the present crisis. Asymmetric information and lack of trust have disrupted the interbank market. In this context, the most important task is to preserve money's role as a reserve asset. Because of asymmetrical information and externalities in the interbank market, banks may be denied access to liquidity, so that they may become illiquid, despite being solvent, and therefore they need assistance. The central bank must, therefore, act as a lender of last resort. The IMF could do so in the international context with respect to international reserve assets. The need for the central bank to act as a lender of last resort was already formulated by Bagehot in 1873[13] and its role has been summarized by Goodhart (2002: 227) in three propositions:

1. lend freely,
2. at a high rate of interest,
3. on good banking securities.

Central banks' practices in recent months have been closer to the monetarist view. They have lent freely, at low interest rates, on bad collateral. The ECB has lost €10 billion by having bought toxic assets and ECB president Jean Claude Trichet has evaluated the bank's balance sheet risk at €600 billion, equivalent to 6 per cent of Euro Area GDP (Trichet 2009). In this situation, government borrowing can become a stabilizing factor, not only because it stimulates demand, but also because it provides banks with low-risk assets and therefore reduces the need for deleveraging in a financial crisis.

Liberal economists and political moralists have asked: should governments bail out banks? Should they rescue other companies, such as car or steel factories? The answers are: yes and no! There is a fundamental distinction between the financial and the 'real' sector. Banks deal with words, the corporate sector with things. Financial contracts are promises and require trust; companies produce goods and services, which depend on the quality of the products. The default of one debtor can affect other debtors like a cascade, and systemic stability, the employment and livelihood of workers, require that this is avoided. Therefore, banks need to be rescued if lack of trust risks bringing down the system.

However, the bankruptcy of a manufacturing or service company is first of all a sign that it did not produce the quality clients desired. From this point of view, such a corporation does not deserve to be rescued by public authorities. In fact, the elimination of uncompetitive companies is welfare augmenting, as it would allow other competitors to take up markets shares with better products. There is, however a sting: when a corporation declares bankruptcy, it will default on part of its debt. This could destabilize its creditors, if it is large enough. Defaults by property companies have brought down American banks. But even if the bankruptcy does not have systemic consequences, it may still affect subcontractors, workers and the activities in regional economies. The political response to such a situation therefore requires differentiated forms of intervention: public authorities must avoid systemic risk and facilitate alternative investment and the implantation of new production units.

Yet, corporate difficulties may also be caused by a lack of effective demand in the economy. One car manufacturer may produce bad cars. But if all car makers are making losses, it is because people do not spend money on cars. In this case, governments must focus on stimulating the economy as a whole, rather than protecting specific sectors.

Conclusion

To summarize, the future of capitalism is its past: credit and interest are the engine of growth in the modern economy, but also the foundation of moral economy of capitalism. Like all morality, the moral economy of money is ambivalent: the functional norms are freedom and equality, the factual reality is material constraint and inequality. Average income per person is today 12 times higher than it was 200 years ago (Clark 2007) and this development of 'real wealth' would not have been possible without the financial sphere. But the system-immanent tendency of capital creating inequality requires an authority capable of leaning against the wind, of correcting social injustice, of providing a stable legal framework.

Capitalism remains a fragile construct: uncertainty makes it potentially unstable and the accumulation of wealth in the hands of few is a permanent challenge to the modern idea of justice, which is based on freedom *and* equality. The modern *democratic state* is the ultimate guarantor for the sustainability of capitalism. The democratic state is not the authoritarian imposition of traditional values on a liberal economy, but the instrument by which free and equal citizens jointly determine their preferences and how they wish to set the balance between liberty and equality; the democratic state integrates externalities of policy decisions, which affect all citizens. But the validity of modern norms does not guarantee their implementation in actual life. In Europe, too many governments behave as authoritarian agents, irresponsive to citizens' preferences and life designs. And European citizens have been denied a European government that would allow all of them together to make choices about the policies that determine their prosperity and future wealth. It is time that this changes.

Notes

1. At the G20 Meeting in London, 2 March 2009.
2. At the United Nations in New York, 23 September 2008.
3. The term 'moral economy' was first coined by Edward Palmer Thompson (1971) and James Scott (1977). For an application to the monetary economy, see also Muldrew 1998.
4. BIS, 2008. OTC derivatives market activity in the second half of 2007; Basle.
5. BIS, 2005. Triennial Central Bank Survey; Basle.
6. As Michael Heseltine, a minister in Margaret Thatcher's government once said, 'Ideally government will meet once a year to hand out the subcontracts'.
7. This is the logical consequence of Walras's Law.
8. Keynes explained his Monetary Theory of Production in the Festschrift for Spiethoff in 1933 (Keynes 1987: 408–412). The neoclassical synthesis was developed by Hicks (1937) and later formalized and popularized by Paul Samuelson.
9. See Popper (1995) for the full development of these ideas.
10. For an overview see Sopart (2005).
11. As G. Tremonti (2008) has superbly formulated: 'People no longer believe in the future, but in tomorrow; they no longer believe in the nation, but in the village.'
12. Speech before the European Parliament on 21 October 2008. http://www.spiegel.de/international/europe/0,1518,585558,00.html
13. See Goodhart and Illing (2002) for excepts of his book.

References

Barro, R.J. (1974). 'Are Government Bonds Net Wealth?', *Journal of Political Economy*, 82(6): 1095–1117.

Berlin, I. (2008 [1958]). 'Two Concepts of Liberty', In Henry Hardy, ed. *Isaiah Berlin: Liberty*, Oxford: Oxford University Press, pp. 166–218.

Buiter, W. (2009). The unfortunate uselessness of most 'state of the art' academic monetary economics. http://blogs.ft.com/maverecon/2009/03/the-unfortunate-uselessness-of-most-state-of-the-art-academic-monetary-economics/ as accessed on 28 January 2010.

Clark, G. (2007). *A Farewell to Alms: A Brief Economic History of the World*, Princeton: Princeton University Press.

Demsetz, H. (1968). 'The cost of transacting', *Quarterly Journal of Economics*, 82: 33–53.

Edwards, J. and Fischer, K. (1994). *Banks, Finance and Investment in Germany*, Cambridge: Cambridge University Press.

Esping Andersen, G. (1990). *The Three Worlds of Welfare Capitalism*, Cambridge and Princeton: Polity Press and Princeton University Press.

Filmer, R. (1991). ' "Patriarcha" and Other Writings', In *Johann Summerville*, ed. Cambridge: Cambridge University Press.

Flood, M.D. (1991). *An Introduction to Complete Markets*, Bulletin of the Federal Reserve Bank of St. Louis, March/April, 32–57.

Goodhart, C. (2002). 'Myths about the Lender of Last Resort', In C. Goodhart and G. Illing, eds. *Financial Crises, Contagion, and the Lender of Last Resort*, Oxford: Oxford University Press.

Goodhart, C. and Illing, G. (eds) (2002). *Financial Crises, Contagion, and the Lender of Last Resort. A Reader*, Oxford: Oxford University Press.

Goodhart, C.A.E. (1989). *Money, Information and Uncertainty*, 2nd ed., London: Macmillan Education Ltd.

Hall, P. and David S. (eds) (2001). *Varieties of Capitalism: the Institutional Foundations of Comparative Advantage*, New York: Oxford University Press.

Hicks, J.R. (1937). 'Mr. Keynes and the "Classics": A Suggested Interpretation', *Econometrica*, 5(2): 147–159.

Israel, J. (2004). 'The intellectual origins of Modern Democratic Republicanism (1660–1720)', *European Journal of Political Theory*, 3(1): 7–36.

Marx, K. (1845). Theses on Feuerbach.

Keynes, J.M. (1930). *A Treatise on Money; Collected Writings V*, London: Macmillan.

Keynes, J.M. (1987). *Collected Writings, XIII. The General Theory and After. Part I. Preparation. 1971*, London: Macmillan.

Kindleberger, C.P. (1984). *The Financial History of Western Europe*, London: George Allen & Unwin.

Leuber, K.R. (ed.) (1987). *The Essence of Friedman*, California: Hoover Institution Press.

Muldrew, C. (1998). *The Economy of Obligation: The Culture of Credit and Social Relations in Early Modern England*, London: Macmillan Publishers.

Peter, L. (ed.) (1988). *Locke, John. Two Treatises of Government*, Cambridge: Cambridge University Press.

Popper, K. (1995). *The Open Society and its Enemies*, London: Routledge.

Riese, H. (2001). *Grundelegungen eines monetären Keynesianismus. Ausgewählte Schriften 1964–1999, in Angewandte Theorie der Geldwirtschaft*, Vol. 2, Marburg: Metropolis Verlag.

Scott, J. (1977). *The Moral Economy of the Peasant: Rebellion and Subsistence in Southeast Asia*, New Haven: Yale University Press.

Searle, J. (1995). *The Construction of Social Reality*, London: Penguin.

Sopart, D. (2005). A state-of-art literature report on Varieties of Capitalism approach. NEZ, Munster, 25.01.2005. Download: http://nez.uni-muenster.de/download/Literaturbericht_Dominik%20mit%20Deckblatt.pdf as accessed on 17 March 2010.

Stiglitz, J.E. and Greenwald, B. (2003). *Towards a New Paradigm in Monetary Economics*, Cambridge: Cambridge University Press.

Thompson, E.P. (1971). 'The Moral Economy of the English Crowd in the 18th Century'. *Past & Present*, 50: 76–136.

Tietmeyer, H. (1999). *The Social Market Economy and Monetary Stability*, London: Economica Ltd.

Tremonti, G. (2008). 'La Paura et la Speranza, Mondadori: Milano.

Trichet, J.-C. (2009). Introductory statement with Q&A, Press conference 5 March 2009 www.ecb.int/press/pressconf/2009/html/is090305.en.html

Vitols, S. (1998). 'Are German Banks different?' *Small Business Economics*, 10: 79–91.

3
Reconsidering the Role of Ideas in Times of Crisis

Erik Jones

Introduction

The cluster of economic problems that emerged from and surrounded the growing defaults in United States sub-prime and Alt-A mortgage lending markets is widely regarded as a 'crisis'. Some have even gone so far as to say that this is the worst economic crisis since the 1930s. But is it a crisis because in some real-world sense it threatens to take down the global financial system, or is it a crisis because policymakers in the US and elsewhere finally decided it is time to make a 'decisive intervention' in the markets?

The distinction here is important. If we side with the real-world interpretation, then the timing of events is exogenous and the policy response is endogenous. Policymakers really have to do something to stop the situation from getting out of hand or else all hell will break loose. If we come down on the 'crisis as narrative' side of the question, then the policy response is exogenous and the timing endogenous. Some clever policy entrepreneur finally succeeded in convincing policymakers to accept his or her view of the situation and so convinced them that now is the time to act.

In general terms, Colin Hay argues for the crisis-as-narrative view (Hay 1994, 1996, 1999, 2001). Although he acknowledges that actual events may make it more likely for a crisis narrative to emerge, he regards material conditions as 'at best a necessary but *insufficient* condition for such an intervention' (Hay 2001: 203, emphasis in original). His stated objective is to force us to re-examine the importance of policy ideas and ideational contestation to the process of institutional change. In turn, this should move us away from an historical institutionalist view of change that seems to imply that policy paradigms or ideologies are introduced instantaneously and fully-formed (Hay 2001: 212–213).

There is obvious merit to Hay's general concern to underscore that 'the institutionalization of a paradigm within the state apparatus and the translation of that paradigm into policy are protracted, unpredictable, and often contested processes' (Hay 2001: 213). What is less obvious is how this justifies the elevation of narrative over material concerns. On the contrary, it is far easier to understand the protracted, unpredictable and often contested process of policy development as part and parcel of the struggle to assert control over events in the material world.

The struggle to master events in the real world is particularly obvious when looking at the financial crisis that has been unfolding since August 2007. There are many narratives that surround why this is happening but their influence on policy has been at best inconsistent. The narratives used by policymakers have been determined by events rather than the other way around. Consider Alan Greenspan's testimony before the Congressional Committee on Government Oversight and Reform:

> It was the failure to properly price such risky assets that precipitated the crisis. In recent decades, a vast risk management and pricing system has evolved, combining the best theoretical insights of mathematicians and finance experts supported by major advances in computer and communications technology. A Nobel Prize was awarded for the discovery of the pricing model that underpins much of the advance in derivatives markets. This modern risk management paradigm held sway for decades. The whole intellectual edifice, however, collapsed in the summer of last year....
>
> (Greenspan 2008: 3)

If we take Greenspan at his word, the crisis is material and not narrative – events have shaped the story rather than the other way around. Moreover, the distinction is non-trivial. Greenspan's implied emphasis on the empirical basis of the current crisis is important for at least two reasons. First, it underscores the relationship between policy actions and real-world outcomes. Politicians and policymakers can have important normative debates about where the priorities for action should lie. But before they can go down that road (and even in the absence of political conflict) there is a real-world question to be answered about what will be the effect of a policy action – and, by extension, whether that effect will be sufficient in material terms to bring the crisis to an end. By placing too much emphasis on narrative over material conditions we run the risk of losing sight of the fact that policies should work – meaning have some material impact – and yet often do not. Even Nobel-prize winning stories about how markets function can suddenly come up short.

The second reason for stressing material rather than narrative forces is to avoid the fallacies and anachronisms associated with what Herbert Butterfield (1931) has immortalized as *The Whig Interpretation of History* – reading the past in light of the present. For example, Hay takes the future of the past as given when he asserts that:

> Crisis can thus be seen as a process; a process in which the tendential unity of the state is discursively renegotiated and potentially (re-)achieved as a developmental trajectory is imposed upon the apparatuses and institutions which comprise it. Crisis is a process in which the site of political decision-making shifts from the disaggregated institutions, policy communities, networks and practices of the state apparatus to the state as a centralised and dynamic agent. The state is constituted anew through crisis.
>
> (Hay 1999: 338)

It is hard to see how contemporary actors would recognize themselves in this process or whether they would agree with his characterization of its inner meaning. More likely, they would see themselves as struggling to keep their fingers in the dike while looking around to find something more permanent to plug the holes. As United States (US) Treasury Secretary Hank Paulson (2008) put it when forced to explain his changing position on the use of funds under the Troubled Asset Relief Program (TARP): 'We adjusted our strategy to reflect the facts of a severe market crisis, always keeping focused on our goal: to stabilize a financial system that is integral to the everyday lives of all Americans.' Writing amidst a major crisis – when the past is the present, so to speak – it is easier to recognize how much the narrative of crisis, and the authors of that narrative, are driven by events on the ground.

This chapter develops an argument about the material basis for the ongoing financial crisis in three sections. The first section sets out different models for policy change and sketches a procedure for telling them apart. The second applies the procedure for choosing between the models using the information we have available about the ongoing financial crisis. The third section extends the argument to more general claims about the importance of experiential learning for the policy process.

Characterizing policy change

Like any analytic concept, it is possible to assign many specialized meanings to the word 'crisis'. All such assignments have their use, none constitutes the essential characteristic or 'true' meaning of the word. For my purposes, I adopt a common-use definition similar to the one provided by the *Oxford English Dictionary* (1971: 1178):

> Crisis: … 3. A vitally important or decisive stage in the progress of anything; a turning point; also, a state of affairs in which a decisive change for better or worse is imminent; now applied esp. in times of difficulty, insecurity, and suspense in politics or commerce.

The crux lies in the notion that change is imminent. If things can continue as they are, there is no crisis. If they must change, there is. Of course since we have human agency involved, we could also add a layer of perception – meaning narrative, probability or intuition. If policymakers think, estimate or believe that things cannot continue as they are, then there is a crisis. If they do not think, estimate or believe that change is imminent, then there is not.

That addition of human agency is where the problem begins. Once we start to define crisis in terms of thoughts, estimates, or beliefs, we expose ourselves to the central role of ideas. Human agents cannot think without ideas, they cannot estimate without models and they cannot believe without conviction. On a basic level, we have to admit that ideas are central to human agency. If human agency is essential to our understanding of crisis then ideas – narratives, stories, what have you – are central to that understanding as well.

This leaves us in a chicken-and-egg situation. Do we focus on the ideas and endogenize human agency or do we focus on our human agency and endogenize ideas? Is the argument that any political leader would have responded in that fashion given the state of the art in policymaking at the time, the advice that was available, or the ideational entrepreneurs who dominated the scene? Or is the argument that these particular leaders were instrumental in promoting this specific policy response and without their presence the outcome would have been very different?

The literature contains examples to suit any response. Although I doubt he would agree with my characterization of his work, Andrew Moravcsik's (1998) *Choice for Europe* would set one end of the spectrum, where policymakers are bound to a course of action dictated by prevailing perceptions of the national interest. By contrast, Craig Parson's (2003) *A Certain Idea of Europe* would lie at the other end of the spectrum, where policymakers are essentially ideational entrepreneurs. Kathleen McNamara's (1998) *Currency of Ideas* fits somewhere in between the two; circumstances conspire to constrain the scope for policy alternatives, but there is still room for individual choice.

The symmetry of this array is beguiling – not least because it omits the possibility that the material conditions underlying perceptions are actually running the show. Despite the weight of professional opinion, the lobbying of vested interests, the skill and access of ideational entrepreneurs and the pre-commitments of the flesh-and-blood agents in power, the policy adopted in a given context is determined by what actually works to change the otherwise unsustainable situation in the real world. Obviously, this possibility is fraught with difficulties. Someone has to recognize that the situation is unsustainable, someone has to propose the new policy, someone has to approve it, someone has to implement it and someone has to assess (and accept) the results. Like it or not, there is bound to be a communication of ideas taking place. Nevertheless, it should be possible to distinguish between different causal trajectories where ideas have differing levels of importance.

At this point it is useful to pull together assumptions into ideal types as a first step in the construction of characterizations for different patterns of crisis-response. Since the goal is to model policy change, the two questions to consider are: Is the stimulus for action material or is it ideational? Is the response mechanical or is it deliberate?

Cybernetic – If the stimulus is material and the response is automatic, then the pattern for policy change is cybernetic and ideas are only important insofar as they relate to the design of the switching mechanism (Steinbruner 1974).

Empirical – If the stimulus is material and the response is deliberate, then the pattern for policymaking is empirical. Policy change takes place because the automatic warning lights flashing in the real world indicate that something is wrong and it continues until the change in material conditions is such that those lights stop flashing. Here ideas are important in the design of the warning mechanism (as in the cybernetic model) and also in the efforts of policymakers to make sense of what is happening in the real world. This is the classical scientific world of Kuhn (1970), as described by Hall (1993).

Narrative – If the stimulus is ideational and the response is deliberate, then the pattern for policymaking is narrative in the sense that policy change is optional and takes place only once human agents are committed to a particular course of action. Moreover, policy change continues so long as the new course of action promises to address the reasons for change and to provide advantages over the plausible alternatives. Here ideas play a vital role in the commitment of human agents that change is necessary and that a particular course of action is the most desirable (Blyth 2001, 2002).

Ideological – If the stimulus is ideational and the response is automatic, then the pattern for policymaking is ideological (or tautological) in the same way that a computer program can simulate the behaviour of complex systems according to predetermined rules. Here ideas permeate every aspect of the policymaking process because they constitute the socially constructed reality (or simulcra) within which policymaking takes place. In methodological terms, this pattern hews closely to the neo-Gramscian approach (Bruff 2008).

The cybernetic and ideological models for policymaking (see Figure 3.1) are interesting, but less obviously relevant to the contemporary debate. We have seen cybernetic systems for economic policymaking in the past – as in the classical Gold Standard or the Bretton Woods System – but the cybernetic approach seems less applicable today. Indeed, what is striking about the present situation is the extent to which the policy apparatus has frozen up rather than swinging into action. The ideological model is also not relevant. Rigidly ideological communism has all but vanished, at least in the policy domain. As for ideological market liberalism, most observers agree that is now to a greater or lesser extent socially embedded (Ruggie 1982). Where it does exist, there is less reliance on market liberalism for policy guidance than there is conviction that something about market liberalism must have failed. Here again it is useful to cite Alan Greenspan's recent testimony before the US Congress:

I made a mistake in presuming that the self-interest of organizations, specifically banks and others, were such is [sic] that they were

<table>
<tr><td></td><td></td><td colspan="2">**Response Mode**</td></tr>
<tr><td></td><td></td><td>*Mechanical*</td><td>*Rational*</td></tr>
<tr><td rowspan="2">**Cause or Stimulus**</td><td>*Material*</td><td>Cybernetic</td><td>Empirical</td></tr>
<tr><td>*Ideational*</td><td>Ideological</td><td>Narrative</td></tr>
</table>

Figure 3.1   Four models for decision-making under crisis.

best capable of protecting their own shareholders and their equity in firms.... So the problem here is something which looked to be a very solid edifice, and, indeed a critical pillar to market competition and free markets, did break down. And I think that, as I said, shocked me. I still do not fully understand why it happened and, obviously, to the extent that I figure out where it happened and why, I will change my views. If the facts change, I will change.

(Hearings 2008: 34–35 [lines 768–772 and 780–786])

We can set aside the cybernetic and ideological patterns in the current context, but that does not make it any easier to distinguish between the empirical and narrative alternatives. Both models involve choices made by sentient (or thinking) individuals who operate in some kind of institutional or social context. Ideas and human agency are inseparable in this regard and so it is as likely that the facts changed and so Greenspan changed his mind, as it is that Greenspan changed his mind and so went out in search of different facts. Indeed, he may not have changed his mind as much as we might think (or he might suggest). Completing the sentence from the first Greenspan citation given above:

The whole intellectual edifice, however, collapsed in the summer of last year because the data inputted into the risk management models generally covered only the past two decades, a period of euphoria. Had instead the models been fitted more appropriately to historic periods of stress, capital requirements would have been much higher and the financial world would be in far better shape today, in my judgment. (Greenspan 2008: 4–5).

Fitting the evidence

We need a testing strategy for recognizing meaningful distinctions between the different models. I propose to focus on four characteristics, each of which can assume one of two possible values. These characteristics relate to the nature of the triggering event, the timing of the response, the strategy for policy evaluation and the structure of any resulting evolution over time. Specifically, my interest is:

Whether the trigger is objective or subjective – does the event require perception to have an impact?
Whether the response timing is automatic or deliberate – do policy-makers have to decide on a response?

Whether the evaluation is end-based or rule based – do results matter more than process?

Whether the policy is adaptive or pre-determined – what is the balance between discretion and path dependence once a particular response is in train?

In focusing on these questions about characteristic features, my priority is that all of the patterns or models have elements in common but each is distinct in its combination of features. For example, the cybernetic and empirical models have objective triggers while the triggers for the narrative and ideological models are subjective. By contrast, where the response timing in the cybernetic and ideological models is automatic, the response timing in the empirical and narrative models is deliberate. Evaluation in the cybernetic and empirical models is based on outcomes; evaluation of the narrative and ideological models are based on adherence to process or rules. Finally, while policy evolution in the cybernetic and ideological models is strongly process-driven (and therefore predetermined or path dependent), the empirical and narrative models are adaptive and the solutions they offer can change significantly over time.

By organizing characteristics in this way (see Figure 3.2), we can generate possible tests about how crisis-response models will manifest in terms of the historical record. For the present case, we should focus on those points of difference between the empirical and narrative models – the nature of the trigger and the basis for policy evaluation. Two questions are relevant:

Can we find evidence to suggest that something bad would have happened even if none of our policymakers recognized its significance?

Characteristics	Models			
	Cybernetic	*Empirical*	*Narrative*	*Ideological*
Trigger (*objective/subjective*)	Objective	Objective	Subjective	Subjective
Timing (*automatic/deliberate*)	Automatic	Deliberate	Deliberate	Automatic
Evaluation (*end-based/rule-based*)	End-based	End-based	Rule-based	Rule-based
Evolution (*predetermined/adaptive*)	Predetermined	Adaptive	Adaptive	Predetermined

Figure 3.2   Four characteristics for decision-making models.

Do we have reason to believe that the situation could worsen no matter how confidently, convincingly or consistently our politicians claim to have mastered events?

The only way to answer these questions is to introduce some economic data and to connect that data to the record of events.

The trigger – objective or subjective?

Most analysts agree that the root cause of the current financial crisis can be found in a combination of three factors.

The first factor was the large-scale creation (origination) of sub-prime and alt-A mortgages in the United States that were in turn chopped up and repackaged in the form of collateralized debt obligations and other asset backed securities to be sold on to investors who were unconnected to the mortgage origination process, thus providing more cash for new mortgages.

The second factor was the inappropriate risk-rating of these mortgage backed securities and the growing availability of over-the-counter quasi-insurance cover against default risk in the form of credit default swaps. The poorly rated securities looked like good deals for large investors with access to cheap credit and the ready availability of credit default swap protection made it more attractive for banks to provide cheap credit to large investors.

The third factor behind the financial crisis was the fact that the compensation schemes used across the industry – from the bounties given to mortgage brokers, to the haircuts earned by the people who repackaged the mortgages into securities, to the fees charged by rating agencies and asset portfolio managers, to the bonuses paid to bank executives – created perverse incentives for each of these different sets of actors to disregard or downplay the risks they faced. Meanwhile, the risks continued to mount as more sub-prime and alt-A mortgages were originated and pushed into the wider financial system.

Borrowing again from Hay, this was a heavy 'weight of contradictions'. It was not, however, a crisis. The crisis came when people started to default on their mortgages. These defaults were most evident in the sub-prime category as a percentage of value. But they were also important among alt-A and prime mortgages, which were less likely to go under in percentage terms but which were much larger in terms of absolute values (IMF 2008: 12). This rise in defaults across all mortgage types presented a number of different problems given each of the three factors listed above.

First, as mortgage defaults and delinquencies start to rise, this puts downward pressure on house prices – because repossessed homes sell at a deep discount and because homeowners who default on their mortgages drop out of the housing market. The effect tended to be localized. It was nevertheless important because the distribution of sub-prime mortgages was localized as well. As a general rule, sub-prime mortgage lending concentrates either in areas where household incomes are universally low (which makes sub-prime mortgages the only route to home-ownership) or in areas where house prices rise quickly enough that the appreciation in nominal home values makes the high cost of borrowing at sub-prime seem worthwhile. When house prices start to fall in those areas where mortgages are most risky, homeowners who are already stretched financially face the prospect that they will not be able to refinance their mortgages or sell out without finding themselves with negative equity, meaning they would owe money to the bank at the end of the process. Hence they become more likely to default as well.

Second, the rise in mortgage delinquencies and defaults cut into the value of the mortgage backed securities and so their prices fell. This happened initially in those securities that were most dependent upon sub-prime mortgages and then spread to other instruments (IMF 2008: 13). In turn, investors who held those securities found themselves short of collateral relative to the loans they had taken out to buy them in the first place and so faced bank-initiated margin calls. This forced them to sell some or all of their investments in a declining market, further pushing down prices – not just for mortgage backed securities but for other financial instruments as well.

Third, the combination of mortgage write-downs and margin calls began to put downward pressure on market prices across the board. Shares in financial industries were particularly vulnerable. To begin with, these industries were themselves large investors and so faced direct losses related to the decline in value of mortgage backed securities. Even if they were not directly exposed, they were indirectly vulnerable because they were the ones who made the loans – either to large investors who were taking direct losses or to other financial firms that were losing directly, indirectly or both. Finally, financial firms were the ones who held most of the instruments used to swap protection against credit default. As the crisis worsened, these instruments not only lost value but also made the firms liable to pay default protection, given up their own cash to cover the loses incurred by someone else.

The crisis emerged when all these forces combined to cause a seizure in the interbank lending market in August 2007 (IMF 2008: 3, 78). As a result, the cost of borrowing on the interbank market suddenly shot up and the possibility of borrowing in any quantity was not guaranteed. Indeed, many banks simply stopped lending to some other banks altogether. This played havoc with those banks that depended upon the interbank market to meet their day-to-day liquidity requirements – like the British regional bank, Northern Rock. Once it became known that Northern Rock would have to depend upon the Bank of England for its liquidity, depositors queued up to withdraw their funds and the government had no choice but to step in.

From this description, it is hard to come to the conclusion that the financial crisis is more about perceptions (and narratives) than reality – at least insofar as the perceptions of policymakers are concerned. Market perceptions may be a different matter. To be sure, banks stopped lending to one another for a reason. Depositors staged a run on Northern Rock for a reason as well. Ideas about solvency and loss clearly played a role in the sudden tightening of the interbank lending market. But these ideas had less to do with any deep understanding of the crisis than with the fear that events were moving outside understanding altogether. The freeze in interbank lending had less to do with credit constraints (the lack of money in the system) than with counter-party risk (the fear that you would not get your money back). Banks simply did not know what was on the balance sheets of potential borrowers and so could not assess their creditworthiness. Rather than gamble on the outcome, they choose to hold onto their cash.

The August/September 2007 crisis was a classic moment of Knightian uncertainty – where probabilities could not be calculated because the data did not fit with the available models (Knight 1964). This uncertainty was not read into the situation. It emerged from the confluence of material forces at play. The crisis was not part of a narrative. As the Greenspan quote above suggests, the crisis came when the narrative broke down.

Evaluation – end-based or rule-based?

At this point it is reasonable to agree with writers like Blyth (2002: 35–37) that only ideas can lead you out of a situation of Knightian uncertainty. If you do not have any idea what is happening and someone tells you to do something, your first consideration would be 'why?' But that would be the case under any circumstance. Purposive action requires a purpose and – to be meaningful – that purpose has to be understood. The more interesting question concerns how long the link between action and purpose can be maintained. Fool me once, shame on you: fool me twice, and you have to consider why I am so easily fooled.

Blyth (2002: 34–44) has a five-part theory for how the link between purpose and action can be maintained. First, ideas help to create certainty in crisis – they tell you what to do when the old formulas for policymaking no longer seem to apply. Second, these same ideas become the focal points for collective action by helping individuals to understand their role in any division of labour as well as their stake in the final outcome. Third, these ideas go on to provide a blueprint for the transformation of the prevailing (or pre-existing) institutional environment, telling actors how to make existing endowments conform to new circumstances. Fourth, ideas stimulate the creation of institutional arrangements that are entirely innovative. Finally, ideas can ensure that interests and expectations conform to the new (and newly reformed) institutional framework.

There are two ways to read Blyth's argument – one trivial, the other novel. The trivial reading is as a description of human agency at work. If humans can only act purposively with some idea in mind, then Blyth's framework is just a litany of the different types or manifestations of human action. The novel interpretation is that Blyth reveals the extent to which human agency is guided by ideas – ideas which possess autonomous causal significance insofar as they not only tell us what to do, but why it is in our interests to do so and, indeed, what those interests are in the first place. Here it is useful to quote at length from another of Blyth's works on the subject:

> Such ideas ['causal stories' about the economy that provide agents with an interpretive framework within which they can define, diagnose, and explain a crisis as an event which necessitates a particular set of actions] do more than alter preferences; they reconstitute agents' interests by providing alternative frameworks through which uncertain situations, and the place of agents within them, can be understood.... By defining how the economy works, and the

place of the individual within the economy, crisis-defining ideas both diagnose the disjuncture and in doing so set limits upon the institutional form that will supposedly solve it. (Blyth 2007: 762, emphasis in original)

For this novel interpretation to make sense, the essential benchmark for evaluating the causal chain effected through human agency has to be 'the idea' itself, no matter how complicated or contested that idea may be. The certainty traces back to the idea. So do the collective action, role conceptualization and even perception of self-interest. Existing institutions must adapt to the idea and new institutions must emerge from it. Finally, any stability must derive from the interaction of idea, certainty, action, concept, perception and institutions taken as a whole. Moreover, it is not just economic or institutional stability that is at stake here; social legitimacy depends upon the resonance of the idea with popular understanding as well (Seabrooke 2007). The idea cannot be 'wrong' in any absolute or material sense; it can only be weak as a framework for problem recognition, collective action and subsequent institutionalization. Political might makes the idea 'right'.

The self-referential character of ideas in this interpretation of Blyth is novel in the sense that it departs from how we usually understand human agency – because the solutions define the people and the problem, rather than the other way around. Indeed, it is hard to imagine that policymakers would recognize themselves in the process or even that they would self-consciously embrace ideational consistency as the most useful frame of reference for evaluating policy choices. This leaves two possibilities. One is that policymakers are unaware of the guiding influence of ideas, much as Keynes complained at the end of his *General Theory*. In this case, ideational consistency should reveal itself in the pattern of policy action. The other possibility is that ideational consistency never reveals itself because policymakers jump from one set of ideas to another. Policymaking stops following a narrative pattern and becomes an empirical concern. To illustrate this point it is useful to consider ongoing debates about a range of different policy instruments: collateral rules for central bank credit, government-sponsored bailouts for the financial industry and deposit insurance for commercial banks and money market accounts. In each case, ideational consistency gives way to events on the ground.

The debate about collateral rules dates back to the Northern Rock crisis. Northern Rock required special liquidity from the Bank of England for two reasons. The first was that it could not get sufficient liquidity from the interbank market. The second was that it did not have adequate collateral to borrow from the Bank of England under the existing rules for central bank lending. Prior to the crisis, the Bank of England would not accept mortgages (or mortgage-backed securities) as collateral for central bank lending because it did not want the risk that such instruments implied on its books. By contrast, the European Central Bank (ECB) had looser collateral rules and so – given enough time to organize the paperwork through its Irish subsidiaries – Northern Rock could have gotten liquidity there. The time simply did not exist and so the chairman of Northern Rock went to the Bank of England for exceptional support. Once the Bank of England made that known, Northern Rock's fate was sealed.

With the collapse of Northern Rock, the Bank of England changed its collateral rules to accept mortgages and related instruments. This brought it more in line with ECB practice. That does not mean, however, that the debate over collateral rules was settled. On the contrary, the ECB began to notice that market participants were (potentially) taking advantage of its willingness to accept relatively risky assets. During the summer of 2008, the ECB worked to tighten its collateral rules to prevent such abuse. This tightening was announced on 4 September 2008, just days before the US Treasury allowed Lehman Brothers to collapse. As interbank lending seized up again, the ECB had to put its changes into reverse. The US Federal Reserve loosened its collateral rules as well.

The Lehman Brothers story underscores the confusion about bank bailouts and defaults. In March 2008, the Federal Reserve Bank of New York opened a special lending facility for the investment bank Bear Stearns and then orchestrated a private sector buyout of Bear Stearns by J.P. Morgan Chase. These actions were intended to shield the market from the consequences of a Bear Stearns collapse. The problem was that they were widely interpreted as nurturing moral hazard. Therefore when another investment bank, Lehman Brothers, threatened to become insolvent in September 2008, US Treasury Secretary Hank Paulson declined to intervene. Instead he tried to orchestrate a wholly private sector solution and when that failed he pivoted in order to prepare the markets for Lehman's inevitable demise.

The consequences of Lehman's default were much greater than foreseen. Although Paulson may have thought he could prepare the markets, he underestimated the challenge that such preparation implied. Not only was Lehman an important counter-party in a number of relationships ranging in terms of complexity from interbank lending to complex over-the-counter derivatives contracts, but it was also subject to a huge volume of credit default protection. Far from acting as a brake on moral hazard, the Lehman default revealed the uncertainty surrounding how big a bank has to be in order to be too big to fail. When Lehman's credit instruments went to auction on 10 October 2008 – a key step in the settlement of credit default swap contracts – the New York Stock Exchange went into a rout. In the aftermath, few policymakers were eager to experiment with another banking collapse.

The remaining illustrations all concern near-misses or policy flips. The extension of deposit insurance to commercial banks and money market accounts illustrates both points. The money market accounts were a near miss. The US Treasury hoped to stop depositors from fleeing their existing money market funds by offering to guarantee them for up to a year. What they did not take into account was that this would make money market funds just as safe as regular deposits, despite the fact that money market accounts pay a higher rate of return. Although it would secure money market accounts, the effect might be to trigger a run on regular deposits. The American Bankers Association intervened and the Treasury included a restriction that it would cover only pre-existing accounts in its policy announcement.

The policy flip comes not from the US but from Ireland, Britain and Germany. On Tuesday, 30 September 2008, the Irish government announced that it would guarantee all deposits in Irish banks. This action drew fire from the British Prime Minister and the German Chancellor. Despite their opposition, however, first one then the other had to increase deposit protection in order to offset the flow of funds from their own institutions into Irish banks and to stave off the prospect of a bank panic at home.

It would be possible to extend this list of illustrations to include central bank term-specific liquidity injections, interest rate reductions, bank recapitalization, fiscal stimulus and a host of other policy instruments. The common theme is experimentation. Not everything works; nothing so far has worked for good. Meanwhile, the economic situation continues to worsen as financial turmoil has undermined real economic performance. Whether we recognized it or not, the August 2007 financial crisis constituted an initial turning point. Failure to respond adequately led to further crises in March and September of 2008. By that time what started as a financial crisis transformed into a crisis of the real economy as well. If we evaluate what has happened so far in material terms, we have to regret that the situation is not better (even if we find comfort in the possibility that it could also be worse). That seems to be what policymakers are saying. They do not have a narrative or a bold idea to get us out of this mess. But they remain determined to do whatever they can until they find something that works.

From bad to worse

The shift from financial crisis to a crisis of the real economy was only a single step in a longer chain. At each stage, policymakers have found themselves at a turning point at which the current situation is unsustainable and a failure to act is likely to make matters worse. The point to note, however, is that this worsening of the crisis was not a narrative condition – instead it played out in the material conditions of the real world. To illustrate this point, I focus on three sets of variables: stock market indexes, long-term sovereign debt yields and exchange rates. In all three cases, the point I want to make is the same. After the deepening of the crisis in the Autumn of 2008, conditions in the real economy infected performance at the international level. As a result, countries that were not exposed to sub-prime lending saw their markets jolted; investment instruments that operate outside the interbank lending market saw their yields diverge; and exchange rates between the major currencies shifted dramatically. Of course each of these events can be traced back to the perceptions of market makers – although how consistently or convincingly is a very different concern. The point is that none of these events can be connected to the perceptions of policymakers (at least not ex ante) and yet each is important to how policymakers ultimately had to respond.

The first illustration concerns the stock market performance in Brazil, Russia, India and China – known collectively as the BRICs – as compared to the US. These countries are not closely tied to the securitization markets that have been at the root of the financial problem in the US and Europe. Nevertheless, they are tied through exports to the real performance of the advanced economies. As that performance deteriorated, the stock markets of these emerging economies collapsed – in some cases losing more than three-quarters of their market capitalization.[1] This can be seen in Figure 3.3, which provides comparable indexes for stock market performance in each of the BRICs that are normalized by setting the average for 2002 equal to 100. As these markets lost value, this not only wiped out the investments of a large number of actors in the developing world, but it also exposed investors from Europe and the US to major loses both directly, where they invested in the market, and indirectly, where they provided loans for local investors to buy stocks on the margin.

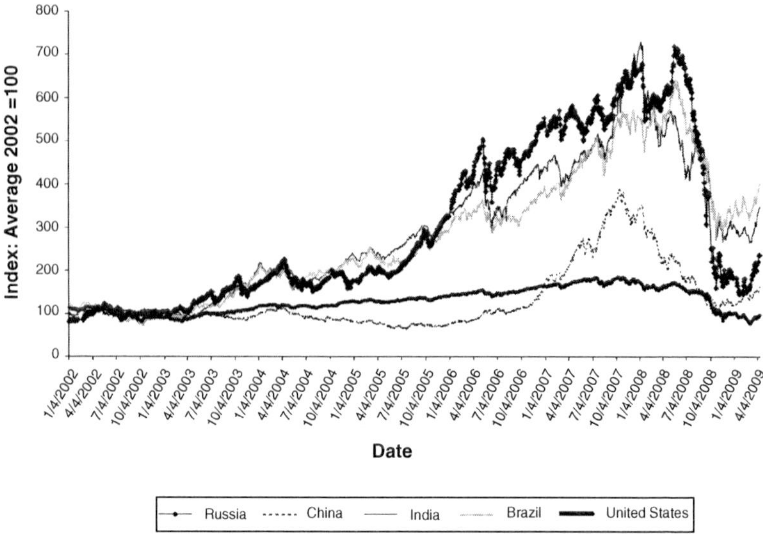

Figure 3.3   Stock market performance.
Source: IHS Global Insight.

The second illustration concerns the yield spreads on long-term sovereign debt issues among highly indebted countries within the euro-zone.[2] As governments across Europe attempted to respond to the sudden economic downturn, they confronted a bond market still confused by the global financial crisis. Within this market, some sovereign debt instruments – like those belonging to Germany – are suddenly very attractive while others – like Ireland or Greece – were the subject of intense speculation. The concern centred on whether a sovereign state in the euro-zone could actually default on its public debt. And while the probability of such an event is low, the pricing implications in the bond market were significant. Where ten-year-long bonds used to have differences of less than one-half of a per cent, suddenly that spread increased by more than a factor of five. This can be seen in Figure 3.4.

The third illustration points to the movement of the dollar, yen and pound against the euro. Exchange rates between the dollar and the euro have long-since departed from anything resembling purchasing power parity and the peak-to-trough movements in that relationship are impossible to explain using macroeconomic 'fundamentals'. Even so, nothing in the first decade of the euro-zone can compare to the wild volatility that erupted during the global financial crisis. Not only did the euro and the dollar move sharply against one another, but

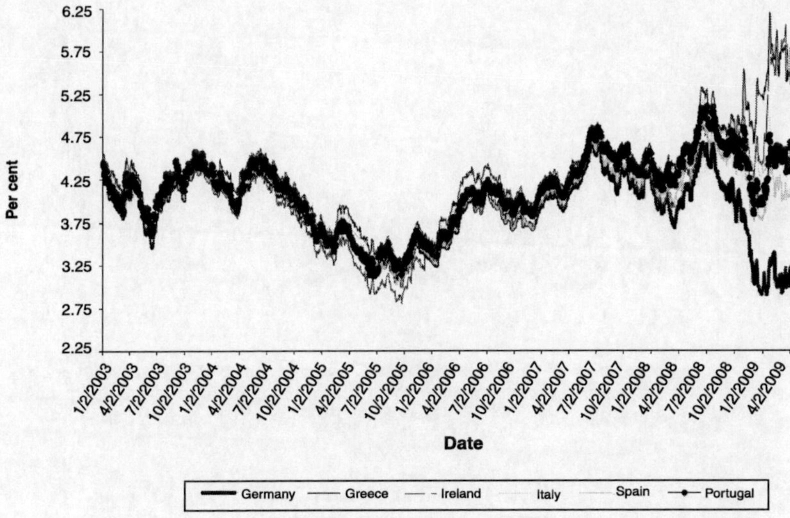

Figure 3.4 Long-term sovereign bond yields.
Source: IHS Global Insight.

the pound–euro and yen–euro exchange rates deviated sharply as well. Explanations for these movements range from portfolio consolidation to an unwinding of the global carry trade. Whatever the cause, however, it is hard to imagine that anyone anticipated these movements before the fact; and it is easy to suggest that policymakers as yet have no idea how best to respond. This exchange rate volatility can be seen in Figure 3.5.

This high degree of exchange rate volatility had a significant impact not only across bilateral currency relationships but across the ensemble of global currency and commodity markets taken as a whole. Once again policymakers faced a bout of uncertainty. The situation could not continue as it was. The question was how should they respond?

The months of March and April 2009 were the worst in terms of financial market performance. Thereafter, stock markets began to recover. Nevertheless, it was clear that the effects on the real economy would continue to accumulate and few were the voices who were quick to declare the problem solved. The prevailing attitude through the end of 2009 was to adopt a wait-and-see approach – hoping that things would continue to get better rather than worse. Underpinning that caution was a fear that the international phase of the crisis was only its most recent manifestation. A political phase may be the next in the round.

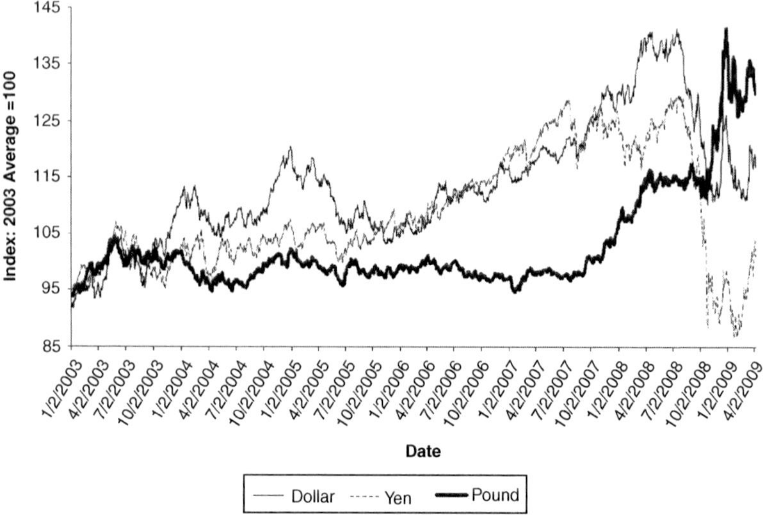

Figure 3.5 Euro exchange rates.
Source: IHS Global Insight.

What does it mean?

If we were going to characterize the pattern of policymaking in the present crisis, the best fit would be that it is empirical rather than narrative. Although real human beings are deliberating about how best to respond and (hopefully) drawing upon the best ideas that the policy and academic communities have to offer, the underlying reality is that the problem they face is a material one and the standards for evaluating policy performance are material as well. Moreover, I think policymakers would easily identify with this characterization.

For social scientists, the implications are more difficult to accept. They not only need to understand how the policy apparatus operates in generating a response to the crisis, but they also need to know how the resulting policies are supposed to work and actually work as well. This means they need to take ideas seriously – not just as the source of policy, but also as the product of interaction between policymakers, policy analysts, academics and the material world.

Of course life would be easier if social scientists only had to take the first element into account. If they could take ideas as exogenous, independent variables, then all they would need to do is show how these ideas penetrate into the political system. Much of the criticism directed at the 'Washington Consensus' in international development seems to go down this route, as does criticism of international responses to the Asian financial crisis. Consider, for example, the contrast between Hall (2003) and Liao (2001).

If ideas really matter, though, they should be treated with greater respect. The burden of proof for those who wish to cast ideas as exogenous variables should be to demonstrate a persistent disconnect from the underlying material reality. This is not an insurmountable obstacle and Blyth (2002), for example, moves at least part way in the right direction. The key is that the tests should be made more explicit. Those who would advocate the causal significance of ideas should claim that material forces were not the trigger for a given crisis only if they can demonstrate their insufficiency. Equally, they should be able to demonstrate that material effects do not form an integral part of policy evaluation as well. No one is denying that politicians are capable of narrating us into crisis. But that is not the same as saying all crisis is narrative, full stop.

Notes

1. For a detailed analysis of the role of emerging markets in the crisis, see Chapter 5.
2. For an analysis of the response to the crisis in the euro-zone, see Chapter 6.

References

Blyth, Mark (2001). 'The Transformation of the Swedish Model: Economic Ideas, Distributional Conflict, and Institutional Change.' *World Politics* 54(October): 1–26.
—— (2002), *Great Transformations: Economic Ideas and Institutional Change in the Twentieth Century*. Cambridge: Cambridge University Press.
Blyth, Mark (2007). 'Powering, Puzzling, or Persuading? The Mechanisms of Building Institutional Orders.' *International Studies Quarterly* 51: 761–777.
Bruff, Ian (2008). *Culture and Consensus in European Varieties of Capitalism: A 'Common Sense' Analysis*. Basingstoke: Palgrave Macmillan.
Butterfield, Herbert (1931). *The Whig Interpretation of History*. Italy: Eliohs Electronic Library of Historiography.
Greenspan, Alan (2008). 'Testimony of Dr Alan Grenspan'. Washington, D.C.: United States House of Representatives, Committee of Government Oversight and Reform (23 October).
Hall, Peter. A. (1993). 'Policy Paradigms, Social Learning, and the State: The Case of Economic Policymaking in Britain.' *Comparative Politics* 25(3): 275–296.
Hall, Rodney Bruce (2003). 'The Discursive Demolition of the Asian Development Model.' *International Studies Quarterly* 47: 71–99.

Hay, Colin (1994). 'Crisis and the Discursive Unification of the State.' In P. Dunleavy and J. Stanyer, eds *Contemporary Political Science 1994*. Belfast: Political Studies Association, pp. 236– 245.

Hay, Colin (1996). 'Narrating Crisis: The Discursive Construction of the "Winter of Discontent".' *Sociology* 30(2): 253–277.

Hay, Colin (1999). 'Crisis and the Structural Transformation of the State: Interrogating the Process of Change.' *British Journal of Politics and International Relations* 1(3): 317–344.

Hay, Colin (2001). 'The Invocation of External Economic Constraint: A Geneology of the Concept of Globalization in the Political Economy of the British Labour Party, 1973–2000.' *The European Legacy* 6(2): 233–249.

Committee on Oversight and Governmental Reform (23 October 2008). 'Hearings: The Financial Crisis and the Role of Federal Regulators.' Washington, DC. Web site: http://oversight.house.gov/index.php?option=com_content&task=view&id=3470&Itemid=2 as accessed on 28 January 2010.

IMF (2008). 'Financial Stress and Deleveraging: Macrofinancial Implications and Policy.' *Global Financial Stability Report*. Washington, DC: International Monetary Fund.

Knight, Frank H. (1964). *Risk, Uncertainty and Profit*. New York: Reprints of Economic Classics, Augustus M. Kelley, Bookseller.

Kuhn, Thomas S. (1970). *The Structure of Scientific Revolutions, Second Edition, Enlarged*. Chicago: University of Chicago Press.

Liao, Kun-jung (2001).'The Developmental State, Economic Bureaucracy and Financial Crisis in Asian Societies.' *Journal of Contingencies and Crisis Management* 9(1): 36–45.

McNamara, Kathleen R. (1998). *The Currency of Ideas: Monetary Politics in the European Union*. Ithaca: Cornell University Press.

Moravcsik, Andrew (1998). *The Choice for Europe: Social Purpose and States Power from Messina to Maastricht*. London: UCL Press.

Oxford English Dictionary (1971). *The Compact Edition*. Oxford: Oxford University Press.

Parsons, Craig (2003). *A Certain Idea of Europe*. Ithaca: Cornell University Press.

Paulson, Henry M., Jr. (2008). 'Fighting the Financial Crisis, One Challenge at a Time.' *New York Times* (18 November).

Ruggie, John Gerard (1982). 'International Regimes, Transactions, and Change: Embedded Liberalism in the Postwar Economic Order.' *International Organization* 36(2): 379–415.

Seabrooke, Leonard (2007). 'The Everyday Social Sources of Economic Crises: From "Great Frustrations" to "Great Revelations" in Interwar Britain.' *International Studies Quarterly* 51: 795–810.

Steinbruner, John D. (1974). *The Cybernetic Theory of Decision: New Dimensions of Political Analysis*. Princeton: Princeton University Press.

4
Challenging the Dollar in International Monetary Relations? The Lost Opportunities of the Euro

Henrik Plaschke

Introduction

As is often claimed, the European Union (EU) remains a huge economic entity in the global political economy but yet has problems in or is incapable of transforming its economic potentials into political influence or power. In terms of its external policies the EU disposes of several instruments – political as well as economical. Monetary policies – and in particular the euro – in this regard remain an interesting case. Money is intrinsically a social and political as well as an economic device and with the euro the EU has created a potentially powerful instrument for shaping and influencing the global political economy, as well as for strengthening the autonomy of Europe in global political and economical affairs. The domestic and the international side of the euro are interlinked. Yet the focus of the present contribution will be limited to the external role of the euro while the domestic side of the euro will only be touched upon when relevant for the external side. In more precise terms we shall deal with the question of whether the euro is increasingly becoming an international currency, that is, a currency increasingly used in international transactions not only between Europe and the rest of the world but also in transactions between third-countries. This inevitably also raises the question of whether the euro may challenge the role of the dollar as the present main reserve currency in the international monetary system.

The international status of the euro has been on the international agenda since the very creation of the euro a decade ago. It has gained even further attention in the wake of the global financial crisis as the latter could have been expected to imply an increased questioning of the global role of the dollar. While the international role of the dollar *is* currently under scrutiny, the EU and its currency have not played any sort of proactive role in this regard. The financial crisis has – if anything – rather exposed the lacking action of the EU with regards to global monetary and financial governance as well as the lack of credibility of the euro as an alternative to the dollar in the global political economy.

The euro as an international currency – why?

There is no simple reply to the question of whether the euro *should* become an increasingly international currency. Correspondingly it is clear that diverging replies to this question exist – among decision-makers, academics and elsewhere. The present text will not attempt to balance the pros and the cons of the debate. Rather we shall start from the premise (to be discussed further below) that the euro may have the potential for becoming an international currency. We will then proceed to argue why an increasing internal role could have an important impact both on the global political economy and on the EU. At least five points are to be emphasized:

Firstly, an increased use of the euro as an international currency may contribute to an easing of the international monetary and financial imbalances and disequilibria linked to the highly unstable status of the current international reserve currency: the dollar. There is nothing new in the unstable nature of the dollar – it dates back to the early 1970s; however, it is also appropriate to note that the present situation of the American economy, characterized by among other things highly significant balance-of-payments as well as budgetary deficits, may prove problematic to the continued international role of the dollar. It may also be noted that we are presently for the first time witnessing a situation in which some kind of an alternative to the dollar – the euro – exists. Compared to the situation in the previous decades of dollar instability this is a radically new situation.

Secondly, the issue of an international reserve currency is far from limited to its monetary and financial dimensions. It is intimately linked to questions of international power and to the political ruling of the international economy. US global dominance and hegemony rest among other things on the international role of its currency. Therefore an increased use of the euro as an international currency may also pose a challenge to US global supremacy.

Thirdly, the international position of the euro could be an important instrument for the strengthening of the international position of the EU. An increased role for the EU in global governance and a relative strengthening of the position of the EU with respect to other international actors may develop not only via, for example, the creation of common foreign and security policies (CFSP), but also via a greater European monetary and financial autonomy. A stronger international position of the euro and a lesser degree of dependence on the dollar would appear to be crucial in this respect.

Fourthly, an increased international role of the euro can hardly be realized without a significant impact on internal European political and economic structures and processes. A greater international role of the euro is hardly thinkable without a clearer political decision making structure with regard to economic policies and without a stronger institutional representation in international institutions linked to international economic policymaking (for example, in the IMF, the G8 and the G20). Currently the EU more often than not speaks with more than one voice – not only in, for example, CFSP matters – but also in issues of international economic policymaking.[1] Similarly a stronger international role of the euro may have a significant economic impact on the European economy: some sort of domestic stability could perhaps be seen as a precondition for the internationalization of the euro and furthermore the latter may have important impacts, for example, on financial markets and public debt. While the cross-border and European dimension of financial markets has been developing drastically, public debts remain fragmented along national lines and the spreads over rates on government bonds testifies to the fact that markets operators or fund owners do not assess the qualities of national public debts in the same way. Currently there is no such thing as a European public debt and it is questionable to what extent the euro may internationalize without a common European public debt.

Fifthly, it seems rather clear that the strengthening of the international role of the euro is a political objective for some member states of the EU. For example, for France an increased role of the euro has often been seen as a means to (counter) balance the dominating position of the dollar and of the USA in the international system – politically and economically. However, hardly all member states share this objective. The aim of strengthening the international role of the euro seems to be shared by the European Parliament and perhaps by the Commission while the European Central Bank (ECB) is much more reluctant in this regard. Governments and other social and economic actors diverge in their conception of European objectives and interests in this area. Thus a strengthening of the international role of the euro is far from politically neutral – neither in global nor in internal European terms.

Tales of the euro – valuation effects and regional dynamics

Since the creation of the euro in 1999 the question of the international status of the euro has been widely discussed and for several years the quantitative role of the euro as an international reserve currency seemed to be increasing. One reason for this development was that the euro took over the role of the previously existing national currencies – in particular that of the German mark. A number of observers have been led to rather optimistic predictions regarding the potential of the euro in the international economy[2] while others took a more cautious or pessimistic position.[3] The optimistic positions have been echoed by more official writings from, for example, the Commission (2008) while, for example, the ECB and the Bank for International Settlements (BIS) have taken a more balanced view.

It would be premature to draw any final conclusions as regards the potential of the euro, but at least we may note that recent developments seem to indicate that this initial international growth of the euro has come to an end or at least to have lost its vigour – particularly since 2003. Developments after 2003, however, have to some extent been blurred by the appreciation of the euro against the dollar. If we exclude valuation effects, the share of the euro in international reserves is at the moment below the share of the currencies presently constituting the euro in the 1980s and early 1990s.[4] Similarly we may note that in political terms the development of the euro hardly seems to have stimulated any form of political action from the European side. The Commission (2008) has also noted that the international role of the euro is limited both by the lack of an international strategy of the euro and by the lack of an international political representation.

There is no simple way of defining and measuring the international role of a currency – and hence of the euro. Both for conceptual and for statistical reasons it is difficult to get a comprehensive picture of the role of different international currencies. These questions will not be dealt with any further in the present paper.[5] However, a few remarks do seem necessary.

It is current in monetary analysis to distinguish between three different functions of a monetary unit: (1) As a medium of exchange; (2) as a unit of account; and (3) as a store of value. Furthermore these three different functions exist both at the level of states (including central banks) and at the level of private actors (firms, banks, funds, investment companies and so on). These three functions are interlinked and cannot be seen in isolation from each other. They may – but they need not – coincide. In principle the same actor may thus choose, for example, one currency for savings (that is, as a store of value) and another currency for payments (that is, as a medium of exchange and/or as a unit of account), while public and private actors in principle may use different currencies for the same purposes. Similarly it may also be noted that the international role of the euro develops in slightly different ways when we look at its three different functions.[6] These points have been extensively discussed in the previously quoted papers and I shall not pursue them any further here. In the following discussion I shall focus on the role of the euro in the foreign exchange reserves of central banks – an indicator frequently used, for example, in publications from the ECB, BIS and the IMF and where comparatively good empirical material is available.[7] Special attention, however, will be given to an aspect mentioned, for example, by both the ECB and the BIS but whose importance remains perhaps somewhat underrated, that is, the significance of valuation effects and composition effects and their relative role in explaining the use of different currencies, for example, as part of international currency reserves.

In order to clarify the significance of this point let me start with a quote from a recent ECB report on the international role of the euro:

> the share of the euro [in the foreign exchange reserves of Central Banks] increased by around 1.5 percentage points between December 2006 and December 2007 when measured at current exchange rates. Corrected for exchange rate fluctuations, however, the share of the euro actually declined by around 1.5 percentage points.
>
> (ECB 2008a, p. 9)

Elsewhere in the same report it is noted that:

> the share of the euro in international reserves rose gradually from 18% in 1999 to around 25% in 2003. Since then, the share of the euro has remained relatively stable, hovering around 24–25% and reaching 26.5% in December 2007 ... this recent increase occurred almost entirely as a result of positive valuation effects. The gradual rise in the share of the euro since its launch in 1999 has been most pronounced in developing countries, where it increased from 18% to 29% in 2007. Among the industrialised countries, the share of the euro in foreign

exchange reserves rose gradually in line with the aggregate trend until early 2003. Thereafter, the share of the euro in industrialised countries declined somewhat until early 2004 and has remained broadly stable at around 20% since then.

These trends are partly driven by valuation effects, notably by the impact of exchange rate changes on the value of euro-denominated reserves. When currency shares in international reserves are measured at constant exchange rates, the overall trends are less pronounced. Developing countries are seen to have increased their holdings of euro-denominated assets relative to other assets until mid-2005 .... Since then, they have somewhat reduced their relative exposure to euro-denominated assets. Constant exchange rate shares for the euro in the reserves held by industrialised countries suggest that these countries, after a period of increasing their exposure to euro-denominated assets, decreased euro-denominated assets relative to other currencies in the first quarter of 2003 and the first quarter of 2004.

(2008a, pp. 60–1)[8]

What is the significance of these observations? In order to clarify the discussion we may refer to Figure 4.1 which shows the developments

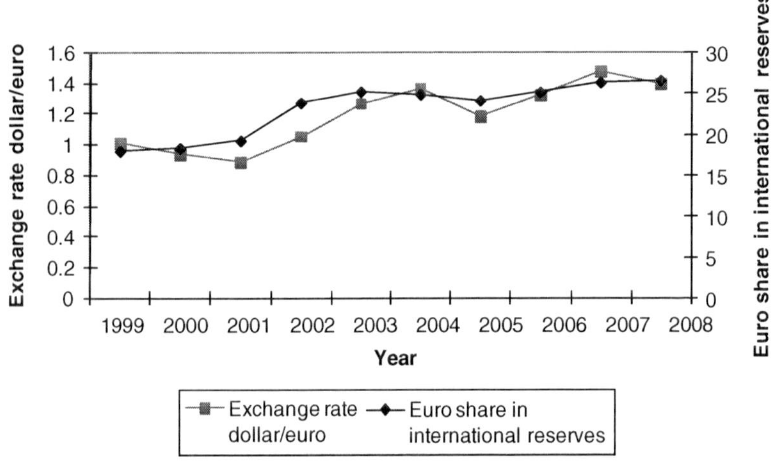

Figure 4.1 Euro share in international reserves and the dollar/euro exchange rate.
Source: Calculated from COFER figures, September 2009.

in, respectively, the exchange rate between the dollar and the euro and the share of the euro (measured in current prices) in the international reserves of central banks as reported by the IMF. Several observations can be made from this figure.

Firstly, we may note – as pointed out previously – the increased international role of the euro since its creation ten years ago – the euro today is the world's second international currency.[9] Secondly, it is striking that the period in which the role of the euro has increased significantly is limited to the first part of the decade. In the period stretching from 1999 to 2003 the share of the euro grew remarkably and this development was not due to valuation effects. In this period one may indeed argue that the increased international role of the euro tends to *precede* developments in the exchange rate of the euro, that is, its appreciation. The peak point of the euro share is reached in 2003. After 2003 the euro share of the euro remains rather stable. Therefore – and this is the third point – in the period after 2003 the rather moderate growth in the international role of the euro can be 'explained' by the increased value of the euro in relation to the dollar. Correspondingly the euro share in 2007 or 2008 is below the euro share of 2002 or 2003 when measured in constant exchange rates (cf. Figure 4.2). Lastly – the fourth point – it is too early to assess the possible impact of the financial crisis on the international euro share in statistical terms. The latest available report by the ECB – published in July 2009 (ECB 2009) – makes the point that

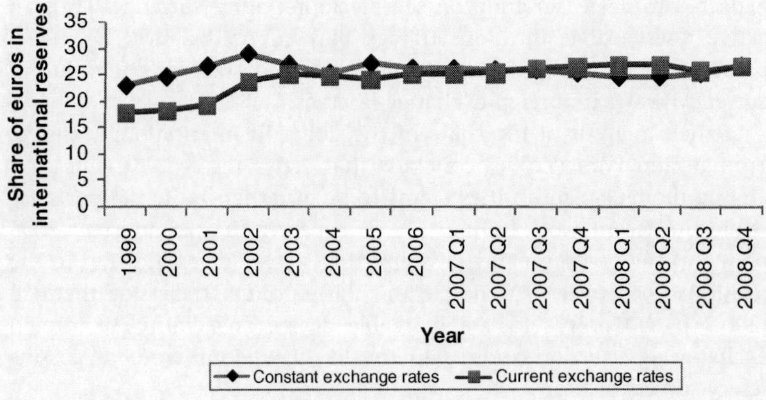

Figure 4.2 Euro share in international reserves-constant and current exchange rates.
Source: ECB 2009, Table 10.

the financial crisis has had no notable impact on the composition of international reserves. The shares of different currencies tend to remain relatively stable over time and this tendency has not been altered by the financial turmoil.

Let us now try to reformulate the significance of the points developed above.

As a convenient starting point we may refer to a distinction between different types or strategies for foreign exchange reserve diversification. Truman and Wang (2006) distinguish between three diversification forms relating to different reactions towards changes in the relative values of the different currencies constituting international reserves: (1) passive reserve diversification; (2) active reserve diversification; and (3) stabilizing reserve diversification or portfolio rebalancing.

Passive diversification implies the absence of a strategy towards changes in the composition of your reserves: if the value of (some of) the currencies constituting your reserves changes, the share of the different currencies constituting your reserve portfolio as defined in value terms may also change even if you do not react to these changes.

Active reserve diversification implies the following of market trends: you purchase a currency whose value is increasing (or expected to increase) and you sell a depreciating currency. Thus active reserve diversification may reinforce the upwards or downwards movement of a currency.

Stabilizing reserve diversification or portfolio rebalancing implies the opposite: you purchase a currency whose value is decreasing (or expected to decrease) and you sell an appreciating currency. Thus an active reserve diversification strategy may counterbalance the movement of the exchange rate of a currency and stabilize the value of currency shares in foreign exchange reserves.

In their analysis of the share of the dollar in international reserves Truman and Wang (2006) conclude that active reserve diversification among monetary authorities seems to be of rather limited importance while the recent work by Lim (2007) covering the period 1999–2005 points to the predominance of stabilizing reserve diversification in the relationship between the dollar and the euro. On their side the ECB (2007, p. 45) points to 'a remarkable degree of stability' of foreign exchange reserves and points to the likely predominance of passive reserve diversification.

It would be premature to draw any final conclusions regarding the respective roles of the three diversification forms in empirical terms. It is striking, however, that active reserve diversification seems to be of quite limited importance while both passive and stabilizing reserve diversification may both play a role, but in different contexts.[10] What these two forms share is, among other things, that they do not contribute to the questioning of the international role of the dollar and the rise of the euro as an alternative reserve currency.

If we were living a process in which the euro was gradually gaining ground with regard to the dollar – the euro slowly catching up with the role of the dollar as the dominating international reserve currency – we should witness a process in which central banks (and perhaps other actors buying and selling international currencies) were gradually acquiring more and more euros and getting less and less dollars as measured in constant prices (that is, corrected for exchange rate fluctuations). And when the exchange rate of the euro is more or less persistently appreciating (this has been the trend since 2002 and until early 2008) central banks should be responding by acquiring more and more euros as measured in constant prices (that is, corrected for exchange rate fluctuations). In the terminology of Truman and Wang this would correspond to an active reserve diversification strategy. But this is seemingly not what is happening. In relative terms market actors are acquiring fewer euros – even if these fewer euros are worth more and more when measured, for example, in dollars. In the terminology of Truman and Wang this would correspond to a portfolio rebalancing strategy.

This point could also be formulated in terms of transaction versus portfolio objectives in the composition of the currency reserves of central banks as discussed by the ECB. When measured in current exchange rates the relative variation in the shares of different currencies in the reserves of central banks is significantly higher than when measured at constant exchange rates. This point, on the one hand, indicates that variations in exchange rates 'explain' a significant part of the changes in the relative share of different currencies and, on the other hand, that transaction motives could be more important than portfolio motives in explaining choices regarding the composition of currency reserves.[11]

Let us close this point by underlining that the fact that the increasing role of the euro essentially reflects valuation effects – the increasing value of the euro exchange rate – does not imply that the process is of no significance. The value – or purchasing power – of a basket of currency reserves is indeed important. If, however, we are interested in investigating whether the euro is developing into a new international reserve currency the share of the euro as measured at current exchange rates constitutes a rather poor – not to say misleading – indicator. This seems to be the position of the ECB also.[12] The publications of the Commission present a somewhat more superficial analysis based on current exchange rate measurements.[13]

We shall return to the question of how to interpret the role of valuation and composition effects and their relative significance below. However, let us first add a few comments on another issue in measurement: the regional dimension of the international use of the euro. We shall close the present section with a couple of remarks in this regard.

Until now the discussion has focused on global developments and aggregate figures. However, as underlined by the ECB, for example, the internationalization of the euro is 'characterised by a strong institutional and regional pattern' (ECB 2007, p. 74). The crux of the matter is that the international spread of the use of the euro is to a significant degree confined to countries having close links to the EU: either in terms of geographical neighbourhood or in terms of political and/or institutional links (for example, EU Member States not being part of the euro-zone and candidate countries). The ECB summarizes this point in the following way: 'One of the most prominent factors [driving the international role of the euro] remains geographical, economic, financial and institutional proximity to the euro area.' (ECB 2008a, p. 9).

This is a remarkable observation: why should proximity play such a crucial role in a world where distance and borders are supposed to be of next to no importance? In the world of money and finance which supposedly is highly globalized? Let us conclude this point by noting that it seems more appropriate to talk about a *regionalization* than about an *internationalization* of the euro.[14] The euro is increasingly taking the character of a regionally dominating currency while it remains subordinate to the dollar in global terms. The increasing role of the euro in regional terms may be characterized as institutionally rather than market-driven[15] while the somewhat more modest development of the euro in global terms may be seen as market-driven rather than institutionally driven.

Learning from theory?

A number of attempts to identify the factors leading a national currency to acquire the status of an international currency have been made in the area of international economics.[16] Thus Chinn and Frankel (2008, pp. 56–59) summarize these factors under the following headings: (1) the relative size of national economies (in terms of output and trade), (2) the organization of national financial markets (for example, size and depth of financial markets), (3) the degree of confidence in the value of the currency, and (4) the phenomena of network externalities (economies of scale and economies of scope). The list of factors suggested by Papaioannou and Portes (2008, pp. 19–20) is roughly similar to that of Chinn and Portes but it has the advantage of focusing more explicitly on economic strength as measured by growth rates. It also explicitly includes a political dimension by its emphasis on political stability and geopolitical strength. It is often pointed out that the above-mentioned factors present a relatively high degree of inertia: they are likely to change only in the long run.

It is hardly questionable that such factors do play a crucial role in promoting the internationalization of national currencies.[17] The problem, however, is whether this list of economic factors can be considered exhaustive. The factors identified above essentially focus on a state of affairs – that is, what characterizes an international currency *once it is established* as such – and not on the *processes* that may be implied in a perhaps contradictory and open-ended process of transition and competition between currencies and their states. They tend to paint a static rather than a dynamic picture.

A more dynamic vision would possibly require a more explicit taking into account of political and other social factors and their impact on the international status of national currencies.[18] Similarly more attention to the potential political and economic contradictions linked to the situation of an international currency might also be relevant: factors such as the (lack of) compatibility between the national and the international roles of a national currency,[19] the relationships between the financial system of a country issuing a currency having an important international role and its long-term process of economic growth and transformation,[20] as well as the relations between, on the one hand, exchange rate and monetary stability and, on the other hand, growth and structural change,[21] are all factors that may merit further attention in this context.

It is, however, beyond the ambitions of the present chapter to suggest a general systemic theoretical analysis of the mechanisms involved in the development of international currencies. We do not have many historical examples of transitions involving the rise and fall of national currencies as international currencies, and generalizations are hence not readily available. On the other hand, when faced with the task of understanding the processes involved in the internationalization of the euro there is hardly any reason not to take inspiration from the theoretical clues briefly surveyed above – supplemented by various critical points alluded to in the previous discussion. These points, however, need further development.

I would thus suggest an added emphasis on (1) a more explicitly institutionalist approach to monetary theory and analysis, (2) processes rather than states of affairs, (3) the role of political and ideological factors, (4) the role of ideas and interpretation and (5) the possible tensions between some of the above-mentioned economic factors – in particular related to the relationship between stability, finance and growth.[22]

Institutionalist economists such as, for example, Keynes and Polanyi have pointed to the social and institutional side of money. Keynes considered money as 'a subtle device for linking the present to the future' (1973[1936], p. 294) and Polanyi (1957[1944]) considered money – along with labour and land – as a fictitious commodity. We may also refer to money as a public good – a point which also emphasizes the non-commodity and institutional nature of money. Political scientists such as Ruggie (1982) and Helleiner (1994) among others have also stressed the social and political nature of international monetary regimes; and Widmaier (2003, 2004) has suggested a constructivist institutionalist approach to the analysis of international monetary affairs. Where do these points lead us in understanding the nature of international currencies?

Several points should be emphasized here: firstly, it is striking that international currencies are usually *national* currencies circulating internationally. In other words we may speak of *national* international currencies rather than of *international* international currencies.[23] International currencies have always been economically and politically backed by their states of origin. Secondly, the fact that international currencies are national involve a potential contradiction between the domestic political-economic priorities of the state issuing the international currency and the perceived needs of the global economic system (or other states) in terms of, for example, liquidity and stability. Thirdly, the question of international currency inevitably has a crucial *political* dimension – it is subject to interests, actors and strategies, and links to other political issues may exist and/or develop – whether functionally or politically. Hence not only market competition (liquidity, stability, economies of scale and so on) but also political interests, strategies and identities may shape and influence the role and status of different currencies. Obviously factors emanating from market competition and factors of a more political and/or social nature may interact. Processes of market competition and currency competition do not unfold in a political and institutional vacuum. They are shaped and influenced by politics, institutions, ideology and culture.

Let me – in order to simplify matters – distinguish between two different modes of internationalizing a currency.[24] On the one hand, a mode based on competition and market selection and, on the other hand, a mode based on institutional and political arrangements. These two modes may be combined and they may also reinforce each other mutually. Nevertheless it is important to distinguish between these two modes.

The market mode implies that market operators should select the currency or currencies to be used internationally without the presence of the visible hands of states and/or central banks. A competitive principle will be involved. The availability of liquidity (for example, for transaction motives) and stability (for example, for portfolio motives) are likely to be the decisive factors in a competitive selection. However, availability of liquidity and stability may not marry that easily. An ample supply of liquidity may imply too little stability while a high degree of stability may imply tight liquidity. In a neoclassical textbook market such a problem would be fixed by the usual demand and supply schedule, but, in view of the non-commodity characteristics of money underlined above, it is hardly justifiable to treat money according to such a model. Money is rather to be seen as a fictitious commodity or as a public good.

One may indeed argue that the currency, or currencies, susceptible to being selected via competitive principles is likely to be a scarce currency, that is, a currency emanating from a country enjoying a balance-of-payments surplus. If not compensated by other means[25] this, however, is likely to imply a deflationary constraint on the international economy. A scarcity-based selection is not conducive to an ample supply of liquidity – in particular when bearing in mind that the supply of liquidity of an international currency is not only for transactions between the country issuing the international currency and other countries but also for transactions and portfolio motives not involving the country issuing the international currency (that is, transactions between third countries).

As an example of a deflationary constraint emanating from such a market selection we may refer to the case of Western Europe in the late 1970s and 1980s where the German Mark, as a consequence of substantial German balance-of-payments surpluses to a certain extent, was selected by market actors as an international currency with little or no support from the visible hands of the German monetary and political authorities. This resulted in strong deflationary consequences on 'non-German' Europe – and in the last instance – also in a political reaction: the strategy of Europeanizing German monetary policies by the creation of a common currency.

An institutional and/or political mode implies some sort of a shared vision and agreement on matters like the rules and regulations of the international monetary and financial system regarding the creation of liquidity, the financing of deficits, the fixing of exchange rates and the balancing between domestic and international needs and priorities. These different elements may be combined in several ways. Among the precondition for an institutional solution to be realized at least the following need to be singled out:

(i)   A sufficient economic strength to supply the international economic system with adequate liquidity or means of payment; this point constitutes a link to the competition based selection principle discussed above. A currency with insufficient economic strength is unlikely to be able to function as an international currency.
(ii) The existence of a political structure governing monetary decisions and policies and facilitating the existence of action in the area of monetary policies; and
(iii) The existence of some sort of a shared vision regarding policies, priorities and economic understandings.

The Bretton Woods system as founded in 1944 may be seen as an example of an institutional solution based on asymmetry, American hegemony and a Keynesian inspired vision of 'embedded liberalism' (Ruggie 1982). It is a well-known fact from analyses of the Bretton Woods Agreements that the post-Second World War international monetary system was the result not only of economic balances of power but also of, for example, negotiations, clashes of visions, diverging political-economic interests and negotiated compromises.[26] Furthermore, the selection of a strong national currency (the dollar) as the international reserve currency was linked to the establishing of a set of institutional mechanisms facilitating the functioning of the Bretton Woods system and partly compensating the asymmetries between Europe and the USA. The deflationary effects of the dollar-scarcity until 1958 were compensated by the European Payments Union, the American acceptance of limits on short-run capital movements and so on.

There is no reason to recall the history of the Bretton Woods system in further detail here. We may simply note that the Bretton Woods system defined a framework for a compromise between the perceived domestic

American needs and the perceived needs of (parts of) the international economic system for a couple of decades. The compromise started to break apart when American priorities (national and/or international) could no more be reconciled with the perceived needs of the international economic system – the dollar based Bretton Woods system was based on a *national* international currency and not on an *international* international currency and the abundance of dollars emanating from US deficits provided not only plenty of liquidity but also increasing instability.

Rather than attempting to draw parallels or precise lessons from the two – very different – cases briefly alluded to above I shall now discuss the question of the internationalization of the euro in the light of the factors discussed until now.

European economic and monetary governance and the internationalization of the euro

In the discussion above I have distinguished between two different modes of internationalizing a currency: a market selection based mode and an institutionally based mode. It has also been noted that the institutionally based mode is unlikely to work unless it is supported by a sufficiently strong economic foundation while the market selection based mode has deflationary consequences. If we use this distinction to characterize the present form of internationalization of the euro we may argue that the euro is essentially internationalized via the market selection mode – at least when we refer to internationalization in general.[27]

If we look at the political and institutional mechanisms framing the internationalization of the euro the following three points should be underlined:

(i) The ECB is explicitly favouring a market selection of international currencies. It has no policy or declared priorities in this regard and wishes neither to promote nor to hinder a possible internationalization of the euro.[28] This attitude may reflect the underlying idea that 'developments in the international use of the euro are the outcome of decisions taken by market participants' as it is formulated by the President of the ECB (ECB 2007, p. 7). It may be discussed whether this idea is supposed to reflect the underlying realities of the international economy, whether it is supposed to represent an underlying normative ideal vision, or whether the two (realities and ideals) in some sense are supposed to coincide. In practice the implications of the viewpoint of the ECB are that the trajectory of the euro is left in the hands not only of market participants but also of other actors in the international economy, including other central banks with more activist and/or offensive attitudes as well as various forms of investment funds.[29]

(ii) Similarly the EU as such has no international strategy for the euro. Thus, Padoa-Schioppa (2004, p. 176) – speaking with the experience of an insider[30] – in 2004 talked about 'a reluctant global actor' and noted that it is 'somewhat paradoxical that, in the process of stipulating ad hoc arrangements on who should speak or act on behalf of euroland, the main advocates of a minimalized role were the Europeans themselves. There were more divisions among them than between them and the Americans' (2004, p. 177). Five years later the passivity of the euro-zone is openly regretted by the Commission in its status report on the euro after ten years: 'the euro area must therefore **build an international strategy** commensurate with the international status of its currency. Following a successful first decade, the euro area…is now called upon to develop a clear and all encompassing strategy on international economic and financial affairs.' (Commission 2008, p. 11, emphasis in the original). In view of the importance that the Commission is seemingly attaching to this issue – we may recall that it is mentioned in the less than one page Foreword to the report – one could have expected it to be thoroughly analysed in the remaining part of the report. What could or would a strategy be like in terms of first steps, actors, objectives, instruments, linkages to other policies and/or issue areas and so on? And yet – after the Foreword and the Introduction – the report never returns to this question. Why attach so much importance to a point and then forget about it? It does in any case remain somewhat obscure how an international strategy is to be developed when the ECB by its emphasis on the neutral stance on the international use of the euro refuses the very idea of a strategy.

(iii) The euro area has no common external representation in international financial and monetary fora such as the IMF – a fact which is equally noted with regrets by the Commission in its status report (Commission 2008, pp. 6 & 11). The euro area speaks with several voices in international monetary and financial matters – a point which complicates the development of common policies and strategies and blocks the euro area in exercising an influence 'commensurate with the international status of its currency' on international monetary and financial issues.[31]

An emphasis on market selection for the international use of the euro, the lack of a strategy for the euro and the lack of an external representation for the euro area – these three factors all point in the same direction: the euro as a *passive* device with regard to issues in the governance of international financial and monetary affairs. To a certain extent these three factors derive from the same fundamental point: the euro is not issued and backed by a state but by the combination of a heterogeneous collection of individual states sharing preferences in some regards but not in others and a common Central Bank. But the problem also has another dimension: the predominance and institutionalization (via the independence of the ECB) of a monetary doctrine favouring the defensive adaptation of the monetary system rather than its active use for framing priorities of global financial and monetary governance. The status report of the Commission (2008) shows a minimal awareness of this problem – it is at least alluded to. On the other hand, the timidity and discretion of the report also show that there is still a long way to go.[32]

Let us now focus on some of the 'domestic' economic and political mechanisms framing the internationalization of the euro.

While it is, on the one hand, clear that the euro financial markets have developed quite substantially (for example, in terms of depth and liquidity) since the introduction of the euro facilitating the international use of the euro, it also seems relevant to point to a couple of important limits to the generalization of the internationalization of the euro.

As noted by many observers, the economic policy formation of the euro-zone is characterized by a centralization of monetary policies and a decentralization of other economic policies, in particular fiscal policies. The common EU-budget remains very modest and no deficit-financing is allowed. The common budget has to be balanced. Thus there are, for example, only week compensatory transfer mechanisms between the different Member States of the euro-zone; if and when counterbalanced by strong external demand (for example, from the US or from Asia) the absence of compensatory mechanisms need not be a problem for the cohesiveness of the euro-zone but when facing a situation combining significantly differentiated developments of unit labour costs and a high or appreciating exchange rate of the euro, this absence indeed constitutes a problem.[33]

The absence of deficit financing emanating from the common budget has other important implications for the present context.

Deficit-financing could stimulate the emergence of some sort of jointly issued European 'Treasury' bonds (that is, not corporate bonds) to finance budgetary deficits. This in turn could enhance the internationalization of the euro: jointly issued bonds could promote a large and liquid market and constitute attractive investment objects to foreign investors We may also note the national segmentation of public debts among the euro-zone countries – we are yet to see the slogan of 'One Money – One Debt' as a follow-up to the 'One Market – One Money' slogan introduced in the context of the single market project of the early 1990s. The ECB cannot facilitate the financing of national budget deficits since it is not allowed to buy the bonds of the Member States. Finally, we may also mention the relatively balanced current account position of the euro-zone as a totality, another factor which does not promote the international use of the euro.[34]

The creation of common European bonds, the Europeanization of national public debts and the development of a European current account deficit could all be steps conducive to an increased international use of the euro. Surplus countries in need of proper instruments for investing their reserves could thus add euros rather than dollars to the reserves of their central banks. However, such steps are not encouraged by current economic policy architecture of the EU. The latter is – in other words – not properly equipped to supply adequate liquidity denominated in euros to the international economy. Inadequate supply of liquidity may explain why periods of dollar instability, leading to an increased demand for euros, seems to translate itself into an appreciation of the euro exchange rate rather than into an increased supply of euros.

Let us now briefly recall some of the most significant characteristics of the present international role of the euro as discussed above: after an initial period of strong growth the international share has been growing moderately when measured in current exchange rates while it has been falling when measured in fixed exchange rates. How can we interpret these tendencies in view of the arguments developed above?

The starting point is the instability of the dollar following from domestic developments in the US economy and rivalry and competition from other economic powers in the global economy. The instability of the dollar leads market actors to search for alternatives to the dollar. Up to a point alternatives to the dollar do exist, but none of them constitute serious alternatives for the present moment. At some remote later stage the Chinese renminbi may become an alternative candidate; and in a long-time perspective we may also imagine an increased role for some sort of Special Drawing Rights from a reformed IMF. Market actors may also choose, for example, gold or oil as investment objects. But at the end of the day – and in view of the size and relative strength of the euro-zone – market actors can hardly avoid focussing on the euro as the main alternative to the dollar. Yet, the currency reserves of the central banks of surplus countries are not being refilled with euros.

I have previously quoted the findings of Lim (2007). These results point to the predominance of stabilizing (or passive) reserve diversification as a dynamic allocation strategy in the management of international currency reserves. The international potentials of the euro are not stimulated by such strategies. One may attempt to interpret the stabilizing (or passive) reserve diversification strategy in microeconomic terms[35] but we may also – at least tentatively – point to the structural, macroeconomic and political framing of currency policies and market processes. We have already alluded to the limited availability of euros for foreign reserves in the discussion above. Here it may be added that it could be the combination of dollar instability and foreign demand for euros as reserves, on the one hand, and the limited availability of euros for reserves, on the other hand, that has lead to an appreciation of the exchange rate of the euro rather than to a growth of euro reserves as measured in constant exchange rates.

Hence it would appear that the form of internationalization of the euro that we are witnessing is the passive consequence of the instability of the dollar rather than anything else. In this regard the euro-zone is passively subjected to rather than actively shaping the globalization of financial and monetary affairs.

Among the consequences of this we may simply note the fact that different Member States of the euro-zone are affected in quite different ways by these processes. Due to a number of factors (including the nature of national productive specialization, market structures and trends in unit labour costs) the impact of the appreciation of the euro varies between the member states of the EU.

And – as mentioned before – this differentiated impact cannot be counterbalanced by a common budget.

Concluding remarks

The international role of the euro has increased considerably in the ten years following its introduction. The euro today constitutes the second most important international currency. A closer study of the dynamics and mechanisms involved in the internationalization of the euro, however, reveals a number of limits to its international role. The strong growth of the international role of the euro is largely confined to the first years of the euro (that is, up to 2002/2003) while subsequent developments are essentially due to valuation effects (the high exchange rate of the euro as measured in dollars) or limited to the bordering countries of the euro-zone; furthermore the political, institutional and ideological framework of economic policy making in the EU is not conducive to furthering the development of the euro as an international currency. The potential of the euro as an international currency and as a rival to the dollar remains limited.

A priori nothing precludes these limits from being modified or removed in a medium- or longer-term perspective. The political agenda as well as the mechanisms and frames within which the international dimension of the euro is developing could in principle be changed – for example, under the impact of a major political, economical or cultural upheaval.

The current global financial and economic crisis indeed invites further reflection on the interplay between the global crisis, the international monetary system and the role of the EU and its currency in global economic governance. While a general analysis of the nature of the current crisis and its various dimensions is beyond the present discussion a couple of points, however, do merit a particular emphasis.

Firstly, and contrary to previous international financial and/or monetary crises, the current crisis originates in the centre of the global capitalist system, that is, the USA; the subsequent international diffusion of the US crisis has been uneven – in terms of speed but particularly in terms of gravity.

Secondly, the development of the crisis is linked to structural changes in the mode of functioning of national and international capitalist economies. What has in recent years increasingly been termed *financialization* (for example, Epstein 2005) would appear to be crucial in this regard. Productive logics have increasingly been crowded out by financial logics in particular in the USA but also in a number of European and other economies – starting with the UK.

Domestically financialization has been linked to the increasingly uneven distribution of incomes within a number of countries – first and foremost the US. On the other hand, a number of Asian economies, including but not limited to China, have pursued processes of intensive growth rather than reaping easy gains from financial speculation, while at the same time accumulating huge dollar reserves following years of substantial external surpluses.

Thirdly, the crisis is linked to changes in the forms of globalizations as these have developed since the Asian crisis of the late 1990s. For the last decade the US has assumed the role of the 'consumer of last resort' of the world economy while China and other Asian countries have financed the corresponding deficits. The polarization between Asian surpluses and an American deficit is the other side of this coin.

The problematic linking of international imbalances and the global supply of a reserve currency is well known since the days of the Triffin dilemma of the early 1960s.[36] In the light of the current global financial and economic crisis we may add that a form of globalization founded on major international imbalances, significantly differentiated processes of growth, financialization and increasing inequalities has proven itself equally shaky. The Triffin dilemma was never 'solved'.

Similarly the current turmoil need not give birth to a new form of structured governance. Indeed the question of how a new viable system is to be constructed remains highly uncertain and politically contested.[37]

From the more limited perspective which has been pursued in the present contribution, a number of observations may be added.

In the early phases of the financial crisis (that is, from September 2008) US weaknesses were rather clearly exposed but, contrary to what one could have expected initially, the weaknesses of the US system have subsequently turned out perhaps to be somewhat less clear cut than one could have expected. Thus, for instance, the financial crisis did not evolve into a currency crisis – and even if the dollar is still somewhat weakened and unstable, rather than exposing the limits of global dollar dominance the crisis has reminded us of the lack both of credible alternatives to US power (monetary and other) and of the intrinsic weaknesses of the European project in influencing or shaping global monetary governance. To the extent that US monetary supremacy is questioned, the challenge does not come from Europe but rather from, for example, China and perhaps a number of oil-exporting countries. Similarly we may note that the most recent ECB Report on the international role of the euro published in July 2009 (ECB 2009) does not point to noticeable effects of the financial crisis on the respective international roles of the euro and the dollar. Furthermore, it may be added that the European responses to the financial crisis have been somewhat erratic; and the EU authorities have not been capable of initiating coordinated responses to the crisis.

While the long-term perspectives of the global role of the US – in monetary as well as in other areas – remain highly uncertain, and while it is indeed very tempting to speculate on the options for long run structural change in the global (dis)order(s), it is equally appropriate to recall the fact that such exercises are bound to remain speculative guesstimates rather than anything else.

From a short- and mid-term perspective it is nevertheless pertinent to point to a number of challenges and issues that the EU and its currency are likely to face in the (long?) transitory period towards whatever is going to emerge from the present turmoil. The EU is badly prepared to face a number of challenges likely to result from current international imbalances, such as a further weakening of the dollar and an increasing turn to export-led growth strategies in most OECD countries likely to result from insufficient domestic demand and the need for deleveraging.

The EU is badly prepared for such challenges among other things because of its weak institutional and political mechanisms: lack of proper coordination mechanisms for economic policymaking in a broad sense, lack of adequate mechanisms for financial regulation, a lack of a proper international strategy for the euro and a general lack of an offensive economic policy strategy.

A further break-down of the global economic system and a strengthening of reform thinking within European political-economic policy-thinking could modify the political agenda as well as the mechanisms and frames within which the international dimension of the euro is developing. On the other hand, in view of the rather timid analysis of the Commission regarding the lack of an international strategy for the euro we may also note that we may still have a long way to go. In this respect it is also appropriate to note that the Lisbon Treaty essentially preserves the present political and institutional framework of economic policy making of the EU – a framework which, as argued above, is inadequate in promoting the increased international presence of the EU in global monetary matters.[38]

Acknowledgements

I am grateful to a numbers of friends and colleagues for comments on earlier drafts of the present text presented to conferences in Sakarya University, University of Tromsø, University of the Agean, Renmin University of China and Warwick University. The comments from Dr Nicolae Iordan-Constantinescu (University of Banking and Finance, Bucharest) and from my colleague Poul Thøis Madsen (Aalborg University) deserve a special mention – even if I have chosen not to follow all of their suggestions.

Notes

1. In economic policymaking the EU essentially speaks with one voice only in the area of international trade.
2. See Chinn and Frankel (2008) for a recent example.
3. See, for example, Cohen (2003, 2007) and Posen (2008).
4. For comprehensive surveys of recent developments in this field, see Galati and Wooldridge (2006), as well as the annual reports of the ECB on the international role of the euro, for example, ECB (2007, 2008a, 2009)
5. See Galati and Wooldridge (2006) and Wooldridge (2006) for useful discussions.
6. See the surveys provided by Galati and Wooldridge (2006, pp. 11–15) and Papaioannou and Portes (2008). In the present context it is, however, worthwhile underlining that such differentiated trends do not appear to be particularly significant.
7. However, these figures do suffer from an important deficiency: not all countries provide information on the composition of their foreign exchange reserves. This is, for instance, the case of China – indeed a rather significant case.
8. These observations are similar to points made in other reports of the ECB as well as to the points made by Galati and Wooldridge (2006).
9. As noted, for example, by the Commission (2008).
10. For example, the ECB could be leaning more towards passive reserve diversification under 'normal' circumstances (that is, if the exchange rate of the euro is seen as sufficiently high) while a too low exchange rate could induce attempts of stabilizing diversification.
11. Cf. ECB (2008a, pp. 63–64).
12. It is in any case striking that the ECB so often notes the fact that changes in the composition of currency reserves are mainly, or to a large extent, due to valuation effects while the Commission is more discreet in this respect.
13. Or as noted by the European Parliament (2008: 60): the EP 'regrets that in its Communication on EMU @ 10 the Commission has not conducted a more detailed and precise analysis of the euro's international role ... '.
14. This observation raises a number of issues which shall not be pursued any further in the present context, such as the meaning of the very concept of a regional currency, the relationship and/or co-existence between regional and global currencies, whether the position of a regional currency is a step towards a global currency and so on.
15. We shall discuss this distinction further later in the present text.
16. Useful summaries of this literature are provided by Chinn and Frankel (2008, pp. 56–59) and Papaioannou and Portes (2008).
17. Even if a number of formulations and specifications may be subject to controversy. I shall not pursue these issues further here, although a few comments will be added below.

18. This point is also mentioned by Papaioannou and Portes (2008) even if they do not discuss it in a very systematic way. Two recent attempts to deal with the political determinants of international currencies are Helleiner (2008) and Posen (2008).
19. The occasionally somewhat uneasy relation between the domestic and the international roles of the dollar should at least provide an illustration of this point. I shall return to it later in connection with the international role of the euro.
20. While a well-functioning financial system indeed appears to be a necessary condition for economic growth, it may also be argued that finance-driven economic systems may imply a problematic focus on short-term profits and speculative gains to the detriment of economic growth and employment as argued in recent research on finance-driven growth and financialization, for example, Palley (2007), Stockhammer (2007) and Toporowski (2008).
21. The relationship between monetary stability and economic growth is indeed far from simple. Firstly, the very notion of stability is far from unambiguous as witnessed, for example, by the problematic relationship between consumer price inflation and asset price inflation. Secondly, it seems obvious that while excessive instability (for example, of the exchange rate or of the inflation rate) is likely to be incompatible with long-term economic growth, it is far more complicated to establish any sort of general linkage between, for example, inflation rates and economic growth. In general terms we cannot claim that monetary stability is a necessary condition for economic growth and under certain circumstances it may equally be claimed that a trade-off between monetary stability and economic growth is likely to exist. See also the survey by Bruno and Easterly (1996).
22. Posen (2008) underlines the role of geostrategic and geopolitical factors for international monetary relations. The present analysis is fully compatible with the geopolitical approach even if the emphasis in the present text is somewhat different.
23. At the Bretton Woods Keynes and the British delegation suggested a plan for an international international currency, that is, the bancor. The plan, however, was never accepted by the USA. The IMF issues another sort of international international currency, the Special Drawing Rights (SDR), but it is only available in rather limited quantities. Recently, however, the Chinese have advocated an increasing issuing and use of the SDR – probably as a way of stabilizing the value of their currency reserves. An increased role of the SDR is likely to raise the delicate and important issue of the voting powers of the different members of the IMF.
24. Such a distinction is also suggested by Arestis and Bain (1995, p. 212).
25. For example, by outflows of foreign direct investment or other ways of creating credits to deficit countries.
26. For example, De Cecco (1979), Ikenberry (1993) and Ruggie (1982).
27. At the regional level institutional mechanisms seem to be of greater significance as briefly touched upon earlier in the present text. This point, however, will not be addressed any further here.
28. 'From a policy perspective, the Eurosystem has adopted a neutral stance on the international use of its currency. It does not pursue the

internationalisation of the euro as a policy goal and neither fosters nor discourages its use by non-residents of the euro area' ECB (2008b, p. 89).
29. We may of course also choose to characterize central banks, hedge funds, sovereign wealth funds and so on as market participants. And in a certain sense they are…however, not in the textbook version of competitive markets.
30. Padoa-Schioppa was a member of the ECB's executive board until 2005.
31. Cf. also Commission 2008, pp. 11, 23, 248–249 and 282. See also McNamara and Meunier (2002) as well as Bini Smaghi (2006).
32. In this regard one may speculate about the possible impact on the global financial and economic crises on the political and institutional architecture of the EMU. We shall briefly return to this point in the conclusion below.
33. The persistent balance-of-payments disequilibria within the EU – Germany maintaining a low level of domestic demand, an export focused economic model and – as a result – a very substantial surplus towards most other member states – illustrates the problem. Developments in recent years (such as the comparatively slow growth of German unit labour costs and the appreciation of the euro) have aggravated the balance problem among the EU member states.
34. We may here add another observation: the development of an external deficit of the EU could lessen the current international balance-of-payments disequilibria (US deficits and Asian surpluses).
35. See Lim (2007), Truman and Wang (2006) as well as the references given therein.
36. How can a country (that is, the US) maintaining a substantial deficit on its balance-of-payments at the same time retain its credibility as the supplier of the international reserve currency and supply adequate liquidity to the global economy via this very deficit?
37. The international ecological imbalances and the climate crisis obviously add to this uncertainty.
38. It may be added that the Lisbon Treaty may strengthen the euro group by giving it a formal status. In a longer time perspective one may imagine the euro group to develop a stronger and more activist position vis-à-vis the ECB. But presently we are rather far away from such a situation.

References

Arestis, Philip and Keith Bain (1995), A European central bank: a necessary evil?, in Arestis, Philip and Victoria Chick (eds), *Finance, Development and Structural Change*, Edward Elgar: London.
Bini Smaghi, Lorenzo (2006), Powerless Europe: why is the euro area still a political dwarf? *International Finance*, vol. 9, no. 2.
Bruno, Michael and William Easterly (1996), Inflation and growth: in search of a stable relationship, *Federal Reserve Bank of St. Louis Review*, vol. 78, no. 3: 139–46.
Chinn, Menzie D. and Jeffrey A. Frankel (2008), Why the euro will rival the dollar, *International Finance*, vol. 11, no. 1.

Cohen, Benjamin (2003), Global currency rivalry: can the euro ever challenge the dollar? *Journal of Common Market Studies*, vol. 41, no. 4.

Cohen, Benjamin (2007), Enlargement and the international role of the euro, *Review of International Political Economy*, vol. 14, no. 5.

Commission of the European Communities (2008), *EMU@10: successes and challenges after 10 years of Economic and Monetary Union*, Brussels, May, COM (2008) 238 final.

De Cecco, Marcello (1979), Origins of the post-war payments system, *Cambridge Journal of Economics*, vol. 3, no. 1.

ECB (2007), *Review of the International Role of the Euro*, European Central Bank, Frankfurt, June.

ECB (2008a), *The International Role of the Euro*, European Central Bank, Frankfurt, July.

ECB (2008b), *Monthly Bulletin*, 10th Anniversary of the ECB, Frankfurt.

ECB (2009), *The International Role of the Euro*, European Central Bank, Frankfurt, July.

Epstein, Gerald (ed.) (2005), *Financialization and the World Economy*, Edward Elgar: London.

European Parliament (2008), *EP resolution of 18 November 2008 on the EMU @ 10: The first ten years of Economic and Monetary Union and future challenges (2008/2156(INI))*.

Galati, Gabriele and Philip Wooldridge (2006), *The Euro as a Reserve Currency: A Challenge to the Pre-Eminence of the US Dollar?* BIS Working Papers, No. 218, October (http://www.bis.org/).

Helleiner, Eric (1994), *States and the Emergence of Global Finance*, Cornell UP: Ithaca.

Helleiner, Eric (2008), Political determinants of international currencies: what future for the US dollar? *Review of International Political Economy*, vol. 15, no. 3.

Ikenberry, John G. (1993), The Political Origins of Bretton Woods, in Bordo, Michael D. and Barry Eichengreen (eds), *Retrospective on the Bretton Woods. Lessons for International Monetary Reform*, University of Chicago Press: Chicago.

Keynes, John Maynard (1973[1936]), *The General Theory of Employment Interest and Money*, MacMillan: London and Cambridge UP: Cambridge.

Lim, Ewe-Ghee (2007), *Do Reserve Portfolios Respond to Exchange Rate Changes Using Portfolio Rebalancing Strategy? An Econometric Study Using COFER Data*, IMF, WP/07/293.

McNamara, Kathleen and Sophie Meunier (2002), Between national sovereignty and international power: what external voice for the euro? *International Affairs*, vol. 78, no. 4.

Padoa-Schioppa, Tomasso (2004), *The Euro and Its Central Bank. Getting United after the Union*, The MIT Press: Cambridge.

Palley, Thomas I. (2007), *Finanzialization: What It Is and Why It Matters*, WP 153, PERI. University of Massachusetts (http://www.peri.umass.edu/).

Papaioannou, Elias and Richard Portes (2008), *The International Role of the Euro: A Status Report*, European Commission, Economic and Financial Affairs DG, Economic Papers 317, Bruxelles, April.

Polanyi, Karl (1957[1944]), *The Great Transformation. The Political and Economic Origins of Our Time*, Beacon Press: Boston.

Posen, Adam S. (2008), Why the euro will not rival the dollar, *International Finance*, vol. 11, no. 1.

Ruggie, John Gerard (1982), International regimes, transactions and change: embedded liberalism in the postwar economic order, *International Organization*, vol. 36, no. 2.

Stockhammer, Engelbert (2007), *Some Stylized Facts on the Finance-Dominated Accumulation Regime*, WP 142, University of Massachusetts (http://www.peri.umass.edu/).

Toporowski, Jan (2008), *The Economics and Culture of Financialisation*, WP 158, SOAS, University of London (http://www.soas.ac.uk/economics/research/workingpapers/).

Truman, Edwin M. and Anna Wong (2006), *The Case for an International Reserve Diversification Standard*, WP 06-02, IIE, Washington (http://www.iie.com/).

Widmaier, Wesley (2003), The Keynesian Bases of a Constructivist Theory of the International Political Economy, *Millennium*, vol. 32, no. 1.

Widmaier, Wesley (2004), The social construction of the 'Impossible Trinity': The intersubjective bases of monetary cooperation, *International Studies Quarterly*, vol. 48.

Wooldridge, Philip (2006), The changing composition of official reserves, *BIS Quarterly Review*, September: 25–38.

5
Emerging Markets and the Global Financial Crisis

Giorgio Fazio

Introduction

Over the 1990s, crises developed in emerging markets and, while they did send shockwaves across the world, their effects were perceived mostly by other emerging markets.[1] The domestic and international policy recommendations that followed focused on strategies to reduce this instability, seen as a threat to the world economy. At the end of the 2000s, the world seems to have gone upside down. The 2008/2009 global financial crisis started earlier in 2007 with a sharp rise in defaults on sub-prime mortgages in one of the most advanced nations, the US, and quickly spread through the interbank market to become an international credit and liquidity squeeze. The credit crisis involved other industrial countries first, while emerging markets initially seemed to have 'decoupled'. Later, however, and expectedly, the crisis developed into a large-scale world crisis and recession.

The plausible list of causes for the crisis is long and presenting them requires an effort that is beyond the scope of this chapter. For our purposes, however, it is sufficient to recall the two main views. The first puts most of the blame on domestic failures in industrial countries, such as lax monetary policy, regulation failure in the subprime market and the inadequacy of financial institutions and rating agencies.[2] Economic theories are also under discussion and it is fashionable to recall Minsky's model (1986) of financial crises and a more active role for the government.

Another interpretation for the crisis is rooted in international macroeconomics and pertains to the concentration of a large pool of savings (mostly in emerging markets) on too few assets. Such global imbalances fuelled asset bubbles in industrial countries, via a reduction in the long-term interest rates. While consensus around the global imbalances hypothesis is not unanimous, Setser (2009) highlights how it would have not been possible for the US to finance the large private deficits without the accumulation of foreign reserves operated mostly by foreign central banks. These stockpiled US bonds preventing the adjustment of interest rates, expected on the grounds of increasing fiscal deficits and increasing short-term rates. According to this view, governments in industrial and emerging markets have to share responsibility for the crisis.

The stand of emerging markets is one of the main novel features of this crisis and deserves further attention. Paradoxically, at the outbreak of the crisis, emerging markets, traditionally cursed by instability, surprised commentators for their resilience. For example, Dallara et al. (2007: 2) comment that:

> By historic standards…the recent re-pricing of risk on emerging markets external debt is a remarkably small blip.

Interestingly, these improved conditions were the by-product of the policy prescriptions for crises in the 1990s, as emerging economies finally seemed to get it right in terms of growth prospects, monetary stability, dependence on external finance and international reserves. Yet, in spite of the early resistance, it is now evident that better fundamentals have not warranted immunity. Shocks have propagated quickly to emerging markets via increased uncertainty and a reversal in risk appetite. Whether these effects are going to be limited to the short run remains an important element for discussion. Early signs suggest that the effects of the crisis have already impacted on growth prospects. The only consolation seems to be that emerging markets are, for once, considered the victims.

This chapter reviews the global crisis with a special focus on emerging markets and Developing Asia in particular. It is argued that it is important to analyse the overlooked role of emerging markets in the development of the crisis. In this direction, it is believed that the large global imbalances that saw emerging market surpluses as the counterpart of the large industrial countries' deficits should be considered more carefully to better understand the crisis and its long-term implications for emerging markets and the global economy. Indeed, while the crisis seems to have reduced these imbalances in the short run, if their fundamental causes persist, they may widen again in the long run once economies recover.

A great irony is embedded in this interpretation: the same policy prescriptions for strengthening developing countries' resistance to crises
may have contributed to the development of a crisis that will likely
impact on them quite heavily. Crisis solutions that do not address the
causes of the fundamental imbalance between developed and developing countries' external positions may be destined to produce effects only
in the short term. Yet, the crisis represents a unique opportunity to build
a more balanced and, hence, more stable world economy.

The rest of the chapter is organized as follows. The next section
describes the international macroeconomic situation in the world economy, at the time of writing. The third section presents the debate on
global imbalances and the role of emerging markets in the crisis. The
fourth section reviews the policy debate, followed by 'Conclusions'.

The impact of the crisis on emerging markets

Emerging markets displayed a remarkable resilience in the wake of the
crisis and, at least in the beginning, there was a widespread opinion that
emerging markets had 'decoupled'. The greater resilience of emerging
markets was considered a consequence of the better policies implemented after the emerging market crises of the second part of the 1990s.
On most accounts, emerging markets, especially Asia, displayed macro-
fundamentals in good shape[3] and better institutions. These, eventually,
were not sufficient to keep emerging markets out of trouble.[4]

Initially, however, commentators concentrated on the short-term
implications for emerging markets. Goswami and Pazarbasioglu (2008)
present the general view of commentators at the 10th Global Bond
Market Forum. In spite of the better policy underpinning in an increasingly integrated world, emerging markets were going to be affected by
increased volatility and perceived risk, and consequently higher spreads
and a reduction in the availability of external funds.[5]

Impact on growth

The depth and the width of the impact of the crisis on advanced and
emerging economies can be gauged from Figure 5.1. This shows the evolution since 1980 and the projections until 2014 of annual growth for
advanced economies, emerging and developing economies and the sub-
group of developing Asian nations,[6] as reported in the World Economic
Outlook (WEO 2009). Developing Asia maintained the best growth
performance over the entire period, with yearly growth falling below

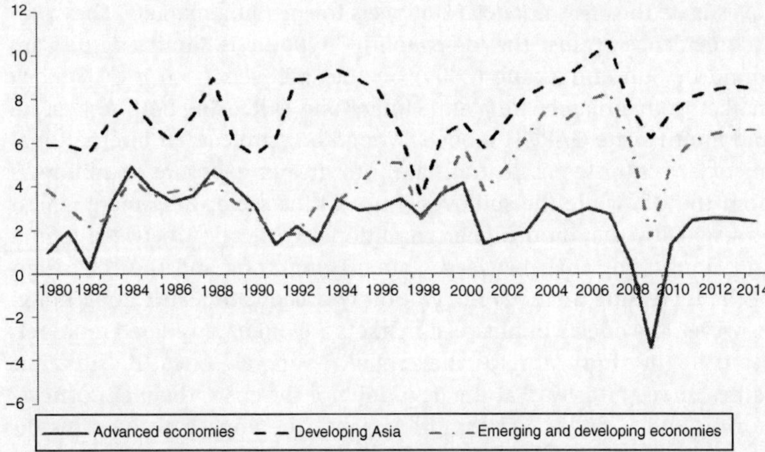

Figure 5.1   Gross domestic product, constant prices, annual percent change.
Source: IMF, World Economic Outlook, October 2009.

4 per cent only at the time of the Asian crisis. Since, they have displayed newly vitalized growth up over 10 per cent.

The global financial crisis caused in 2008 a large drop for all three groups. While advanced economies, typically slow growers, have moved into negative growth after a slide of around 6 percentage points, emerging and developing markets in general have maintained positive growth, but have experienced a drop similar to that of advanced economies. Developing Asian nations seem to show a reduction in growth smaller than the other groups and slightly smaller than the one they experienced at the time of the Asian crisis.

Many potential channels can explain the transmission to emerging markets. Among the others, particularly important are the trade and the financial channel, operating through international banking and direct and indirect investment reversals, reductions in foreign debt servicing, and stops in international transfers, such as remittances. While here we consider the overall impact on Emerging and Developing countries, the impact of each channel may differ across countries.

Impact on financial markets

Financial markets were the first to feel the effects of the crisis in the US. Frank and Hesse (2009) use multivariate GARCH techniques to measure the extent of co-movements of financial variables across markets and investigate the crisis financial spillovers to emerging markets. They provide evidence against the 'de-coupling' hypothesis. Similar results are found by Sun and Zhang (2009) on the spillovers from the US stock markets to mainland China and Hong Kong SAR, using both univariate and multivariate GARCH models. Hong Kong's role as an international financial centre seems to translate into greater exposure to spillovers from the US, while the spillovers onto China seem to be more persistent. Finally, they find higher conditional correlation between China and Hong Kong than between China, Hong Kong and the US, a sign of the increasing financial integration between China and Hong Kong. However, the effects in financial markets are often considered more relevant in the short term, as they should evaporate once the situation settles. Indeed this was, at the beginning of the crisis, the main conclusion in policy circles. On the other hand, the impact of the crisis on trade, direct investment and commodity prices seems more relevant for the long-term implications of the crisis.

Impact on international trade and investment

The impact of the crisis on trade and investment can be seen in Figures 5.2 and 5.3. Trade is clearly one of the main channels of transmission: a crisis in the industrial North necessarily will affect the demand for exports from the developing South, impacting on both

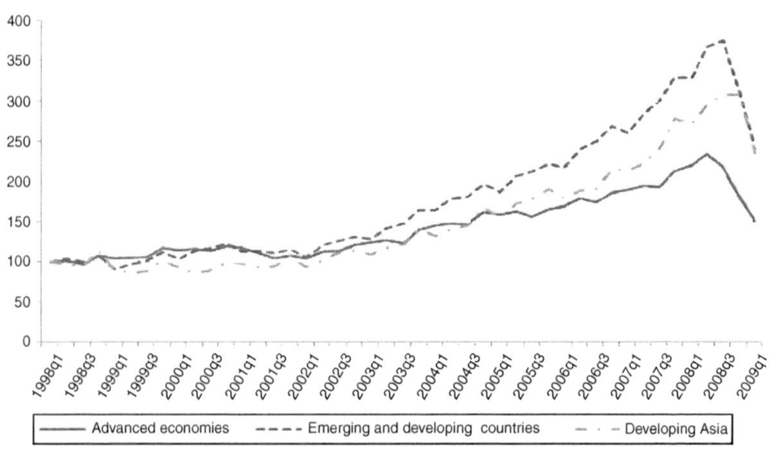

Figure 5.2 Exports disaggregated by region (1998q1 = 100).
Source: IMF Direction of Trade Statistics, October 2009.

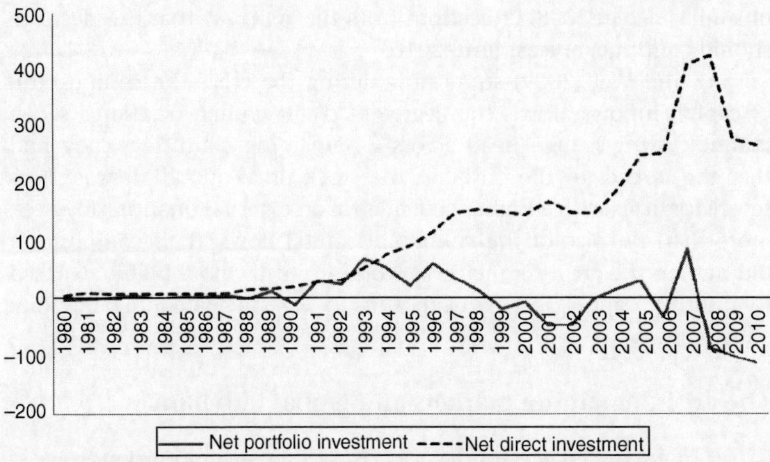

Figure 5.3 Emerging and developing countries, Net Direct and portfolio investment billions of US$.

Source: IMF, World Economic Outlook, October 2009.

prices and volumes. Figure 5.2 shows the large drop in exports of advanced economies, emerging and developing economies and Developing Asia around the second quarter of 2008.

Willenbockel and Robinson (2009) use simulations of a world trade model to compare pre- and post-crisis trade patterns and assess the impact of the crisis on the exports and welfare of less developed and emerging markets. Expectedly, they find that size and consequences of the crisis vary depending on the country group characteristics and, in particular, their export composition. Countries with less diversified export structure, such as fuel exporters in sub-Saharan Africa, should suffer the most. Among those countries with similar degree of exports diversification, those with higher trade openness should be hit harder. In absolute values, however, the losses merely related to trade are relatively small, especially compared to the cost of bail-outs in developed countries.

It is also interesting to look at the dynamics of Net Direct and Portfolio inflows to emerging and developing markets. Figure 5.3 shows that while direct investment inflows have steadily increased even after the main 1990s crises, portfolio flows have been decreasing at least until 2001 and have become more volatile. While the two series exhibit very different behaviour in the period between 1997 and 2001, they show again similar trends afterwards. In particular, they both experience drops of similar size in 2008. Projections from the WEO say that this decrease should continue, at least until 2010.

Tong and Wei (2009) study how during the crisis the composition of capital inflows affects the degree of credit crunch of a large set of manufacturing firms spread across 24 emerging countries. They find that the impact of the crisis on the stock price quotation was more severe for firms with a higher dependence on external finance. However, more than the size of the volume of capital flows, their composition did matter: the credit crunch was worse for firms more highly exposed to non-FDI capital inflows. Exposure to FDI alleviated the liquidity constraint.

The crisis, emerging markets and global imbalances

Crises in advanced economies vs. crises in emerging markets

As mentioned above, the global financial crisis presents features unseen for many decades in economic history. Frenkel and Rapetti (2009) argue that the crisis has sent shockwaves not just through the economy, but also in economic paradigms. In particular, this seems to have led to a revamping of Minsky's interpretation of financial crises. However, even this reading needs to account for some fundamental differences between developed and developing economies. Frenkel and Rapetti (2009) discuss these differences in the context of Minsky's interpretation of financial crises. In particular, they argue that while crises in advanced economies are usually endogenously determined in the domestic financial system, crises in emerging markets are more likely borne out of macroeconomic mismanagement.

In Minsky's model the financial system is subject to a cycle. The cycle begins when economy is in equilibrium with a booming phase, where excessive optimism leads to greater risk appetite, to the creation of new financial instruments and to excess consumption of goods and assets. Expectations generate positive feedback and contribute to creating a more fragile financial system. In the second phase, after some negative event, investors enter in distress and start reducing consumption and demanding low risk and highly liquid assets. The bubble bursts and deflates assets sending liquidity constrained agents into bankruptcy. Expectations generate negative feedback, further depressing spending and investment. According to Frenkel and Rapetti (2009), instead the booming phase in emerging markets does not begin within the financial system, but with the implementation of a new macroeconomic policy. In this direction, the list of culprits for crises in the 1990s includes, among others, the fast deregulation of undeveloped financial markets and the adoption of regulated exchange rates. These may have induced in international investors a false sense of security and generated the large expansion of capital flows, investment and output usually observed in the period before the crisis. Later, the real exchange rate appreciates, the trade balance worsens, productivity slows down and the current account deteriorates reducing the credibility of the exchange rate rule and raising the probability of devaluation. In the case of the Asian crisis, this generated the Balance Sheet effects, and the typical third generation models dynamics, that led to the currency and financial crisis. In this context, the implementation of a new macroeconomic rule represents an exogenous shock on the domestic financial system.

In the recent events, the new macroeconomic rule could be represented by the desire after the crises in the late 1990s to hold international reserves as a measure of self-protection.

The global saving glut

One of the dominant explanations for the global crisis is the so called world 'saving glut', firstly suggested by Bernanke (2005). This interpretation is particularly interesting because it gives a role to emerging markets in the development of global imbalances and, hence, the crisis. On one side of these imbalances, there is the large US current account deficit. This is represented in Figure 5.4 together with the government balance and annual growth. The large US current account deficit is clearly a long-term phenomenon, starting in the early 1990s and reaching its peak in 2006. The IMF projects a reduction in the deficit for the period 2008–2014. Before the crisis, the deficit was interpreted by some as a 'made in the USA' phenomenon, and in particular as depending on the growing fiscal deficit and the reduction in private savings caused by the bubble. Bernanke argues that this is only part of the story, since the US external deficit seems to follow a long-term trend, quite independently from fiscal imbalances (see, again, Figure 5.4).

Instead, he points to the excess global saving generated, in small proportion, by demographics and ageing population in industrial countries and to a greater extent by excess saving in emerging markets and Asia in particular. Specifically, he highlights how the reaction of emerging economies to crises in the 1990s included, together with efforts towards better internal macroeconomic management, a change in attitude towards external borrowing in international capital markets. As a measure of self-protection from capital flow reversals, these countries accumulated foreign exchange reserves, as a self insurance. This caused

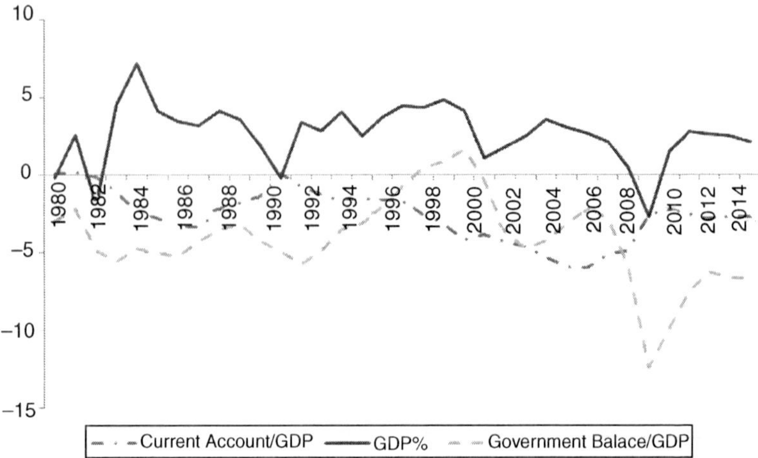

Figure 5.4   US macroeconomic outlook.
Source: IMF, World Economic Outlook, October 2009.

a shift of emerging markets from a status of net borrowers to one of net lenders to industrial countries.

This is reflected in Figure 5.5, where national saving and invest-ment are reported for advanced economies, emerging and developing

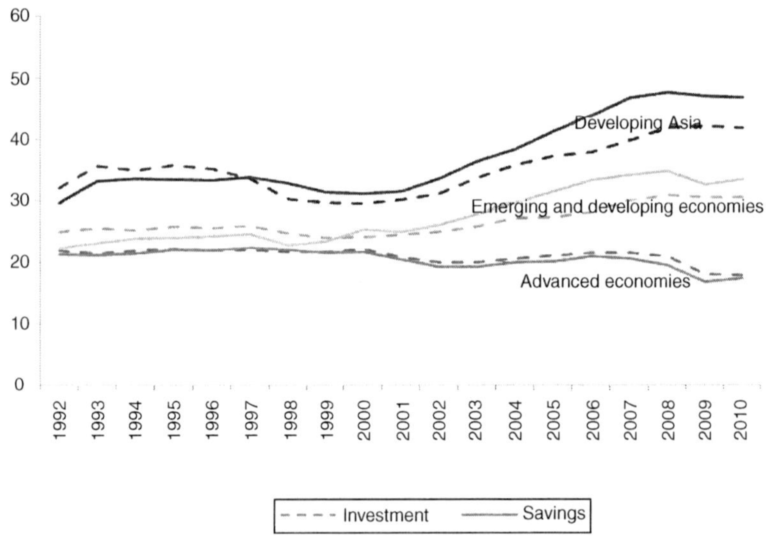

Figure 5.5   National saving and investment as a share of GDP.
Source: IMF, World Economic Outlook, October 2009.

economies and Developing Asia more specifically. Three facts emerge. First, Developing Asia shows higher share of investment and savings compared to both other emerging markets and advanced economies. Second, while advanced economies show a long trend of a shortage of saving, Developing Asia has developed after the Asian countries, exactly as suggested by Bernanke, an excess of savings. Emerging and developing economies follow slightly later.

In this respect, the rise of China and India in the world economy has played a particular role. Growth performance and economic reforms have led the citizens of these countries to have higher propensity to save. Chamon and Prasad (2008), for example, investigate the increase in average urban household saving rate in China. Using micro-level data, they do not identify any significant level of consumption smoothing over the life cycle. The increase in saving rate is present in all age groups, but it is highest among the youngest and the oldest groups. They explain this with the rising private burden of expenditure on housing, health and education, supposedly due to economic reforms.

According to Bernanke, the governments of these countries used these excess savings to accumulate international reserves, as a measure of self protection. This is evident in Figure 5.6, where international reserves (excluding gold) are disaggregated by geographical area. Again, Developing Asia shows an exponential increase in reserves higher than overall emerging markets. Figure 5.7 disaggregates bilateral trade balances of

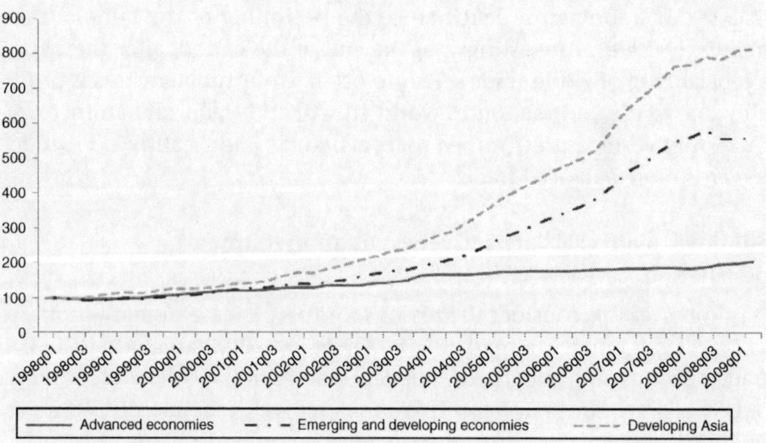

Figure 5.6   International reserves of advanced and emerging economies 1998q1–2009q2 (1998q1 = 100).
Source: IMF International Financial Statistics.

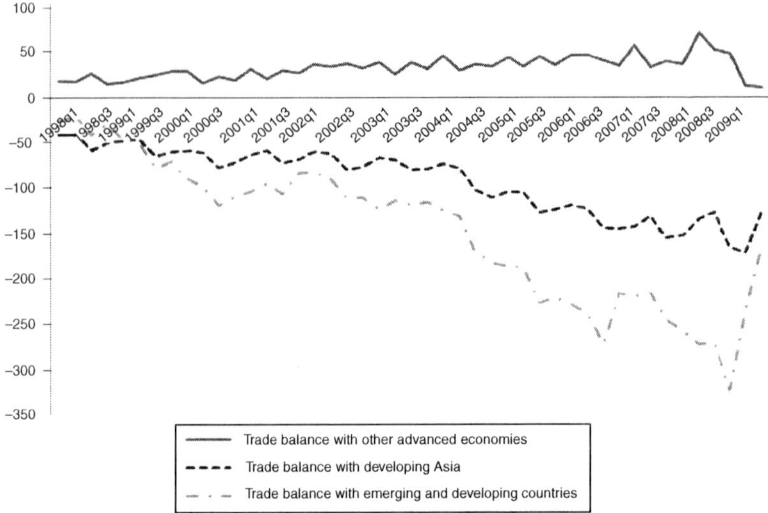

Figure 5.7 Trade balance of advanced economies disaggregated by region (1998q1–2009q1) billions of US$.
Source: IMF Direction of Trade Statistics, 2009.

advanced economies into balances with other advanced economies, with emerging and developing economies in general, and with Developing Asia, in particular. While trade among advanced economies is generally in surplus, trade with emerging economies and Developing Asia shows a long-term deficit since the beginning of the sample (first quarter of 1998). Interestingly, at the end of the period, after the crisis, a rebalancing of world trade seems to occur. Unfortunately, this is probably due to the contraction in world growth and trade, and an increase in restrictive measures, rather than a natural and healthy correction towards more balanced trade.

Flight to quality: US attractiveness as an investment destination

It is important to consider the reasons for this increase in precautionary savings from emerging markets. Dooley et al. (2005) argue that the US trade deficit is equivalent to a supply of international collateral in terms of US dollars to the periphery. This grants access to (supposedly) efficient financial markets to countries hampered by underdeveloped domestic financial markets. These countries export their gross savings and have it redirected back through more efficient channels, such as FDI.

The self-precautionary nature of reserves is probably more likely for countries like China, who used these reserves to avoid unwanted currency appreciation and pursue export-led growth.

Mendoza (2009) investigates the hypothesis that the Asian crisis in 1997–1998 indeed generated the desire to hold international reserves as a measure of self-protection. In particular, he estimates the elasticity of developing countries reserves to a number of vulnerability indicators before and after the Asian crisis and finds a higher propensity to hold reserves in the latter period. This result seems stronger for countries more prone to 'sudden stops'. No significant difference is, instead, detected in the behaviour of China, a country with a particularly large trade surplus.

The 'attractiveness' of the US as an investment destination and the lack of investment opportunities in other industrial and emerging markets can potentially explain why excess saving has inflated mainly US assets.

According to Bernanke (2005), emerging markets adopted the strategy to increase international reserves by issuing domestic debt and using the proceeds to buy US public and private assets. Governments in emerging markets essentially acted as financial intermediaries channelling private domestic savings into international capital markets and the US in particular. According to Bernanke, this translated during the period 1996–2000 into the observed dollar appreciation and stock market bubble. Both effects raised the willingness of US citizens to reduce saving and increase consumption, especially in foreign goods, widening the trade imbalance. After the stock market collapse in 2000, the saving glut was the root of low real interest rates and the so called Greenspan's 'conundrum'.[7] Low interest rates kept US saving low and financed excessive residential construction.[8]

Theoretical rationalizations for this interpretation have been recently advanced by Caballero (2006) and Caballero et al. (2008, 2009), who develop formal models where an equilibrium entails the current account deficit, low interest rates and the shift in global portfolios towards US assets. Empirical support to the view that foreign holdings may have kept long-term US interest rates down, has been found by Craine and Martin (2009) and Warnock and Warnock (2009).

Cova et al. (2009) discuss the role of Emerging Asia in generating the large global imbalances antecedent to the crisis. In particular, using simulations in a general equilibrium model of the world economy, they argue that emerging markets in Asia have experienced both a slowdown in productivity and an increase in the desired level of net foreign assets since 2001. The latter has significant spillovers onto the US. In a similar fashion, Chinn and Ito (2007) try to explain the move of emerging Asia into net lending position and find support for the view that the current account improvement of these countries was generated by a lack of investment opportunities rather than excess saving.

The role of primary commodity prices

Since the early contributions of Prebisch (1950) and Singer (1950) and, more recently, Grilli and Yang (1988), the prices of primary commodities have been considered a particularly important indicator for developing economies. This is usually due to the relevance of these goods for the terms of trade of emerging markets. An issue that has attracted a lot of attention has been the substantial increase in primary commodities around the early 2000s. Oil and primary commodity prices have been increasing exponentially since the beginning of the 2000s until 2008. Three main explanations have been advanced for the surge in commodity prices: speculation, increase in demand and resource shortage. According to Frankel (2006), low interest rates have provided an incentive for speculation in storable commodities. Similarly, Calvo (2008) argues that low central bank interest rates and the growth of sovereign wealth funds have reduced the demand for liquid assets and increased the demand for primary commodities. Wolf (2008), instead, highlights the role of increasing world demand due to the rise in world trade of new emerging markets like China and India. Krugman (2008) argues that since no increase in inventories can be detected, speculation is the less likely explanation. Instead, he blames resource shortage.

Increasing oil and commodity prices are a further explanation for the shift of emerging markets from the status of net borrowers to that of net lenders. This increase is shown in Figure 5.8, where the quarterly price index of UK brent and non-fuel commodity prices are plotted for the period from the first quarter of 1998 to the second quarter of 2009. Oil exporters are in the group of countries that have experienced large current account surpluses contributing significantly to the development of global imbalances. Arezki and Hasanov (2009) argue that oil exporters have played an important part in the development of global imbalances and may play an important part in the crisis resolution, especially if oil prices will increase in the long run. In particular, they estimate current account regressions for oil and non-oil exporters, using alternative estimators. They find that the current accounts of oil exporters are more responsive to fiscal policy and also less persistent than those of non-oil exporters.

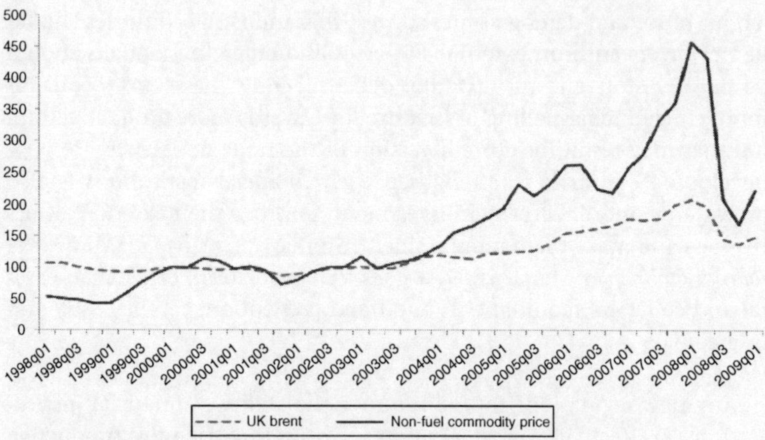

Figure 5.8   UK Brent and non-fuel commodity prices (1998q1–2009q2).
Source: IMF, International Financial Statistics.

It is interesting to note in Figure 5.8 how the crisis has determined the large slide in the price of non fuel commodities and oil. At the end of 2008, however, both series have already started to pick up again.

The crisis and the policy debate

The policy debate on the remedies to the crisis is obviously affected by the heat of the moment. Interestingly, the immediate action taken from national economies has been the adoption of expansionary policies.[9] At the international level, however, very little has been done to coordinate the efforts, beside a predicament against anti-protectionist policies that does not seem to have achieved strong effects. Indeed, according to Bown (2009), the global economy has recently seen an 18 per cent rise in protectionist measures.

For the longer term, there seems to be a stronger focus on regulatory policies for the financial system of advanced economies, rather than for the global economy and emerging markets. However, according to the above discussion, a good part of the blame for the crisis should be on global imbalances. To the extent that these imbalances are responsible for the crisis, long-lasting solutions and the prevention of future trouble should address the issue. This warning was already contained in Bernanke (2005), who lamented the undesirability of an unbalanced international position in the long run. Intrinsically, he argues, capital labour ratios and demographics suggest that industrial countries should be net savers and run external surpluses and emerging markets should be net investors and run external deficits. Mildly, he seems to call for more efficient channelling of investment towards more productive capital that may result in future inversion of the trade imbalance. Helping developing countries to strengthen their financial institutions is also important, since it can foster investment, improve their external attractiveness and make them more resilient. Similarly, Greenspan (*Wall Street Journal Online*, 11 March 2009) argues that regulation, other than capital and collateral requirements and fraud prevention, can be costly and ineffective:

> Any new regulations should improve the ability of financial institutions to effectively direct a nation's savings into the most productive investments.

Frenkel and Rapetti (2009) stress the relevance of loosely regulated domestic financial systems for the development of crises in industrial economies. While the same policy prescription is valid for emerging markets, here the impact of macroeconomic policies should also be considered, in particular with respect to the consistency between the exchange rate policy and the sustainability of the current account. They suggest a crisis preventive macroeconomic regime based on three fundamental policies regarding: flexible exchange rate regime; capital account management; robust external accounts (again through the accumulation of foreign exchange reserves). With respect to the improvement of financial regulation, Frenkel and Rapetti (2009) stress that any reform should take account of emerging markets' specificities.

Berglof (2008) claims that while the adequacy of international institutions was not relevant in preventing the crisis, it is important to resolve it and calls for a review of the international financial architecture to avoid further problems. At the outbreak of the crisis, international crisis lending was severely underfunded and national rescue packages generated adverse spillovers. A more coordinated action is needed between the East and the West to avoid these problems.

Rodrik (2009) argues that the global financial crisis entails a unique opportunity for developing nations, who can claim greater participation in multilateral organizations and contribute to the governance of globalization. Clearly, this participation brings both benefits and responsibilities. In particular, Rodrik calls for improvements on three fronts. First, he claims that under imperfect global capital markets, better counter-cyclical capital-account management policies should be set in place:

> the '[…] discouraging foreign borrowing in good times, and preventing capital flight in bad'. (Rodrik, Vox 28 January, 2009)

Second, he calls for greater transparency, especially on tax evasion. Third, he encourages developing nations to adopt a type of Tobin-tax on global foreign currency transactions, which, in his view, at a small efficiency cost would discourage speculation and allow raising revenues to be spent on public goods and development assistance, health and environment. Finally, he argues that to ensure successful globalization developing nations should call for the preservation of the notion of 'policy space', a space where important social and political policies can be pursued, within the World Trade Organization. However, the counter side of a greater role is greater responsibility and cooperation. In return developing nations should ensure greater transparency in the use of sovereign wealth funds, liability in the reduction of greenhouse gases and eliminate trade protectionism.

In terms of future scenarios, according to Setser (2009) the fall in oil prices will reduce saving in oil exporters and increase saving in the US. This is evidenced already in the reserves drop that can also be observed in Figure 5.6 at the end of 2008. Setser (2009) discusses two scenarios. In the first scenario, the fiscal deficit expansion in the US drains the increase in household saving and once the effects of the positive oil shock have vanished, the fiscal stimulus should worsen again the US current account. Again, the current accounts of emerging and Asian economies will improve and capital accounts deteriorate. If countries will show, as in the past, reluctance to let the exchange rate appreciate, we will observe again a piling up of foreign reserves. The path to recovery will see the US as the only locomotive of the world economy with no improved strength of the international financial system. In the second scenario, the US fiscal stimulus helps the US economy, but does not help the world economy. Now, surplus countries will have to provide greater economic stimulus to their economies and will find it more difficult to resist appreciation pressures. In this case, the outcome will see smaller imbalances.

As commodity prices are already picking up, prompt action in terms of greater policy coordination may not be procrastinated too long.

This coordination may also involve some form of international monetary coordination. Edwards (2007), for example, argues a reduction of global imbalances could be less painfully achieved through some form of exchange rate rebalancing, especially from China, rather than growth rebalancing.

Conclusions

The apparent decoupling of emerging markets at the beginning of the 2008/2009 crisis has led many to initially underestimate its impact on developing economies. Consequently, most attention in academic and policy circles has initially been devoted to domestic and regulatory explanations, and relevant solutions, for the crisis in the advanced economies. In this essay, we have reviewed the global financial crisis from the standpoint of emerging markets and in an international perspective. In particular, we have first discussed the effects of the crisis on emerging and developing economies and Developing Asia in relation to the advanced economies with respect to growth, trade and investment. Then, we have focused on the role played by the international concentration of excess savings (mostly in emerging markets) on too few assets (mostly in advanced economies, and the US in particular). Paradoxically, this situation seems to have occurred as emerging markets tried to take stock of the crises experienced in the 1990s and improve their internal and external macroeconomic environment. According to this hypothesis, the governments of emerging markets and their 'mercantilist' approach share responsibility for the crisis with the governments of industrial economies. Therefore, understanding the causes of the large global imbalances that see emerging market surpluses as the counterpart of the large industrial countries' deficits is important in order to devise long-lasting solutions to the crisis not just for emerging markets, but for the global economy in general. Crisis solutions that do not address the roots of such fundamental imbalance between developed and developing countries external positions may be destined to produce effects only in the short term. In this respect, the crisis may also represent an opportunity to build a more balanced and, hence more stable, world economy. Then, together with policies aiming at achieving domestic equilibrium and financial stability, it seems necessary to encourage greater international cooperation in terms of domestic policies, but also in the direction of achieving more balanced terms of trade and aligned real exchange rates.

Data appendix: country groups

Advanced economies include

Australia; Austria; Belgium; Canada; Czech Republic; Cyprus; Denmark; Finland; France; Germany; Greece; Hong Kong SAR; Iceland; Ireland; Israel; Italy; Japan; Korea; Luxembourg; Malta; Netherlands; New Zealand; Norway; Portugal; Singapore; Slovak Republic; Slovenia; Spain; Sweden; Switzerland; Taiwan Province of China; UK; US.

Emerging and developing economies

Afghanistan, Rep. of; Albania; Algeria; Angola; Antigua and Barbuda; Argentina; Armenia; Azerbaijan; Bahamas, the; Bahrain; Bangladesh; Barbados; Belarus; Belize; Benin; Bhutan; Bolivia; Botswana; Bosnia and Herzegovina; Brazil; Brunei Darussalam; Bulgaria; Burkina Faso; Burundi; Cambodia; Cameroon; Cape Verde; Central African Republic; Chad; Chile; China; Colombia; Comoros; Congo, Dem. Rep. of; Congo, Rep. of; Costa Rica; Cote d'Ivoire; Croatia; Djibouti; Dominica; Dominican Republic; Ecuador; Egypt; El Salvador; Equatorial Guinea; Estonia; Eritrea; Ethiopia; Fiji; Gabon; Gambia, The; Georgia; Ghana; Grenada; Guatemala; Guinea; Guinea-Bissau; Guyana; Haiti; Honduras; Hungary; India; Indonesia; Iran, I.R. of; Iraq; Jamaica; Jordan; Kazakhstan; Kenya; Kiribati; Kuwait; Kyrgyz Republic; Lao PDR; Latvia; Lebanon; Lesotho; Liberia; Libya; Lithuania; Macedonia, FYR; Madagascar; Malawi; Malaysia; Maldives; Mali; Mauritania; Mauritius; Mexico; Moldova; Mongolia; Montenegro, Rep. of; Morocco; Mozambique, Rep. of; Myanmar; Namibia; Nepal; Nicaragua; Niger; Nigeria; Oman; Pakistan; Panama; Papua New Guinea; Paraguay; Peru; Philippines; Poland; Qatar; Romania; Russia; Rwanda; Samoa; Sao Tome and Principe; Saudi Arabia; Senegal; Serbia; Seychelles; Sierra Leone; Solomon Islands; South Africa; Sri Lanka; St. Kitts and Nevis; St. Lucia; St. Vincent and the Grenadines; Sudan; Suriname; Swaziland; Syrian Arab Republic; Tajikistan; Tanzania; Thailand; Timor-Leste, Dem. Rep. of; Togo; Tonga; Trinidad and Tobago; Tunisia; Turkey; Turkmenistan; Uganda; Ukraine; United Arab Emirates; Uruguay; Uzbekistan; Vanuatu; Venezuela, Rep. Boliv. de; Vietnam; Yemen; Zambia; Zimbabwe.

Developing Asia

Afghanistan, Rep. of; Bangladesh; Bhutan; Brunei Darussalam; Cambodia; China; Fiji; India; Indonesia; Kiribati; Lao PDR; Malaysia;

Maldives; Myanmar; Nepal; Pakistan; Papua New Guinea; Philippines; Samoa; Solomon Islands; Sri Lanka; Thailand; Timor-Leste, Dem. Rep. of; Tonga; Vanuatu; Vietnam.

Notes

1. See, among others, Bayoumi et al. (2007) and Fazio (2007).
2. At the international level, failure in the regulation of the market for structured products has been blamed. In this respect, a special mention has been dedicated to the (in)ability of international institutions to deal with a systemic crisis, both in terms of mandate and funds availability.
3. Clearly, good fundamentals were not distributed equally across regions. Many Central and Eastern European countries, for example, suffered from current account deficits.
4. See, among the others, Bartram and Bodnar (2009) for a discussion of the impact of the crisis on global investment.
5. See Reisen (2008) for an early discussion of the impact of the financial crisis on emerging markets.
6. Most notably, this group includes China and India.
7. Greenspan (2005) defined a *conundrum* the low levels of long-term interest rates in the mid of the 2000s in spite of increasing short term rates.
8. The relationship between worsening current accounts and house price appreciation seems to hold for other industrial countries, as well. Germany and Japan, instead, experienced large surpluses and very little house price increases.
9. In this respect, policymakers seem to have taken stock of the lessons of the Great Crisis in 1929.

References

Arezki, Rabah and Fuad Hasanov (2009). Global Imbalances and Petrodollars. IMF Working Paper, WP/09/89, International Monetary Fund, Washington D.C., USA.

Bartram Sohnke M. and Gordon M. Bodnar (2009). No place to hide: the global crisis in equity markets in 2008/2009. Online at http://mpra.ub.uni-muenchen.de/15955/ as accessed on 28 January 2010 MPRA Paper No. 15955, posted 28 June 2009/13:36.

Bayoumi, Tamim, Giorgio Fazio, Manmohan Kumar and Ronald MacDonald (2007). Fatal attraction: Using distance to measure contagion in good times as well as bad. *Review of Financial Economics, Elsevier*, 16(3), 259–273.

Berglof, Erik (2008). The financial crisis in emerging markets: lessons for global and not-so-global financial architecture. Presentation at the conference 'Preventing the Next Financial Crisis', Columbia University, 11 December.

Bernanke, Ben S. (2005). The Global Saving Glut and the U.S. Current Account Deficit. Sandridge Lecture at the Virginia Association of Economics, 10 March.

Bown, Chad P. (2009). Protectionism increases and spreads: global use of trade remedies rises by 18.8% in first quarter 2009. A monitoring update to the global antidumping database, Brandeis University and The Brookings Institutions, mimeo.

Caballero, Ricardo J. (2006). On the Macroeconomics of Asset Shortages, MIT Department of Economics Working Paper No. 06–30.

Caballero, Ricardo J., Emanuek Farhi and Pierre-Olivier Gourinchas (2008). An equilibrium model of 'global imbalances' and low interest rates. *American Economic Review* 98, 358–393.

Caballero, Ricardo J. and Arvind Krishnamurthy (2009). Global imbalances and financial fragility. *American Economic Review* 99(2), 584–588.

Calvo, G. (2008). Exploding commodity prices, lax monetary policy and sovereign wealth funds. VoxEU, 20 June.

Chamon, Marcos and Eswar Prasad (2008). Why are Saving Rates of Urban Households in China Rising?. IMF Working Paper, WP/08/145, International Monetary Fund, Washington D.C., USA.

Chinn, Menzie D. and Hiro Ito (2007). Current account balances, financial development and institutions: Assaying the world 'saving glut'. *Journal of International Money and Finance* 59(1), 47–76.

Cova, Pietro, Massimiliano Pisani and Alessandro Rebucci (2009). Global Imbalances: the Role of Emerging Asia. IMF Working Paper, WP/09/64, International Monetary Fund, Washington D.C., USA.

Craine, Roger and Vance Martin (2009). Interest rate conundrum. *The B.E. Journal of Macroeconomics* 9(1) (contributions), article 8.

Dallara, Charles, Yusuke Horiguchi and Philip Suttle (2007). The U.S. Mortgage Crisis and Emerging Markets. Institute of International Finance, Special Briefing, 27 August.

Dooley, Michael, David Folkerts-Landau and Peter Garber (2005). International financial stability: Asia, interest rates and the dollar. Deutsche Bank Global Markets Research, http://econ.ucsc.edu/_mpd/Int%20Fin%20Stab.pdf

Edwards, Sebastian (2007). On current account surpluses and the correction of global imbalances, National Bureau of Economic Research Working Paper No. 12904.

Fazio, Giorgio (2007). Extreme contagion and extreme interdependence between emerging markets. *Journal of International Money and Finance* 26(8), 1261–1291.

Frank, Nathaniel and Heiko Hesse (2009). Financial Spillovers to Emerging Markets During the Global Financial Crisis. IMF Working Paper, WP/09/104, International Monetary Fund, Washington D.C., USA.

Frankel, J. Alexander (2006). The effect of monetary policy on real commodity prices, NBER Working Paper 12713.

Frenkel, Roberto and Martin Rapetti (2009). A developing country view of the current global crisis: what should not be forgotten and what should be done. *Cambridge Journal of Economics* 33, 685–702.

Goswami, Mangal and Ceyla Pazarbasioglu (2008). Emerging markets weather fallout from financial crisis. *International Monetary Fund Survey Magazine*, 8 May Web site: http://imf.org/external/pubs/ft/survey/so/2008/NEW050808A.htm as accessed on 28 January 2010.

Greenspan, Alan (2005). Statement to the Senate Committee on Banking, Housing, and Urban Affairs, presenting the Federal Reserve Board's Monetary Policy Report to the Congress. 16 February, www.federalreserve.gov/boarddocs/hh/2005/february/testimony.htm

Greenspan, Alan (2009). The Fed didn't cause the housing bubble. *Wall Street Journal Online*, 11 March. Web site: http://online.wsj.com/article/SB123672965066989281.html as accessed on 28 January 2010.

Grilli, Enzo R. and Yang M. Cheng (1988). Primary commodity prices, manufactured goods prices, and the terms of trade of developing countries: what the long run shows. *The World Bank Economic Review* 2, 1–47.

International Monetary Fund (IMF), Directions of Trade Statistics, October 2009, ESDS International, (Mimas) University of Manchester.

International Monetary Fund (IMF), International Financial Statistics, October 2009, ESDS International, (Mimas) University of Manchester.

International Monetary Fund (IMF), World Economic Outlook, October 2009, ESDS International, (Mimas) University of Manchester.

Krugman, Paul (2008). Running Out of Planet to Exploit, 21 April, New York Times Op-Ed Columnist.

Mendoza, Ronald U. (2009). Was the Asian crisis a wake-up call? *Journal of Asian Economics* 21(1) February 2010, 1–19.

Minsky, Hyman (1986). *Stabilising and Unstable Economy*. New Haven, CT: Yale University Press.

Prebisch, Raul (1950). The Economic Development of Latin America and its Principal Problems. Reprinted in: *Economic Bulletin for Latin America* 7, 1962, 1–22.

Reisen, Helmut (2008). The fallout from the financial crisis: Emerging markets under Stress, OECD Development Centre, Policy Insight, No. 83, December 2008, Paris.

Rodrik, Dani (2009). Let Developing Nations Rule, VOX, 28 January.

Setser, Brad (2009). Debating the global roots of the current crisis, VOX, 28 January.

Singer, Hans (1950). The distribution of gains between investing and borrowing countries. *American Economic Review* 40, 473–485.

Sun, Tao and Xiaojing Zhang (2009). Spillovers of the U.S. Subprime Financial Turmoil to Mainland China and Hong Kong SAR: Evidence from Stock Markets. IMF Working Paper, WP/09/166, International Monetary Fund, Washington D.C., USA.

Tong, Hui and Shang-Jin Wei (2009). The Composition Matters: Capital Inflows and Liquidity Crunch During a Global Economic Crisis. IMF Working Paper, WP/09/164, International Monetary Fund, Washington D.C., USA.

Warnock, Francis E. and Veronica C. Warnock (forthcoming). International capital flows and U.S. interest rates. *Journal of International Money and Finance*.

Willenbockel, Dirk and Sherman Robinson (2009). The Global Financial Crisis, LDC Exports and Welfare: Analysis with a World Trade Model, Munich Personal Repec Archive No. 15377, May.

Wolf, Martin (2008). Life in a tough world of high commodity prices. *Financial Times*, 4 March.

6
The Global Financial Crisis and the Crisis of European Neoliberalism

Alan W. Cafruny

Introduction

The global financial crisis has devastated Europe's economy and greatly damaged its prospects for closer integration. Europe's plunge into the worst recession since the Second World War abruptly terminated the mood of triumphalism that accompanied the introduction of European Monetary Union (EMU) and the rather modest gains in productivity, growth and employment that had been achieved during the period of 2005–2007 after years of stagnation.[1] By demonstrating that Europe remains especially vulnerable to external financial shocks and the contraction of global trade the crisis has shattered dreams of de-coupling from the US. It has also brought into sharper relief a number of underlying problems that have bedeviled the EU throughout its neoliberal phase of development: overemphasis on price stability and flexible labour and capital markets to generate employment and growth; uneven development and mounting financial imbalances; and German mercantilism.

This chapter examines the EU's response to the global financial crisis. The crisis broke out in the US banking sector, but the underlying cause was stagnation and the mutually reinforcing cycle of declining real incomes and ultimately unsustainable increases in household indebtedness beginning in the 1980s. Prior to the crisis, it was possible to argue that the member states of the EU – and especially the euro-zone – had achieved sufficient regional autonomy under the shelter of the euro so as to be at least partially insulated from the effects of global recession (IMF 2007). But this argument underestimated the extent to which the European economy had become integrated within global financial markets and dependent on flexible labour markets, outsourcing and, especially in the case of Germany, export-led growth. European banks were heavily exposed to the US sub-prime meltdown that started in early 2007, and the continent was hit hard by plummeting global demand that followed the crash of Lehman Brothers bank in September 2008.

During the third quarter of 2009 the EU technically emerged from recession. However, the fragile and anaemic recovery excluded the UK, Ireland and many southern and eastern European member states. A global depression was arguably averted primarily by the expansionary policies of the US Federal Reserve Bank, the US Treasury and the Bank of China, and secondarily by the interventions of European national governments and the ECB. Brussels, by contrast, was relegated to the sidelines. Even before the crisis Europe's global economic and political influence was waning and its project of integration was in disarray. Europe's prospects and global stature will continue to diminish unless it finds a way to resolve the problem of asymmetry between the economic and political dimensions of integration.

Origins of the crisis

The tendency towards financialization and growing indebtedness in the US lies at the heart of the global crisis. The expansion of debt was made possible by the emergence of the dollar as a fiat currency after 1971. Debt levels and the size of ensuing global imbalances increased gradually in the second half of the 1980s and 1990s, and then exponentially in the aftermath of the Asian financial crisis of 1997, when developing countries sought to prevent speculative attacks and IMF structural adjustment programmes by accumulating massive dollar reserves.

Financialization and stagnation

The turn towards financialization in the US came about in the context of the crisis of Fordism and the collapse of the Bretton Woods regime. The Volcker shocks of 1979, under which high interest rates imposed harsh monetary discipline throughout the world, laid the basis for the emergence of the 'Dollar Wall Street regime' with the dollar as lynchpin (Gowan 1999, Sarai 2008). As a result of global capital market liberalization US financial institutions could attract massive inflows of capital, greatly enhancing their capacity to restructure the US society along neoliberal lines (Felder 2008). Financialization gathered steam throughout the 1980s and 1990s as the regulatory framework that had been established during the New Deal was reconfigured by the Clinton and Bush administrations under the close supervision of money centre banks and the US Treasury. In the 1980s US savings and loan institutions were deregulated. In 1999 the Gramm-Leach-Bliley Act repealed the last remnants of the Glass-Steagall Act, which had prohibited investment banks from owning commercial banking institutions whose accounts were ensured by the FDIC. The Commodities Futures Modernization Act (CFMA) of 2000 eliminated Federal and state regulation of important banking activities, including derivatives contracts. These measures led to the explosive growth of credit and increasingly reckless speculation on asset-price increases, necessitating a succession of privately organized or government bailouts. Their impact on the financial system was magnified by lax SEC enforcement, increases in the amount of leverage allowed to investment banks and permissive monetary policies supported by the claim that the 'irrational exuberance' of markets was self-correcting. Rather than relying on their traditional house-bank linkages at home, Asian and European corporations increasingly turned to the US stock market to raise capital. All of these factors allowed the US to finance growing balance of payments and government deficits and opened up vast and lucrative new markets for the US financial services industry.

The causes of the financial crisis have generally been understood to have arisen within the sphere of finance and regulatory policies. However, a deeper and more comprehensive explanation for the crisis points to changes in the 'real political economy' that precipitated speculation and deregulation. Underlying financialization and deregulation was a long-run trend towards stagnation (Foster and Magdoff 2008; Harvey 2005), expressed through declining rates of growth and corporate profitability. As Table 6.1 indicates, the rate of growth of real US GDP has decreased throughout the post-Second World War period.

A further indication of stagnation has been the long-range decline of capacity utilization in manufacturing, a reflection in part of the problem of the US domestic automobile industry. Since the late 1970s the rate of return on domestic investment in the US has declined in absolute terms as well as in relation to foreign direct investment (Dumenil and Levy 2004). The decline was especially dramatic for the decade 1997–2007 (Mandel 2009).

The neoliberal offensive represented capital's attempt to reverse these tendencies by imposing new legal restrictions on trade unions, scaling back levels of progressive taxation, increasing rates of immigration and subjecting labour to increased global competition through trade liberalization and outsourcing. These measures led to declining real wages,

Table 6.1   Average annual percent growth in real GDP, 1930–2007.

1930s	1.3
1940s	5.9
1950s	4.1
1960s	4.4
1970s	3.3
1980s	3.1
1990s	3.1
2000–2008	2.2

Source: National Income and Products Accounts, 'Current Dollar and Real GDP,' Table 1.1.1. Bureau of Economic Analysis, www.bea.gov/national/xls/gdplev.xls.

steep reduction in the share of wages in GDP and growing inequality (Piketty and Saez 2003; OECD 2009; Saez 2009; Weisbrot 2009). Between 1979 and 2006 real incomes for the top 1 per cent of households rose by 256 per cent compared to 21 per cent for the middle fifth; and 11 per cent for the bottom fifth. The share of national after-tax income of the top 1 per cent of households rose from 7.5 per cent to 16.3 per cent (Schmitt 2009). Having peaked in 1945, trade union membership declined from 31 per cent of the workforce in 1960 to 11 per cent in 2007, approximating the level of 1929.

These data provide the context for understanding the explosive growth of the financial services 'industry', including not only the expansion of existing banks and financial institutions but also the growing involvement of industrial corporations in finance and investment. Between 1998 and 2006 the financial services industry doubled in size, from 4 per cent to 8 per cent of GDP. In 2006 it produced no less than 41 per cent of the profits of the US domestic economy (Johnson 2009). Finance capital arguably ascended to a position of structural dominance in the US during the first two decades of the twentieth century. But the contemporary crisis and terms of its resolution suggest that a further 'quiet coup' (Johnson 2008) has taken place whereby the structural power of finance capital in the American state has become instrumentalized among a small oligarchy of leading money centre banks that are 'too big to fail' and whose interests and outlook now entirely transcend party politics and electoral cycles.

The stagnation of real incomes reinforced the tendency towards financialization as an expanding pool of investment resources outpaced opportunities available in the 'real economy'. At the same time, working and middle-class households sought to maintain levels of consumption by working longer hours and accumulating rising debt on credit cards, automobiles and mortgages, encouraged by a burgeoning shadow banking system seeking to expand credit to progressively less qualified borrowers. The ability of the Federal Reserve to keep credit flowing was facilitated by the status of the dollar as international reserve currency and the determination of export-led emerging markets, especially in Asia, to maintain large dollar balances and depreciated currencies. Americans became the world's 'consumers of last resort', but continuing high levels of consumption depended on a succession of bubbles and ultimately unsustainable levels of household debt. Mounting global imbalances are raising increasingly urgent questions concerning the contingent status of the dollar as international reserve currency. If in the aftermath of the immediate crisis these questions remain unanswered they nevertheless appear to be placing limits on the extent to which traditional Keynesian policies of public debt could replace an exhausted 'private debt-Keyensianism' as unemployment has soared to unprecedented post-Second World War levels. At the same time, the foregoing suggests the limits of an approach to crisis resolution that is restricted to the sphere of finance: if in fact financial instability is rooted in the growing inequalities resulting from the neoliberal offensive then a comprehensive solution to the long-run crisis would require substantial wealth redistribution (Ivanova 2009). Yet, there is little evidence that the requisite social forces for such a radical political transformation can be mobilized at the present time. In this sense, capital's own long-range interests have not been well-served by labour's virtually unconditional surrender.

Europe's structural position within the US-led global financial system

If the US has been its epicentre, the trend towards financialization has nevertheless played out globally and in the EU (Konings 2008). In part, this has resulted from an active process of emulation of, and linkage to, an allegedly superior 'American model' thought until recently to be capable of generating higher growth and productivity rates (Cafruny and Ryner 2007a). The growing role of finance in Europe may also reflect tendencies that are internal to the process of capital accumulation in all mature economies (Sablowski 2008). Financial market liberalization in continental Europe has made considerable progress, albeit more incrementally than in London and New York. As a result of the Financial Services Action Plan (FSAP) of 1999 the goal of a unified market for financial services was established. EU–US financial market integration has proceeded rapidly during the past decade as part of a broader process of transatlantic economic integration (for example, Quinlan 2003). While 'Rhineland capitalism' continues to display distinctive features, a profound transformation in Germany has nevertheless been set in motion not only with respect to corporate finance but also to labour markets. During the last two decades capital markets have become increasingly more important for German firms as the shift towards investment banking has disrupted traditional ties between banks and industry. Large German banks have severed their ties with industrial companies. Hedge funds, insurance companies and foreign investors have gained influence. As Thomas Sablowski (2008: p. 148) writes, 'Even if, compared to other countries, the role of the new institutional investors is still limited, the large banks and insurance companies in Germany have set up their own investment companies which are pursuing the same short-term shareholder value orientation as Anglo-Saxon institutional investors.'

Financialization rendered Europe highly vulnerable to the effects of the US sub-prime crisis. Not only British, Swiss and French, but also German banks were heavily exposed. At the start of the crisis German banks had the largest leverage rates among OECD countries. IKB Dutwsche Industriebank suffered a near collapse in 2007 as a result of its participation in US sub-prime mortgages, compelling it to write off $20 billion and obtain massive aid from the government. Several other German banks, including regional *Landesbanks*, suffered significant losses, including HSH Nordbank, Commerzbank, Bayern LB and Deutsche Bank which listed 50 private Goldman Sachs deals for sub-prime bonds, mostly issued through the Cayman Islands, of which 80 per cent held AAA ratings (Gordon 2009). At the end of 2009 European banks were estimated to hold more than $1 trillion in toxic assets, more than two-thirds of which was held by German banks (Carrington et al. 2009).

The volume of financial transactions between the US and Europe increased exponentially over the decade 1997–2007. At the end of 2007 the share of EU securities in foreign holdings by US individuals amounted to 42 per cent for equities and 53 per cent for asset-backed securities, amounting by the end of 2006 to $1.8 trillion of equity holdings and 0.87 of debt holdings. Similarly, the share of EU investments in US equity amounted to 39 per cent of total foreign investments, while that of asset-backed securities was 32 per cent. EU holdings of US debt and equity amounted to $2.1 trillion and $1.2 trillion, following growth rates of approximately 20 per cent per year (Deutsche Bank research 2008. By 2007 the US accounted for 40 per cent of global stock market capitalization; 26 per cent of European asset price variation (50 per cent in the case of equity markets) was due to developments in the US. (IMF 2007: Chapter 4).

The mutually reinforcing tendency of growing financialization and labour market flexibility that has characterized the US is also evident throughout Europe and most consequentially in Germany. At the level of the EU it has been encouraged by the Lisbon Strategy with its emphasis on competitiveness and labour market flexibility, the anti-growth bias of the ECB and a succession of intergovernmental pacts mandating fiscal austerity. During the last decade a succession of reform programs and 'employers offensives' (Kinderman 2005) undertaken by both the CDU/CDS and SDP has dramatically decreased unit labour costs. In 1997 the Kohl government implemented 'the largest cutbacks in social policy in the Federal Republic's history (Siegel 2004: p. 118)'. Unwilling to challenge fiscal austerity and 'sound money', the Schroeder government pursued further welfare state retrenchment. Agenda 2010 resulted in further sweeping changes in employment protection and social assistance. Alongside these reforms, German corporations have pursued extensive outsourcing strategies, especially in Eastern Europe (Lorentowicz et al. 2002). These developments have resulted in significant increases in levels of poverty, inequality and part-time and precarious work. (OECD 2009; Weinkopf 2009). As a consequence of these measures the link between export-led growth and the internal market that characterized Germany's post-war growth miracle has been severed (Hugh 2007; IMF 2007). Germany's growing dependence on exports has important implications for the stability of the euro-zone.

EU policies and the crisis

If the thesis of 'de-coupling' with respect to 'emerging markets' retains some plausibility, especially with respect to China (for example, El Erian 2009), the global financial crisis has refuted claims that the European economy is capable of generating an autonomous growth trajectory. Since the outset of the crisis, Europe has suffered greater declines in production and growth than any other region. The euro-zone has experienced larger declines in GDP even than Britain and the US. Exports fell by 24 per cent during 2008 as the EU's share of global exports fell from 31 per cent in 2004 to 28 per cent in 2008. During 2009 the euro-zone's GDP was forecast to fall by 4.1 per cent, with German GDP falling by 4.3 per cent, Italy at 4.7 per cent, Spain at 3.7 per cent and France at 2.3 per cent (Eurostat 2009). By the end of September 2009 European banks had written off $685 billion in losses in securities and loans but were estimated to have yet to acknowledge a further $934 billion (IMF 2009, Figure 1.9). Levels of unemployment began rising in the first quarter of 2008 and increased by 5.8 million between March 2008 and September 2009 (Eurostat 2009); and were expected to increase substantially throughout 2010.

This is the context in which the EU technically exited from recession in the third quarter of 2009, led by Germany and France with GDP increases of 0.7 per cent and 0.3 per cent respectively. Yet even this tepid recovery (from a very low base) masked the profound structural problems facing the euro-zone: continuing corporate downturns; a massive credit crunch affecting households and the private sector; declining industrial output; lagging productivity even in relation to the US; and the growing role of exports as key driver of growth. High levels of excess capacity suggested a longer-run danger of deflation. As Europe embarks on its own process of labour flexibility, the problem of sustaining demand – and hence productivity – becomes more difficult (Bertola 2009). At the end of 2009 it was possible that the anaemic recovery would not last; in the aftermath of the September 2009 elections a new wave of corporate restructuring and large increases in unemployment was widely anticipated (Atkins and Benoit 2009;). 'Automatic stabilizers' in the form of transfer payments and short-term work schemes were vulnerable to fiscal retrenchment and the ECB's proposed exit strategy. Europe's periphery is experiencing much worse. While a full-scale meltdown may have been averted, real GDP in much of Eastern Europe in 2009 was expected to reduce by 5–10 per cent, including falls of 14–18 per cent in the Baltic States and over 20 per cent in the Ukraine.

Washington and Brussels

The financial crisis hit Europe just as it was attempting to emerge from years of ECB-led monetary austerity, slow growth and weak productivity gains. In response to modest recovery beginning in 2005 the ECB embarked on a programme of interest rate increases. Indeed, as late as July 2008, long after the crisis had erupted, interest rates were raised from 3.75 per cent to 4.25 per cent. In similar fashion, fiscal austerity remained a central goal of EU policy; under the terms of the GSP, public deficits in the euro-zone were reduced from 1.3 per cent in 2006 to 0.6 per cent in 2007. Of course, ECB policies changed dramatically after the crash of Lehman. The ECB then provided massive liquidity to troubled banks. By May 2009 it had lowered the lead interest rate to 1 per cent (still above US rates). In June, 2009 the ECB further stated that it would meet banks' demands for reserves by offering 12-month loans. European governments also injected large amounts of liquidity into major banks and offered guarantees for inter-bank lending. As a result governments became major shareholders in a number of large banks, including BNP Paribas, Societe Generale, Lloyds, RBS and Commerzbank; Northern Rock, Hypo Real Estate, Anglo-Irish and Fortis were nationalized.

Despite these policies the meltdown was averted primarily as a result of the extraordinarily aggressive intervention of the US Treasury and Federal Reserve Bank, recoiling at the spectre of global depression. Such intervention included the injection of $2 trillion in reserves in the 6 weeks following the collapse of Lehman; a $787 billion stimulus package equal to 3 per cent of GDP in 2009 and 2010; conventional and innovative measures designed to ease credit for money centre banks to nominal zero and *de facto* negative interest rates; unprecedented provision of liquidity and guarantees (US commitments of approximately $12 trillion overall); dramatic expansion of IMF, EBRD, EIB, Federal Reserve Bank swaps to the ECB, Japan and emerging markets totalling $585 billion (Martensen 2009). In addition, China implemented a stimulus package of $689 billion, although much of it was devoted to export infrastructure. Notwithstanding the stimulus package, the response of the Obama Administration and Democratic-led Congress has been focused primarily on repairing the balance sheets of Wall Street banks.

Financial regulation and state aid

Focusing primarily on liberalization of labour and product markets and financial deregulation, prior to the crisis neither the ECB nor the Commission addressed Europe's own speculative banking practices, including the deepening involvement of Western European banks in the US sub-prime market and similar overexposure in Eastern European property markets, in which Austrian (Eastern Europe) and Swedish (Baltics) banks played a prominent role. Following the collapse of Lehman Brothers, significant structural reforms to the European financial system were widely anticipated. However, as the immediate impact of the crisis receded, the impetus for reform diminished. The de Larosiere

Report, publishing in February 2009, made several proposals for reforms, including the establishment of a European Systemic Risk Council. Sharp conflicts of interest over the future scope of banking regulation have paralyzed the Commission. The European banking sector continues to be organized along national lines. Member states have been unwilling to accept pan-European supervisory principles and boards. As the immediate crisis has receded banks have lobbied more forcefully against tighter controls (for example, Guha 2009). There have been several clashes between the British government and the 'Franco-German alliance' concerning the regulation of hedge funds and accounting rules for banks. But fundamental changes in existing rules are unlikely to be carried out against the wishes of the City of London. These conflicts are reproduced at the global level with reference to the actions of the G-20 regarding financial reform. The main achievement of the G-20 has been expansion of IMF resources, albeit largely in response to the EU desire to use these resources to avoid financial collapse along its own periphery and bail out its own banks.

While European national governments have embarked on extensive stimulus programmes, these have not been coordinated on a European basis: stimulus programmes have been entirely national in scope, structural rather than counter-cyclical and lacking an exit strategy. The failure to coordinate state aid has been most notable with respect to Germany and France. Even as Chancellor Merkel eventually stepped back from Finance Minister Peer Steinbruck's dismissal of 'crass Keynesianism' she made it clear that there was 'no sensible alternative' (*Wall Street Journal* 2009) to exports as a foundation for German growth and prosperity. Germany has established a €115 billion 'Deutschland Fund'. It has responded to French state aid in the automobile industry with its own 'cash for clunkers' programme and a proposed extensive (€4.5 billion) state aid for Opel as part of a deal with Magna that was clearly structured to export surplus capacity to other member states, thereby contradicting single market rules and solidarity norms (GM's rejection of the deal has precipitated a new bidding auction among member states).

France and Germany appear to be on a collision course with respect to fiscal policy. In September 2009 Germany changed its constitution to prevent the federal deficit from exceeding 0.35 per cent of GDP over the economic cycle, implying a long-run debt-to-GDP ratio of 10 per cent. Although the cap is to take effect in 2016 it will require significant fiscal retrenchment prior to that date. Even without taking into account the 'grand loan' France has stated it will not reduce its budget deficit to 3 per cent of GDP before 2015 at the earliest and its budget deficit is slated to peak at 8.5 per cent of GDP in 2010. At that time its debt-to-GDP ratio is expected to exceed 90 per cent. Italy's debt-to-GDP ratio will exceed 125 per cent by the end of 2010 (Plender 2009). By October 2009 the Commission had initiated 'excessive deficit' procedures against no less than 18 countries, including Germany. The sizes of the deficits (and surpluses) are a symptom of the financial crisis and its immediate aftermath but, more fundamentally, a reflection of the chronic and growing problem of uneven development.

Uneven development and German mercantilism

Conflicts over industrial and fiscal policies underline the limitations of the euro as an international reserve currency. The euro-zone remains a politically motivated construct; 10 years after its advent, even as the euro itself has demonstrated impressive 'stability' and taken its place as a secondary international reserve currency the euro-zone has in important respects arguably moved farther away from an 'optimal currency area'. The divergence in growth rates has increased; unemployment in the euro-zone has exceeded that in the 'opt-out' countries and labour productivity has slowed in absolute and relative terms. Current account imbalances following the introduction of the euro have risen twice as fast as during the prior decade (Lund and Roxburgh 2009). Labour mobility continues to be limited by cultural and linguistic attachments. By encouraging structural labour reform the ECB's anti-inflationary mandate has thus far buttressed Germany's position as surplus country and export powerhouse (Flassbeck 2008). Given its concentration on high-technology exports and ability to reduce unit labour costs Germany has thus far been able to increase its share of global exports even as the euro has appreciated substantially against the Renminbi and Dollar. However, Germany's structural position as a surplus country does not appear compatible with an increasing global role for the euro.[2]

By permanently eliminating the depreciation option, EMU took the euro-zone countries into uncharted waters. The EU has no centralized fiscal policy and, as the history of the fiscal pacts makes clear, over the long haul no intergovernmental pact can compensate for the absence of a genuine polity. The disciplinary and pro-cyclical features of a succession of fiscal pacts have reflected the interests of the stronger economies, most notably Germany, in institutionalizing fiscal austerity. The absence of a Union budget does not allow for the extensive redistributive policies necessary to minimize uneven development by compensating weaker

Figure 6.1 Italy and Germany shares of world exports 1995–2006.
Source: Banca d'Italia (2006b).

economies that have lost the option of devaluation. It is widely assumed that the imperatives of monetary union mean there is no alternative to flexible labour markets. If structural labour reform is a feasible short-term solution to Germany's predicament it is a highly problematic strategy for the euro-zone as a whole.

The policy of 'competitive austerity' (Albo 1994) as the means of (internal) adjustment to a one-size-fits-all exchange rate is thus ultimately a strategy of German mercantilism (Cafruny and Ryner 2007b, esp. Chapter 3; de Grauwe 2006a, 2006b). German exports have shown remarkable resilience; exports constitute a growing share of GDP alongside a secular decline in the rate of household consumption growth (Hugh 2007). Germany's trade surplus with its euro-zone partners has increased dramatically in the last decade. In 2008 Germany's current account surplus with the rest of the world reached $235 billion representing 6.4 per cent of GDP, of which 85 per cent was with the rest of the EU. By contrast, Spain's current account deficit was $154 billion, equal to 10 per cent of GDP. Greece and Portugal had even larger current account deficits in relation to GDP (Lund and Roxburgh 2009). Figure 6.1 documents the contrasting trajectories of Italy and Germany with respect to shares of world exports beginning in 1995.

Klaus Mueller has aptly summarized the implications of these developments (2009: p. 5):

Germany, now behind the protective shield of the common currency, could devalue its unit labour cost without having to fear the sanctioning mechanism of the past: a revaluation of the German Mark.

Germany *free rides* in the euro-zone by restricting domestic consumption while expecting demand for its highly competitive goods from all other countries; it expects global demand without demanding itself.

Because the deficit economies cannot depreciate their currencies and can only achieve productivity gains in the long run, they are compelled to adopt wage cuts and deflation, a strategy that exacerbates the problem of fiscal deficits and produces political instability. Germany has begun to define its national interests as distinctive from the demands of European integration, a development that is also evident in growing political and commercial linkages with Moscow, especially in the energy sector.

Crisis in Europe's periphery

The effects of the crisis on Southern and Eastern Europe have been especially acute. On the eve of crisis the new member states already were struggling with a model of development based on foreign direct investment in search of cheap labour and trade dependence on Western Europe, especially Germany (Bohle 2006; Ivanova 2009). Strategic sectors of the Central and Eastern European economies, including banking, telecommunications and utilities had been privatized and sold to Western firms. Many Central and Eastern European economies were heavily exposed to borrowing in foreign currencies and vulnerable to global financial disorder by virtue of massive current account deficits. By 2004 debt service payments accounted for 25 per cent of Hungary's, 27 per cent of Croatia's and 35 per cent of Poland's exports. Western European banks, especially Austrian, German, Italian and Swedish, are heavily exposed as a result of their participation in the property bubble; the exposure of Austrian banks is equivalent to 70 per cent of GDP (Raviv 2007). As noted above, with the exception of Poland, which has benefited from substantial currency devaluation and foreign remittances, Eastern and Central European member states have suffered massive decreases in GDP since 2007 and large spikes in unemployment. Abandoning its stated commitment to solidarity, the EU has deployed the IMF as the key arbiter of emergency funding (Verhofstadt 2009). Since November 2008 the IMF has concluded agreements with 11 countries in the region, starting with Latvia, Hungary and Ukraine. Yet, these agreements are essentially pro-cyclical structural adjustment programmes, designed in part to bail out heavily exposed Western European banks (Weisbrot 2009).

The situation within the euro-zone itself is even more problematic. The gap between the surplus countries of the north and debtor countries of the south has grown substantially since the outbreak of the financial crisis, threatening the integrity of the monetary union. Membership in EMU protected debtor countries from currency crises even as it kept their borrowing costs low. At the same time, of course, it precluded devaluation as a means of regaining competitiveness. Given that Italy, Spain and Greece would each require devaluation in the range of 30 per cent in the real effective exchange rate to regain competiveness (Plender 2009: 20), the only other option is massive fiscal retrenchment and reduction of wages. Hence the possibility of default on rising public sector debt in Europe's periphery remains acute. A debt crisis would present three possible alternatives: first, a 'nuclear option' of default followed by exit from the euro-zone for one country. This action, which will become increasingly attractive as the ECB begins its exit strategy, could trigger a chain reaction and ultimately lead to a break-up of the monetary union. A second scenario is a transition to a political union under which government bonds could be issued centrally by the ECB, thereby enabling the redistribution of resources from surplus to debtor countries. If the second scenario is idealistic, the first does not appear likely at the present time. In February 2009 German finance minister Peer Steinbruck signalled that Germany, either on its own or in conjunction with the ECB, would be willing to bail out debtor countries (and, by implication, German banks). But this third scenario would be politically unpopular in Germany. German or ECB bail outs would certainly entail significant austerity and conditionality, perhaps even under the auspices of the IMF, further exacerbating tensions within the eurozone.

The inherent tension between a monetary union and fiscal intergovernmentalism has led to calls for a 'Stability Pact for External Balances' for the euro-zone (for example, Dullien and Schwarzer 2009; Goodhart 2007). Such a pact would mandate that euro-zone governments monitor deficits and use fiscal and wage policies to achieve external balance. A pact of this sort would inevitably promote conflicts over burden-sharing; it presupposes that which is lacking: a European polity.

Conclusion

The global financial crisis struck Europe long after the project of political integration had been effectively abandoned. The fate of the 'Constitutional Treaty', proposed as a means of resuscitating the project, confirmed the deep underlying crisis of political legitimacy of the Union. The referenda of 2005 in the Netherlands and France illustrated the difficulties of neoliberalism as a viable articulating principle for further integration (van Apeldoorn 2008). The subsequent Lisbon Treaty was sanitized of all concrete and symbolic references to European statehood. Its eventual passage after years of negotiation, facilitated by numerous opt-outs, bribes, threats and a *de facto* prohibition on future enlargement, further exposed the divide between the EU's institutions and people. Even the Lisbon Treaty was considered by the German Constitutional Court – in a decision suffused with references to German sovereignty – to be incompatible with basic democracy. After all this, the new posts of council president and high representative for foreign affairs, widely celebrated innovations designed to enhance the supranational identity of the Union, were given to minor politicians who would be kept on a very short leash by Paris, Berlin and London.

As the dream of political integration has faded, the neoliberal project, spearheaded by the *monetary constitution*, has taken its place. The EMU, governed by a central bank explicitly removed from democratic control, has thus by default become, in Commissioner Almunia's words, 'a potent symbol of our growing *political* unity'. (European Commission 2009). 'Europeanization' has become little more than an expression of market liberalization, driven forward by the Lisbon Strategy designed to promote a 'new economy' based on deregulated markets for capital, labour and products. Indeed, Europeanization has become virtually synonymous with the crisis to which it left Europe exposed. Because the Lisbon Strategy has been discredited by the global financial crisis and the travails of the American economy which it sought to emulate the global financial crisis has thus raised, in Mario Monti's words, the possibility of a 'quasi-existential crisis' for Europe: 'The special role played by the Commission in EU integration is based on the market' but 'the market economy itself is in crisis... this threatens to tip the Community into disintegration' (*Daily Telegraph* 2009).

The contemporary predicament of the EU does not therefore arise from a general or abstract problem of *integration per se* or the growing pains that might be expected to arise as the a union enlarges and governance is gradually shifted from the national state to supranational institutions. To be sure, nationalism, institutional paralysis and failures of leadership – the usual suspects – have become more pronounced in the context of the global economic crisis. The crisis has thrown into sharper relief the deeper, structural problem: the exhaustion of a two-decade long phase of neoliberal economic integration, one that has condemned Europe to slow growth and mass unemployment, has weakened traditional forms of political and social solidarity at the national and regional levels and has further exposed Europe to the uncertainties of an increasingly unstable US imperium.

Europe's subordinate participation within the transatlantic order, as structured by finance, pre-empts the possibility of resolving structural problems associated with contemporary capitalism in a way that is compatible with traditional European notions of social and regional solidarity. And if the crisis has thrown a spotlight on Europe's *disintegrative* tendencies, it has also accelerated Europe's global decline. As the London Summit of April 2009 showed, there has been an extraordinarily transformation, both symbolic and tangible, in international economic diplomacy. The G-7 has given way to the G-20, which is itself in at least some respects yielding to a *de facto* G-2 US–China condominium.

Even if financial meltdown and global depression have been averted – an assumption that by no means inspires confidence – Europe faces massive problems in the coming years. Confronted with growing political and economic disarray, European policymakers can be expected to search for pragmatic consensus toward future EU policies. While a modest version of incrementalism has obvious appeal, it does not fully comprehend the political and economic implications of the neoliberal project and thus underestimates the depth and meaning of a broader crisis. The formation of a single market and single currency embedded in little more than a competitiveness project has represented a radical and destabilizing development. The failure to construct a *polity* – which would necessarily take Europe well beyond the present mix of market liberalization and mercantilism – portends continuing social and economic instability, political fragmentation and international marginalization.

Notes

1. For a sampling of what now seems a rather quaint triumphalism see, *inter alia*, Haseler (2004); Hemerijck (2002); Kupchan (2002); Leonard (2005); McCormick (2007); Reid (2005); Rhodes (2002). For a critique see Cafruny and Ryner (2007); Ryner (2008).
2. As the EU's economy commissioner Almunia stated, 'Everybody agrees that the present world reserve currency, the dollar, is there and will continue to be there for a long period of time.' (Associated Press 2009, Web site: http://www.ap.org/)

References

Albo, G. (1994) ' "Competitive Austerity" and the Impasse of Capitalist Employment Policy' in Miliband, R. and Panitch, L., eds, *Between Globalism and Nationalism: The Socialist Register*, London: Merlin Press.

Atkins, R. and Benoit, B. (2009) 'Swabian Housekeeping Forced to Adapt,' *Financial Times*, November 30, p. 21.

Bertola, G. (2009) 'Labour Markets on the Verge of a Regulation Crisis,' http://www.voxeu.org

Bohle, D. (2006) 'Neoliberal Hegemony, Transnational Capital and the Terms of EU Enlargement,' *Capital and Class*, 88, 57–86.

Cafruny, A. and Ryner, M. (2007a) *Europe at Bay: In the Shadow of US Hegemony*, Boulder, Co.: Lynne Rienner.

——— (2007b) 'Monetary Union and the Transatlantic and Social Dimensions of Europe's Crisis,' *New Political Economy*, 12, 2.

Carrington, C. (2009) 'The International Impact of the Subprime Mortgage Meltdown' Dallas, Web site: http://www.docstoc.com/docs/16138008/The-International-Impact-of-the-Subprime-Mortgage-Meltdown as accessed on 28 January 2010.

Daily Telegraph (2009) 'EU Faces 'Existential Danger from Economic Crisis,' 13 September.

de Grauwe, P. (2006a) 'What Have We Learnt About Monetary Integration Since the Maastricht Treaty?' *Journal of Common Market Studies* 44, 4.

——— (2006b) 'Germany's Pay Policy Points to a Euro-zone Design Flaw,' *Financial Times*, May 5.

Delegation of the European Commission to the USA, http://www.eurunion.org/eu as accessed on March 17, 2010.

Deutsche Bank Research (2008) *EU-US Financial Market Integration – A Work in Progress*, EU Monitor 56, 4 June.

Dullien, S. and Schwarzer, D. (2009) 'An External Stability Pact for Europe,' *Project Syndicate*, http://www.project-syndicate.org

Dumenil, G. and Levy, D. (2004) 'The Economics of U.S. Imperialism at the Turn of the 21st Century,' *Review of International Political Economy* 11, 4, 657–676.

El Erian, M. (2009) 'Analysis over Decoupling Must Focus on Specifics' *Financial Times*, 15 August.

European Commission (2009) *Focus—EU Economic and Monetary Union*, Delegation to the USA, Brussels.

Eurostat (2009) 'Statistics Database,' European Commission, Brussels.

Felder, R. (2008) 'From Bretton Woods to Neoliberal Reforms: the International Financial Institutions and American Power,' in Panitch, L. and Koningns, M., eds, *The American Empire and the Political Economy of Global Finance*, New York: Palgrave.

Foster, J, and Magdoff, F. (2008) 'Financial Implosion and Stagnation: Back to the Real Economy' *Monthly Review*, December.

Goodhart, C. (2007) 'Replacing the Stability and Growth Pact?' in Bibow, J. and Terzi, A., eds, *Euroland and the World Economy – Global Player or Global Drag?* New York: Palgrave.

Gordon, G. (2009) 'Goldman Left Foreign Investors Holding the Subprime Bag,' McClatchy Newspapers, 3 November.

Gowan, P. (1999) *The Global Gamble: Washington's Faustian Bid for Global Dominance*, London: Verso.

Guha, K. (2009) 'Top Bankers Launch Fightback Against Feared Regulatory Overkill,' *Financial Times*, 3/4 October.

Harvey, D. (2005) *A Brief History of Neoliberalism*, Oxford: Oxford University Press.

Haseler, S. (2004) *Superstate: The New Europe and its Challenge to America*, London: I.B. Taurus.

Hemerijck, A. (2002) 'The Self-Transformation of the European Social Model(s),' *International Politics and Society*, 4.

Hugh, E. (2007) 'Structural Aspects of German Export Dependence Part II,' Edward.Hugh.blog, www.edward.hugh.blogspot.com/2007

International Monetary Fund (2007) 'De-Coupling the Train? Spillovers and Cycles in the Global Economy,' *World Economic Outlook*, Chapter 4, Washington, DC, Web site: http://www.imf.org/external/pubs/ft/weo/2007/01/index.htm as accessed on 28 January 2010.

———— (2009) *Global Financial Stability Report*, October 2009, Figure 1.9, Washington, DC.

Ivanova, M. (2009) 'Back to the Future: Can American-Style Consumer Capitalism Be Saved? Should it Be Saved?' paper presented at the European Sociological Association, Critical Political Economy Network, Lisbon, Portugal.

Johnson, S. (2009) 'The Quiet Coup' *The Atlantic*, May. Web site: http://www.theatlantic.com/doc/200905/imf-advice as accessed on January 28, 2010.

Konings, M. (2008) 'European Finance in the American Mirror: Financial Change and the Reconfiguration of Competitiveness,' *Contemporary Politics*, 14, 3, 253–275.

Kinderman, D. (2005) 'Pressure from Without: Subversion from Within: The Two-pronged Germany Employer Offensive,' *Comparative European Politics*, 3, 432–463.

Kupchan, C. (2002) *The End of the American Era: U.S. Foreign Policy and the Geopolitics of the Twenty-First Century*, New York: Vintage.

Leonard, M. (2005) *Why Europe Will Run the Twenty-First Century*, London: Fourth Estate.

Lorentowicz, A., Marin, A. and Raubold, A. (2002) *Ownership, Capital, or Outsourcing: What Drives German Investment in Eastern Europe?* Munich: Center for Economic Policy Research.

Lund, S. and Roxburgh, C. (2009) 'Imbalances that Strain the Euro-zone,' *Business Week*, 18 November.

Mandel, M. (2009) 'A Bad Decade for Non-financial Profits,' *Business Week Economics Unbound*, 4 March.

Martensen, C. (2009) 'Currency Swaps, U.S. Dollar, and a Tilted Playing Field,' 28 September, www.seekingalpha.com

McCormick, J. (2007) *The European Superpower*, New York: Palgrave.

Mueller, K. (2009) 'Disintegrative Tendencies in the European Monetary Union,' European Sociological Association, Critical Political Economy Network, Lisbon, Portugal.

OECD (2009) 'Inequality Measures, mid-1980s to mid-2000s,' Social Policy Division, Table C07.1, Paris: OECD.

Piketty, T. and Saez, E. (2003) 'Income Inequality in the United States, 1913–1998,' *Quarterly Journal of Economics*, 118.

Plender, J. (2009) 'Will Rising Debt Trigger Euro-zone Break-up?' *Financial Times*, 30 November, p. 20.

Quinlan, J. (2003) *Drifting Apart or Growing Together? The Primacy of the Transatlantic Economy*, Baltimore, Md. Paul H. Nitze School of Advanced International Relations, Johns Hopkins University.

Raviv, O. (2007) 'Central Europe in the EU Financial Embrace,' in Assassi, L., Wigan, D. and Nesvetailova, A., eds, *Global Finance in the New Century – Beyond Regulation*, London: Palgrave.

Reid, T. (2005) *The United States of Europe: The Superpower No-One Talks About*, New York: Penguin.

Rhodes, M. (2002) 'Why EMU Is – Or May Be – Good for European Welfare States,' in Dyson, K., ed., *European States and the Euro*, Oxford: Oxford University Press.

Ryner, M. (2008) 'Neoliberal European Governance and the Politics of Welfare State Retrenchment: A Critique of the New Malthusians,' in van Apeldoorn, B., Drahokoupil, J. and Horn, L., eds., *Contradictions and Limits of Neoliberal European Governance – From Lisbon to Lisbon*, New York: Palgrave.

Sablowski, T. (2008) 'Towards the Americanization of European Finance? The Case of Finance-Led Accumulation in Germany' in Panitch, L. and Konings, M., eds, *American Empire and the Political Economy of Global Finance*, New York: Palgrave.

Saez, E. (2009), 'Striking it Richer: The Evolution of Top Incomes in the United States (update with 2007 estimates)' http://www.elsa.berkeley.edu/saez/

Sarai, D. (2008) 'US Structural Power and the Internationalization of the US Treasury' in Panitch, L. and Konings, M., eds, *American Empire and the Political Economy of Global Finance*, New York: Palgrave.

Schmitt, J. (2009) 'Inequality as Policy: The United States Since 1979,' Center for Economic and Policy Research,' October, www.cepr.net

Siegel, N. (2004) 'EMU and German Welfare Capitalism' in Martin, A. and Ross, G., eds, *Euros and Europeans*, Cambridge, UK: Cambridge University Press.

van Apeldoorn, B. (2008) 'A National Case Study of Embedded Neoliberalism and its Limits: The Dutch Political Economy and the "No" to the European Constitution,' in van Apeldoorn, B., Drahokoupil, J. and Horn, L., eds, *Contradictions and Limits of Neoliberal European Governance – From Lisbon to Lisbon*, New York: Palgrave.

Verhofstadt, G. (2009) 'Euro Solidarity With Eastern Europe: It's a Shame that Assistance Efforts for the New Member States are not EU-led but Spearheaded by the IMF,' *Wall Street Journal*, November 18.

Wall Street Journal (2009) 'Merkel Slams Cycles,' 3 July.

Weinkopf, C. (2009) 'Germany: Precarious Employment and the Rise of Mini-jobs' in Vosko, L., McDonald, M. and Cambbell, I., eds *Gender and the Contours of Precarious Employment*, London: Routledge.

Weisbrot, M. (2009) 'IMF-Supported Macro-economic Policies and the World Recession: A Look at Forty-one Borrowing Countries,' Center for Economic and Policy Research, Washington, DC, www.cepr.net

7
The Impact of the Global Financial Crisis on the City of London: Will the UK Finally Decide to Join the EMU?

Leila Simona Talani

Introduction

The European Economic and Monetary Union (EMU) is already ten years old and the UK still have not decided to join it. Despite some timid attempts to revamp the debate about British entry into the EMU made by the early Labour administration, the issue has been left aside for a long time, to surge again to the attention of the public only with the explosion of the global financial crisis.

Is there a link between the renewed interest in the British academic and political quarters towards EMU and the crisis of the financial sector? What is the relation between the City of London and EMU? Is this relation rooted in the structure of British capitalism?

This Chapter answers the above questions starting from the 'exceptional' nature of British capitalism development.

The British system is 'exceptional', because of the persistence of aristocratic, pre-industrial elements in British polity (Stanworth and Giddens 1974: 100). In Anderson's conceptualization (Anderson 1964) this 'exceptionalism' is owed to structural considerations about the development of British capitalism: namely the dual nature of British capitalism, that is, the divide between the financial fraction of capital and the industrial one, and the dominance of the former over the latter.

The separation between the industrial and the financial fractions of British capital and the prevalence of City's interests over industrial macroeconomic preferences, has also been recognized as an important factor of the British decision to keep the UK outside the EMU (Talani 2000).

This chapter seeks to understand whether the global financial crisis, and the subsequent, alleged crisis of the City of London is likely to modify the relation between the industrial and the financial components of the British capitalist elite and put an end to British 'exceptionalism'. The final aim is to ascertain whether the preferences of the British capitalist elite with respect to the euro have changed as a consequence of the global financial crisis and whether this will finally convince the UK to join the EMU. The author argues that the crisis mostly impacted on the labour force of the British and global financial sector and produced a restructuring that consolidated and enhanced the political economy relevance of the City of London. By no means, the crisis resulted in a decrease of the hegemonic power of the City of London. If anything, it confirmed its capacity to influence the decision making process of the British Government in favour of its preferences. These preferences, however, still do not include entry of the UK into the EMU.

The chapter is divided into three sections. In the first section the author analyses the case for entry into the EMU recently put forward in the British public debate as a consequence of the impact of the global financial crisis on the City of London. After reviewing the events leading up to the crisis, the chapter will identify the arguments proposed in the public debate by leading academics and public opinion makers in favour of British entry into the euro-area. In the second section the author reviews the reasons why the UK decided not to join the EMU in the first place with reference to the theoretical debate on British exceptionalism. Conclusions will be drawn on whether the impact of the global financial crisis on the City of London justifies a rethinking of the British decision not to enter the EMU.

Should the UK adopt the euro? Analysis with reference to the impact of the global financial crisis on the City of London

What happened? The global financial crisis

Already in February 2007, there were warnings that the situation of the American sub-prime lender industry was unsustainable. However, it was only in August 2007 that it became clear that the crisis had moved from the American mortgage sector to the global financial and banking ones (ILO 2009).

In the UK, Northern Rock became the first institution to witness a bank run for about 150 years. The situation was solved only thanks to the intervention of the Bank of England, first bailing it out and then nationalizing it.

In the meantime the global banking sector started experiencing huge losses; on 5 October 2007 Merrill Lynch reported a loss of US$5.5 billion and three weeks later came back with a figure over $8 (ILO 2009). The losses in mortgage derivative market also triggered a massive run on Bear Stearns liabilities. On 13 and 14 March 2008; they fell by $17 billion (Orlowski 2008: 10).

At the beginning of 2008, with the massive loss incurred by financial institutions on mortgage backed securities and other derivatives, they started investing in commodity futures, especially the crude oil futures markets. As a consequence, NYMEX oil futures prices experienced almost a 100 per cent increase from $75 per barrel in the beginning of October 2007 to their peak of $147 on 11 July 2008 (Orlowski 2008: 11).

On 15 September 2008, Lehman Brothers filed for bankruptcy and the Bank of America agreed a $50 billion rescue bid for Merrill Lynch.[1] On Tuesday 16 September HBOS shares halved in value to a low of 88 pence and Wall Street giant Goldman Sachs reported 70 per cent drop in profits.[2] On the 17th, the US Government agreed to give AIG $85 billion to keep afloat, in return for control of the company; Lloyds TSB finalized its takeover of HBOS and Russia suspended stock market trading. In the meantime the Bank of England extended its special liquidity scheme, after pressure from banks, and Morgan Stanley shares fell 30 per cent, as it became the latest bank under fire and looked for salvation through a merger with Wachovia.[3] The Russian stock markets remained closed for a second day on the 18th while the panic spread in Asia, where the Nikkei dropped 260 points to 11,489. On the same day central banks around the world pumped $180 billion into the system in a concerted effort to end the crisis, but London's relief did not last, as the FTSE 100 closed 32.4 points lower at 4880.0. At 6 p.m. the UK's Financial Services Authority (FSA) announced a ban on the short-selling of bank shares. The US treasury secretary, Henry Paulson, spent the weekend of the 20th of September trying to thrash out his $700billion 'bad bank' plan but political opposition to the $700billion bail-out plan grew in Washington during the following week, pushing shares prices lower.[4] During the same week, Morgan Stanley and Goldman Sachs gave up their status as investment banks to become

traditional commercial banks that accept deposits from ordinary people and businesses, marking a dramatic change in the make-up of Wall
Street.[5]

The peak of the crisis was reached on 29 September, when George
Bush took the podium to urge the House of Representatives to pass the
$700 billion bail-out plan. His short speech fell on deaf ears and a few
hours later the House of Representatives voted the bail-out down. The
Dow Jones plunged 777 points, its biggest ever fall in points terms. In
the meantime in Iceland, the government was forced to take control
of one of the nation's biggest banks. The Asian stock markets were the
first to react to the shock news that the $700 billion Wall Street bailout
had failed. When London opened it was disaster, with banking shares
destroyed. Anyone who did have savings was trying desperately to find
a safe haven with government-backed National Savings & Investments
swamped by savers. The banks themselves were finding it increasingly
difficult to raise financing with the cost of inter-bank borrowing experiencing its biggest ever one-day rise. Dominique Strauss-Kahn, the
managing director of the IMF, believed a bail-out was the only option
for the US economy and on 2 October the US Senate voted in favour of
the Wall Street bail-out. In the meantime, European leaders were considering their own bail-out, which could cost up to €300 billion (£237
billion). The French president, Nicolas Sarkozy, led the talks.[6]

On 4 October , Gordon Brown attended an emergency summit in
Paris to discuss the crisis with his French, German and Italian counterparts. On 7 October , the Icelandic internet bank Icesave blocked savers
from withdrawing money and the following day Icesave accounts were
declared in default. This move triggered Financial Services Compensation Scheme which will return 100 per cent of savers' money. The same
day the Treasury announced what amounts to a £500 billion bank rescue package to stop the country's financial system from melting down.
Most bank shares fell again. At 12 p.m. the Bank of England, the US Federal Reserve and the European Central Bank all cut half a point off their
key interest rates in the first unscheduled rate moves since the aftermath
of 9/11. At first, Stock markets calmed after the turmoil.[7] The FTSE 100
jumped 61 points by midday. Banks continued to recover following the
UK Government's £500 billion rescue plan announced the previous day.
However, the London market failed to hold on to early gains. With Wall
Street in decline yet again on the 10th the FTSE 100 closed 8.85 per cent
lower at 3932.1 – a 381.7 point fall, destroying about £89.5 billion off
the value of Britain's biggest companies. This was the worst daily fall

since the crash of 1987. On 11 October, Alistair Darling attended meetings in Washington with the G7 finance ministers and the IMF. The G7 came up with a five-point plan, which includes spending billions of taxpayers' money to rebuild the global banking system and reopen the flow of credit.[8]

On the 12th, Gordon Brown travelled to Paris where European officials were desperate to prevent a continent-wide meltdown of the banking sector. He succeeded in persuading the EU's core countries to adopt a plan along the lines of his £500 billion banking system bail-out.[9] On the 13th, the 15 members of the euro-zone, led by Germany and France, unveiled large, coordinated plans along British lines to provide their banks with capital funding. In the meantime, the British Government announced it would put £37 billion of emergency recapitalization into the RBS, HBOS and Lloyds TSB. The prospect of governments pumping vast sums into banks on both sides of the Atlantic cheered up financial markets. The FTSE 100 closed 325 points higher at 4256.9, a rise of 8.3 per cent. The Dow Jones rocketed by 936 points to 9387, its biggest one-day gain by points. It closed up 11 per cent, the largest daily jump in percentage terms since 1933.[10]

It seems that the decision to pump an enormous amount of public money into the global financial markets avoided the global catastrophe. But which is the impact of these events on the City of London? Lord Adair Turner, the Financial Service Authority chairman, during this tragic week told *The Guardian* that the days of soft-touch regulation were over, warning the City that higher-paid regulators would ask tougher questions in the wake of the credit crisis. However, up to now the consequences of the crisis have been felt mainly by the workers of the British and the global financial sector and there are hints that the British financial elite was able to cash on the crisis itself.[11]

The impact of the global financial crisis on the City of London

At the onset of the crisis, in 2007, the financial and professional services sector accounted for around 11 per cent of UK GDP. The UK trade surplus in financial services was £35.6 billion. In terms of banking, the UK was the world's largest source of international bank lending, with total banking assets of £7.5 trillion in September 2008, and 20 per cent of cross-border lending, that is the world's biggest share.[12]

In 2007, London had 250 foreign banks with branches or subsidiaries almost double the number in New York. Besides, London had been the fastest-growing market for assets management with $400 billion of assets under management at the end of 2007. This accounted for 80 per cent of hedge funds managed in Europe and 20 per cent of the world's hedge fund assets. The value of global hedge fund assets peaked at $2250 billion at the end of 2007.

Always in 2007, the UK was the world's leading market for international insurance, with UK worldwide premium income totalling £262.6 billion. The UK financial sector was responsible for 25 per cent of insurance business written in Europe and the UK accounted for 11 per cent of global premium income with £262.6 billion in premiums in 2007.[13] The UK capital markets were thriving as well. The market value of UK Government securities (Gilts) totalled £390 billion in March 2007, up 19 per cent from the end of the previous year. The UK's share of cross-border derivatives turnover was 47 per cent in 2007. In 2007, 1224 million futures and options contracts were traded in London. London still accounts for over 30 per cent of world foreign exchange business, 80 per cent of the £4 billion EU Emissions Trading Scheme and 20 per cent of cross-border lending. In the first nine months of 2008 London's share of European Initial Public Offerings (IPOs) was 63 per cent of the total value and 32 per cent of the number of all European IPOs.[14]

With respect to professional services, in 2007 exports of accounting services increased by 4 per cent to reach £1012 million. Moreover, the UK is a leading international law centre, with the largest three legal companies in the world and over 200 foreign firms. This sector contributes £14.9 billion to the UK's GDP. International law firms based in London account for nearly 50 per cent of UK law firms' gross fees. The UK is the top centre for international arbitration with 98 per cent of commercial cases handled by London law firms for an international party. Management consultancy within the financial sector generated £2.8 billion in 2007.

London has offices, branches or headquarters of almost every major international bank and financial institution in the world, including the European headquarters of over a third of all *Fortune* 500 firms. It also hosts the largest share of six out of eight key international financial markets. It is the world's most important marketplace for over-the-counter (OTC) derivatives with 43 per cent of global trades. Moreover, London had 46 per cent share of global foreign equity trading and over 70 per cent of global trading in international bonds in 2007. London also hosts Europe's largest international banking centre, with an estimated 41 per cent of all the EU's financial services and a 6 per cent share of the global equity market capitalization totalling £42.8 trillion in September 2008. Moreover, the London Stock Exchange has over 1500 companies trading on the main market and in 2007, IPOs raised £26.1 trillion. The AIM[15] is the most successful growth market in the world with over 1600 companies trading. Since opening in 1995, over £60 billion has been raised through IPOs and further issues. Since opening in 2005, the London Carbon Trading Exchange trades £40 million each day. Over 43 million contracts were traded in London on the European Derivatives Exchange (EDX) in 2007. Trading on LIFFE[16] totalled 949 million contracts in 2007 and 814 million in the first nine months of 2008. London is the global clearing centre for the global trading of gold and silver, trading on average $24.9 billion of gold and £3.02 billion of silver each day.[17]

Even more important for our discussion, the City of London has so far acted as the off-shore centre of euro-zone capital. In 2007, inflows from the euro-area were £1020 billion and outflows were £981 billion. The impressive amount of these figures, much higher than the British GDP, not only graphically demonstrates the relevance of the City of London as a global financial centre, but more crucially its role as the financial centre of the euro-zone (Bishop in Bishop et al. 2009: 31).

Summing up, when in 2003 Gordon Brown revised the case for British entry into EMU applying his 'five tests'[18] there was no evidence of any negative impact on the City of London if the UK did not join. A large proportion of the UK banking system was by then accounted for by euro-area based banks. Moreover, most firms in London were counterparties of the ECB. Indeed, London had become the main financial centre for euro-denominated business (Green 2009).

Will all this be put under discussion and disrupted by the global financial crisis? This is debatable, especially in the light of the historical analysis of the development of the City reported below. What is evident, at the moment, is only the impact that the crisis had on the workers of the British financial sector (ILO 2009: 14). Also here, however, it is worth noting that many of the job losses experienced in the City of London are the consequence of decisions taken in distant headquarters of major foreign financial institutions. Employment decisions of Nomura of Japan, Deutsche Bank of Germany, UBS and Credit Suisse of Switzerland will impact workers in the City of London. This is not to deny, however, the extent to which job losses in the UK's Lloyds TSB Group, RBS and Barclays will affect jobs not only in the UK but also in Europe, Asia, Africa, Latin America, Eastern Europe and so on.

It is undeniable indeed that the main consequence of the global financial crisis has been a remarkable loss of jobs in the global financial sector. The ILO estimates total announced layoffs of 325,000 between August

2007 and 12 February 2009 (ILO 2009: 14). This figure underestimates the real number of jobs lost as, on one side not all institutions announce their employment decisions in advance and also it does not include independent mortgage brokers, other independent contractors or the myriad of small financial firms which are likely to disappear as a consequence of the crisis. In the UK, not so surprisingly, one of the most hit is the mortgage broking industry, also as a consequence of the Bank of England's decision to restrict access to its best rates to the biggest players in the market. The mortgage industry lost 15 per cent of its members between the start of the credit crunch in August 2007 and mid-2008. Moreover, the number of mortgage advisers fell about 30,000 to 26,000 during the same period. This is particularly serious considering that before the crisis almost three-quarters of the £15 billion in UK mortgages were sold through brokers, according to the UK Council of Mortgage Lenders.[19]

The ILO lists some of the 325,000 announced job cuts by banks, asset managers and insurers around the world from August 2007 to 12 February 2009 in Table 7.1.

As already elaborated above, the peak of the global financial crisis happened in October 2008. Indeed, 40 per cent of the job losses, around 130,000 jobs, were announced from October 2008 to 12 February 2009. It seems, however, that the restructuring of the global financial sector will lead to a further concentration of its different industries, with many jobs lost in the process. The ILO confirms that the investment banking industry, for example, is expected to see thousands of job cuts following a wave of mergers and acquisitions (ILO 2009: 16). Even in IT supports, merging firms are expected to cut out overlapping roles. Analysts expect more than 50,000 layoffs of IT professionals in banking by the end of 2009. IT expenditure for 2009 by European investment banks was projected to drop 9 per cent and 15 per cent for Europe and the US, respectively.[20]

In the City of London, restructuring decisions by financial institutions, including those headquartered abroad, have significant job implications for the UK. For example, the decision by Credit Suisse to reduce its employees by 5300 (11 per cent of its worldwide staff) should lead to 650 posts lost in London. Also Nomura Holdings is expected to cut 1000 jobs in London, a fifth of its local workforce, after acquiring Lehman Brothers' European arm. According to an independent economic consultancy, Oxford Analytica, London-based financial institutions should reduce their employment by 30,000 jobs in 2008, whereas in 2009 figures are expected to be at least 30 per cent higher. The repercussion on the broader London economic sector would

Table 7.1 Number of job cuts from banks, insurers and funds since August 2007.

Company	Jobs cut	Headcount before August 2007	Latest headcount	Remarks
PNC Financial Services	5,800	28,054	59,595, 3 February	Includes jobs from merger with National City Corp. on 31 December job cuts at the combined group due to be completed by 2011
Bank of America	45,500	195,675	243,075, 31 December	Includes 30,000–35,000 jobs to be cut over 3 years after the purchase of Merrill Lynch and 7,500 jobs to be cut over 2 years after Countrywide Financial Corp acquisition
Barclays	9,050	127,700	150,000, 15 January	Includes 3000 cuts after the acquisiton of Lehman Brothers businesses
Bear Stearns	1,500	N/A	N/A	Layoffs August 2007–April 2008, before takeover by JPMorgan
Citigroup	75,000	361,000	323,000, 3 December	
Commerzbank	9,000	35,384	42,983, 30 September	All layoffs announced after the acquisition of Dresdner Bank
Credit Suisse	7,320	45,600	50,300, 30 September	
Deutsche Bank	1,380	75,140	81,308, 30 September	
Fidelity investments	4,000	Unavailable	44,400, 12 November	
Fidelity National Financial Inc.	4,100	Unavailable	Unavailable	
First American	4,250	38,000	34,000, 30 October	Includes 1500 cuts after purchase of three title insurers in December 2008
Goldman Sachs	4,800	29,905	30,067, 28 November	Estimate

HSBC	2,850	312,577	335,000, 4 August	
ING	Over 7,000	119,097	130,000, 27 January	
JP Morgan	15,900	179,664	224,961, 31 December	Includes 7500 cuts announced after purchase of Bear Stearns and 9200 layoffs at former Washington Mutual Inc., bought by JP Morgan
Lehman Brothers	12,570	N/A	N/A	Includes about 5000 job cuts made before the bank collapsed in September and an estimated 10,500 left jobless after the bank collapsed – about 8000 others were transferred to Nomura and 10,000 to Barclays
Merrill Lynch	3,300	61,900	N/A	Layoffs before takeover by Bank of America based on 1 January
Morgan Stanley	8,680	45,845	45,964, 30 November	
National City Corp.	7,400	32,445	N/A	Layoffs before National City Corp. merged with PNC on 31 December
Nomura	1,480	15,854	25,318, 31 December	Includes 1000 jobs cut after acquisition of Lehman Brothers units
Santander	2,500	135,922	170,961, 31 December	
RBS	3,950	135,400	170,000, 14 November	Includes employees from ABN-AMRO, acquired in October 2007
UBS	11,000	81,557	77,783, 31 December	
UniCredit	9,000	135,880	177,393, 30 September	Includes staff from Ukrsolsbank, acquired in January 2009

Source: ILO (2009), p. 14.

be significant with a projection of 194,000 jobs lost and total London jobs declining from 4.71 million in 2008 to just over 4.51 million in 2010 (ILO 2009: 16).

Another aspect of the crisis is the rise in corporate and individual bankruptcies in the financial sector. Its 51.6 per cent year-to-year increase in England and Wales is doomed to have significant employment consequences. For example, the incorporation of HBOS into the Lloyds Banking Group, following a Government-backed takeover of HBOS by Lloyds, has endangered 30,000 jobs in the combined company, now 43 per cent government-owned. It is expected that Lloyds will save £790 million from cuts in the merged banks' retail operations and £235 million by putting together their insurance and investment businesses. Overlapping branches, call centres and IT are going to close. In wholesale and international banking savings for up to £430 million should be realized. As the takeover involved a loss of over £11 billion, the bank is determined to save as much as possible from rationalizing operations.[21]

Although this is a pretty dire picture, London is by no means the only global financial centre to be hit by the crisis. Other cities around the US, the UK and other countries with major financial services centres experienced a similar impact of the crisis on their jobs. In September 2008, the Belgian Government bailed out the Franco-Belgian banking group Dexia. The latter has announced relevant layoffs all around the globe with 700–800 positions cut, about half of them from its Belgian operations. This should lead to around 15 per cent cost savings over three years (ILO 2009: 17).

Very serious was the situation in Ireland. The Anglo Irish Bank has been nationalized and strategic shareholding positions have been taken in Bank of Ireland and Allied Irish Banks. Another 750 jobs, (up to 550 in the Republic of Ireland and 200 in Northern Ireland) are being cut with the closure by Ulster Bank, a subsidiary of the UK's Royal Bank of Scotland (RBS), now 70 per cent owned by the British Government, of its First Active subsidiary (ILO 2009: 17). Forty-five First Active branches will be closed while the remaining 15 will be transferred to Ulster Bank. This is just the start of a substantial restructuring of Irish banking. The Bank of Ireland itself is reducing its 4000 workforce in the UK by 600 units. The Irish mortgage lender and life pensions company, Irish Life Permanent, is offering up to €35,000 to take career breaks. The Irish banking sector is witnessing a dramatic reduction of activity which will inevitably lead to more redundancies. Currently it employs 41,000 people, with 94,000 for the overall financial services (ILO 2009: 17).

The outlook in Japan is not much more reassuring. Japan is experiencing the steepest fall in economic output since the 1974 oil shock. The situation for the banking sector is even worse with rising costs of bad loans and heavy losses on stock portfolios in client companies. The level of job cuts in the Japanese financial industry is not yet comparable to that of the US and the UK. However, there has already been a downsizing in property-related areas and reductions in fixed-income workforce as banks cut back their bond trading to reflect the fact that the current crisis was largely caused by a lack of risk and credit control in fixed-income products (ILO 2009: 18).

The situation of Australian financial companies is different as they remain highly profitable despite rising bad loans. However, they too are cutting the workforce. In September 2008, Macquarie reduced its global workforce by 1047 to 12,851. This was the result of two write-downs totalling $2 billion and of the halving of its profitability. Also Babcock & Brown announced that by 2010, its workforce will be cut by two-thirds, 850 jobs, leaving only 650 employees (ILO 2009: 18). The Australian Finance Sector Union (FSU) estimates that in 2008 there were almost 5000 job losses in the financial industry, but on the basis of company briefings to analysts and media reports it is possible to claim that the losses were closer to 19,000.[22] A similar picture is envisaged for 2009.[23]

Even Africa, which was initially supposed to emerge untouched from the financial crisis, given its small, local dimension and its little exposure to toxic assets, faced problems. Despite the lack of reliable figures, observers now say that the continent will experience substantial job reductions in its financial service sector. The reasons are various. First, this could be the consequence of the failure of parent banks outside. Second, this could be related to the reduction of capital flows, including remittances from migrants which make up much of the GDP of many African countries. Moreover, foreign aid, another relevant part of the African GDP may fall as a consequence of the impact of the crisis in donor countries. Another reason could be the decline in commodity prices. Finally, pre-existing macroeconomic imbalances may require stronger action and produce a negative impact on employment (ILO 2009: 18).

However, the country experiencing the worst impact of the global financial crisis was the US and, quintessentially, New York City. The Governor of New York State believes that only in Wall Street job losses should reach 45,000. Other observers put this figure as high as 80,000 or half the projected total private sector job losses in the state. The economic spillover of these redundancies will be substantial as the finance, insurance and real estate sectors account for one-third of personal income earned in New York City. It is projected that up to 100,000 financial services jobs will be lost in the wider NY financial sector. Also Boston will experience relevant job cuts. Only in January 2009 the US financial services cut 42,000 jobs. In the last three months of 2008, 17,600 jobs were lost in the US securities industry. It is forecasted that job reductions will mount in 2009. For example, American Express, has already declared that a manoeuvre to save $1.8 billion in 2009 should reduce its workforce by 7000 (about 10 per cent) as part of cost reductions (ILO 2009: 16).

Finally, as it might be expected, there are serious gender imbalances in the redundancies of the financial sector. In the US, women tend to be over-represented in such occupations as receptionists and clerical workers in sectors that have suffered heavy reductions, and therefore many have faced above-average levels of job loss. In American financial services, for example, women held about 59 per cent of the jobs, but accounted for a staggering 76 per cent (102,000 posts) of the 134,000 job losses. The situation is not likely to improve in the future.[24] In the UK the latest unemployment statistics showed the number of women full-time workers to have fallen by 53,000 in the fourth quarter 2008 compared with a drop of 36,000 for men.[25]

Summing up, although no conclusive evidence can still be provided on the impact of the global financial crisis, it seems clear that the loss of jobs experienced by the City of London parallels similar layoffs in all the other major financial centres. This means that the position of the City of London as one of the most important global financial players needs not to be put under discussion. Moreover, much of the restructuring which is leading to the rationalization of the workforce, including some nationalizations, is the result of consolidations based on mergers and acquisitions which do not necessarily mean a reduction of the overall importance of the financial sector neither globally nor within the UK. Finally, there is no evidence that the City of London lost its market share and leadership in the European financial sector, whereas there is plenty of evidence that many of its competitors might be in an even worse shape. Overall the City not only survived the blow but there is also plenty of evidence[26] that it turned it to its advantage. In this climate, which are the arguments in favour of joining EMU that have been put forward as a consequence of the financial crisis?

The case for the UK to join the EMU after the global financial crisis

The case for joining the EMU has never been as pressing as since the global financial crisis started. Leading scholars and public opinion makers in the UK joined the debate promoting accession on various occasions (Bishop et al. 2009).

Mike Artis,[27] quoting Keynes, attributes to the changed economic climate the need to rethink the British position towards the euro (Artis 2009). When the euro was launched, the British economy enjoyed a long period of economic growth with almost no inflationary pressures compounded by a strong pound. None of these circumstances applies today. Moreover, contrary to what the City of London believed, the European Central Bank policy has been well-considered and well-conducted and effectively sheltered euro-area countries from the worse consequences of the crisis (Artis 2009: 12). Iceland's fate is an instructive example for the UK not to follow. Although certainly Iceland is smaller than the UK, the British GDP has certainly fallen in recent years. And even more certainly, the financial globalization rendered smaller countries more vulnerable than ever. Concluding, joining the euro-area will allow the British economy to enjoy all the advantages of a big economy in a world economic climate which is more unstable and uncertain than before (Artis 2009: 13).

The need to overcome the rhetoric about the five economic tests is advocated by Iain Begg.[28] The 'current febrile economic environment' (Begg 2009: 20) should open up the debate on whether they are still appropriate. The five tests were set out in 1997 by the then Chancellor, Gordon Brown, to assess whether or not the economic benefits of euro membership exceeded the costs and therefore justified joining. However, their purpose was also a political one, namely to avoid taking a decision until 'the time is ripe'. In 2003, an in-depth assessment of the five economic tests ruled out the possibility of joining 'for the time being'. However, the tests could not forecast the current financial and economic crisis and crucially overlooked the connection between the currency regime and financial stability. The credit crunch has made clear that this approach is inappropriate and that in a situation in which financial markets are globally interconnected, membership of the euro-area would shelter the British economy (Begg 2009: 22). Not to mention the fact that the much needed regulatory reforms that will have to ensue from the crisis could require a much higher level of governance than the national one, and therefore the UK could be left outside of key decision making (Begg 2009: 22).

Also, according to Willem Buiter,[29] the economic case for the UK to adopt the euro in the present circumstances is overwhelming (Buiter 2009: 40). Indeed, reviewing the five economic tests in the light of the global financial crisis, there is no doubt, in the opinion of Buiter, that they are all fulfilled. Leaving aside the third test (investment) and the fifth test (growth, stability employment), which would be satisfied if and only if the other three are satisfied, he assesses the first, second and fourth tests. The main new finding of this analysis is that the global financial crisis is in itself a powerful and sufficient argument for the UK to enter the EMU as soon as possible. This is because it adds a financial stability dimension to the already strong optimal currency ones (Buiter 2009: 40). Concluding, the author advocates immediate UK membership to the euro-zone. This is supported by, on the one hand, the conventional optimal currency area criteria (convergence, flexibility, labour mobility, fiscal flexibility). Moreover, with the global crisis a new financial stability criterion has emerged. Membership of the euro-zone is essential for the UK to avoid a triple financial crisis (a banking, currency and sovereign debt crisis). These crises would be inevitable otherwise because the UK belongs to a group of countries characterized by a new inconsistent quartet: (1) a small country with (2) a large internationally exposed banking sector, (3) a currency that is not a global reserve currency and (4) limited fiscal capacity relative to the possible size of the banking sector solvency gap. Euro-zone membership would eliminate the third member of the quartet and by reducing liquidity risk *premia*, could even reduce the impact of the fourth element (Buiter 2009: 57).

The fall in the value of the pound is what most worries Graham Bishop[30] in his statement in support of British entry. The three questions to answer are, for the author:

1. Why has Sterling fallen so much in the last 15 months?
2. Does it matter?
3. What can be done about sterling? (Bishop 2009: 26).

The point is that the value of sterling is a reliable indicator of the sustainability of the British economic stance. A loss of value of 27 per cent against a broad basket of currencies since summer 2007 can only mean that the credibility of the British administration's economic policy is judged to be very low by foreign observers. Although the government does not seem to have understood the message yet, the only solution is for the UK to finally join the EMU (Bishop 2009: 27). The issue is whether the rest of the euro-zone countries feel like taking the risk of accepting the UK in such dire economic circumstances (Bishop 2009: 27).

According to David Lea,[31] saving the pound means making it the 'Euro Pound' (Lea 2009: 126). The free fall of the pound should be considered unacceptable even by the most chauvinist of Britons. The reason why it is happening is according to him, first, the role of financial services in the UK's economic structure and then, after the banking collapse, the inevitable fiscal expansionary policy. To give stability to the British economy it is imperative to stabilize the exchange rate with the main trade partner of the UK, which is the euro-area. Consequently the British government has to admit that the five economic tests have been met and allow the country to enter the euro-zone (Lea 2009: 135).

The question is therefore only to decide whether to join the euro by a rational decision or through a crisis, believes John Palmer (Palmer 2009: 142).[32] The devaluation of the pound is unsustainable, but London still has the possibility to open the debate now before the crisis reaches its final height. The British Government can still make a calm case for joining the euro, and is still in a position to negotiate the terms for fixing the sterling rate against the euro and to shape the future policy strategies of the euro-area as a whole. But this is a political decision (Palmer 2009: 146).

Stefan Collignon[33] re-introduces to the debate the political dimension addressing the issue of how sovereignty and democracy can help in promoting the case of British membership of the euro-area (Collignon 2009: 61). His argument is based on the need to guarantee European democracy as the next step of European integration after the adoption of the single currency. Entry of the UK into the EMU would contribute to increasing the level of European democracy legitimizing the process of European integration further (Collignon 2009: 68).

Even more political is the argument put forward by Nick Crosby[34] although the relevant political dimension is, in this case, not only the European one, but also the British one (Crosby 2009: 70). As the chances for the Conservative Party to win the next elections and, consequently, for David Cameron to become the next British Prime Minister are high, the problem is how to guarantee the UK's European credentials. The Tories, indeed, have moved to a more and more radical opposition to the EU, and their seizing the power could represent a fatal blow for the process of EU integration. Under Cameron, the Conservatives would oppose Britain joining the euro, would oppose strengthening of the EU's foreign policy machine and would seek a major political confrontation over the Lisbon Treaty reforms. All this would happen in a moment of serious economic crisis. The UK cannot afford it. This is why the Labour government should enhance the UK's credibility and power in the EU by joining the euro-area as soon as possible (Crosby 2009: 77).

Politics is at the heart of Brendan Donnelly's[35] intervention in the debate (Donnelly 2009: 78). The silence of all British political parties regarding EMU in the face of the global financial crisis is yet another proof of the dysfunctionalism of the British political system where European questions are concerned. The case proposed by the then Chancellor of the Exchequer, Gordon Brown, that British distinctiveness and economic and financial superiority made it unthinkable to join the euro, has been blatantly disproved by the events ensuing from the crisis. British distinctiveness as an economic model has proved to be fraught with dangerous errors, which will bring the UK to a more severe recession than that of any of its neighbours. It is debatable whether the British financial sector will ever recover, providing the same level of jobs, income and tax revenue as before the crisis. Not to speak about the decline in the British property market, the fall of the external value of the pound and the difficulty in financing British governmental debt (Donnelly 2009: 79). In a similar situation it would have been appropriate for Mr Brown to reconsider his refusal to join the euro. The fact that this did not happen demonstrates the incapacity of the British political elite to deal with all what is 'Europe' (Donnelly 2009: 85).

Also, in the opinion of Nicolas Stevenson,[36] there is no doubt that the myth of the superiority of the UK economic performance, on the basis of which the decision not to join the EMU in 1998 was taken, should be abandoned (Stevenson 2009: 169).

In his analysis Niels Thygesen[37] demonstrates to what extent this idea that the UK could not join the euro area by virtue of a superior framework for macroeconomic policy was wrong, especially in the light of the most recent events. Besides, political considerations in the UK public debate weighing against any such participation cannot be discarded (Thygesen 2009: 198).

For Richard Basset (Basset 2009: 13) the issue of British membership of the euro-area is indeed mainly a political one. The problem is to obtain public opinion (PO) consensus on a policy which is badly needed in the light of the global financial crisis. The gravity of the crisis, the dramatic devaluation of the pound and, again, the Icelandic experience, suggest that a change of opinion of the British public is desirable (Basset 2009: 15). Moreover, it is apparent to the author that the Bank of England has misjudged the situation and is endangering

British economic future with its too low interest rate policy. And this is apparent even to the 'man in the street' (Basset 2009: 16). However, there is a major obstacle to British entry: at present a referendum held on euro membership would offer little guarantee of success for the pro-euro cause. The media are not helping the cause with Murdoch positively boycotting it. But even they could be convinced by a sufficient protracted period of economic deterioration. None of the critics of the euro membership can indeed deny that the fiscal solvency of the UK cannot any longer be taken for granted. Regrettably, the catalyst for this issue to be re-examined is a full-blown Sterling crisis; which for the author is looming. This would and will result in a destruction of British assets with its corollary of inflation. As a result the country would be desperate for stability and everyone, PO and media included, will be advocating entry into the EMU (Basset 2009: 17).

However, not all British media are currently against joining the single currency. David Seymour, a former Political Editor of the Mirror Group, is an enthusiastic supporter of UK entry to the euro. He also believes that a referendum on the subject could be won. Indeed, although only months before the referendum of 1975 on continued membership of the Common Market polls indicated that the British PO was opposed, the result was almost two to one in favour (Seymour 2009: 148).

One of the hottest topics of discussion in the wake of the global financial crisis is that of banking supervision. The need for global economic governance of the banking and financial sector has been underlined in a number of international forums and enjoys the support of leading world politicians.[38] David Green, former Head of International Policy at the FSA (Financial Services Authority) assesses to what extent it matters for the UK to be out of the euro and European supervision (Green 2009). When the euro was launched, the idea of having a pan-European banking and financial supervision seemed pretty theoretical and therefore it really didn't matter if the single market coincided with the single currency area. In fact, even in the euro-area banking and financial supervision remained in the hands of the national central banks. Moreover, when, after some discussions, a separate banking supervision committee at EU-wide level was created, the Committee of European Banking Supervisors, this was not only outside the ECB but was also physically located in London, on the model of the UK's FSA. Moreover, as London clearly became the dominant financial centre of Europe, the UK was substantially involved in the drafting of the Financial Services Action Plan, and never marginalized for not being part of the EMU (Green 2009: 99). The current crisis might put under discussion the assumption that being outside the EMU does not matter for supervision. Indeed the role of the Central Bank as the lender of last resort which has been highlighted by the current situation has also put in evidence the need for the Central Bank to exert a closer control on the banking and financial institutions. An idle clause in the Maastricht treaty gives the ECB a formal role in banking supervisory policy. Although this has not yet been activated, it is evident that euro-area central banks have a forum to co-ordinate their interventions in the banking systems from which the UK is excluded. Also many euro-area banks have been active in London and their supervisory authorities have noticed how much of the business leading to the crisis was conducted in the British capital where, however, they do not have a jurisdiction. This might propose again the need for the UK to join the euro-area to have a say on the future outlook of banking and financial supervision in Europe (Green 2009: 101).

A parallel argument is proposed by Dirk Hazell.[39] Financial services regulation failed to move with the times, provoking the current disaster. However, this gives Europe a historically unprecedented opportunity to build an exceptionally strong and effective capital market by enacting proper common regulation. If the British Government wants to keep the centrality of the City of London as the financial market of Europe, it cannot afford to remain outside this process and needs to take the decision to join the EMU (Hazell 2009: 110).

According to Will Hutton[40] it is finally 'Time to be brave' (Hutton 2009: 112). The idea that Britain is doing fine outside the euro and will continue to do so, has been put under discussion by the recent financial events. His argument is that euro membership must be considered as a strategic move allowing Britain to keep its leadership of the international financial markets and, equally, to boost its knowledge intensive manufacturing and service sectors. Britain would finally be at the heart of a major currency block, which will increasingly shape the world's international financial system. Moreover, it would support its industrial sector by adopting the euro at a favourable exchange rate and stabilizing its interest rate policy (Hutton 2009: 118).

The excessive risk taking attitude of global financial markets in general and the City of London in particular is also at the heart of Richard Laming's[41] intervention in the debate over the UK's entry into the EMU. The scale and nature of the recent crash in the financial markets should indeed lead to a rethink of the British model of economics and regulation as the one adopted so far has proved unsustainable and a failure (Laming 2009: 120). The British economic model was to remain outside the euro and its requirements of sustainable budgetary policy and prudent financial regulation. The UK preferred to become an offshore commercial paradise based on debt. Low regulation on low business costs, paralleled by high exchange rates and disposable incomes were the rule, and the increase in house prices the sign of success. As the bubble exploded the UK has only one shelter left: the euro (Laming 2009: 124).

Let's face it, adds Peter Sutherland,[42] adopting a counterfactual analysis, the UK would have less problems during the financial crisis if it had entered the EMU in 1998 (Sutherland 2009: 184). And even if the UK was better off staying outside during the first ten years of the euro, it is now time to rethink this decision (Munchau 2009: 136) according to the opinion of Wolfang Munchau.[43] Economic circumstances over the next ten years are doomed to change so profoundly that the balance between the benefits of joining and the costs will be overturned. First of all, finance will no longer be the main specialization of Britain and the country will have to find a new one. Second, the era of global free-floating exchange rates will come to an end slowly as floating exchange rates have not aided current account adjustment. In Europe, this would mean that accession to the euro-zone will continue, and all of East Europe EU, plus Denmark and Iceland will join. This would leave the UK in the unsustainable position of being an independent exchange rate country at the fringes of a stable exchange rate block. The exchange rate of the pound will be more volatile; investors would ask higher interest rates. Membership of the euro would help to reduce those risks. Concluding, the external situation will change so dramatically, that the past benefits of staying out will be wiped out. This change will ultimately be reflected by change in the public opinion (Munchau 2009: 140).

The majority of the analyses reported above insist on the changes that the global financial crisis will have not only on the British economic strategy, but, more importantly, on the structure itself of the British economy. It seems almost inevitable that the role of the financial sector will decline, although it does not emerge clearly what would take its place. Moreover, the centrality of the City of London as the 'European' financial capital or as a global financial power has been allegedly put in danger by the crisis. This has led the economists and commentators above to identify as a solution that of joining the euro-area. Indeed it is not the first time more integration of the UK into Europe has been advocated as the panacea of sudden and seemingly otherwise irresolvable problems of the British economy. This happened already, notably when the UK, having decided to enter the Exchange Rate Mechanism (ERM) of the European Monetary System (EMS) in October 1990, decided to leave it shortly thereafter in September 1992. And there have also already been, according to the scholars, moments in the development of the British capitalist structure in which it seemed as if the power of the City had been finally overcome. But somehow the City has always been able to emerge again as the dominant actor of the British socio-economic scene. Will this happen again? Maybe it is too soon to say, but having a look at the way in which British capitalism developed may give useful insights on the future of the British economy and of the British position towards the EMU.

Why the UK did not join the EMU on the first place? The theoretical debate over the development of British capitalism and the definition of the City of London

Theoretical concerns: exceptionalism in British capitalist development

'Exceptionalism' is the term mostly used by the scholars to define the development of British capitalism and, accordingly, to describe the present characteristics of its economic, political and social organization.

The British system is 'exceptional', as Ingham points out (Ingham 1984: 17), to the extent that in Britain no *bourgeois* revolution, of the kind in France, ever happened and thus British society, especially the political system and its ideological supports, retained markedly traditional and to an extent 'aristocratic' characteristics. Several writers[44] agree with this interpretation: Britain is 'exceptional' in relation to other advanced capitalist societies where the old order has perished or, in some cases, never existed. However, despite the agreement amongst the majority of the authors over the recognition of the peculiar, 'exceptional' nature of British capitalism, the hypotheses proposed to explain this phenomenon, as well as the very definition of British 'exceptionalism', differ in a variety of ways.

In the most widely accepted explanation of British 'exceptionalism', this coincides with British 'traditionalism'. In turn, the persistence of pre-industrial elements is seen to be the ideological outcome of a mutually advantageous compromise between bourgeois and aristocratic forces which, later in the nineteenth century, resulted in a complete social integration of the two classes (Stanworth and Giddens 1974: 100). In this view there is no doubt that Britain has become a truly *bourgeois* society, but it is one into which the aristocratic and traditional ideological elements have successfully established themselves (Ingham 1984: 18; Perkin 1969).

However, there is also another fairly well established, but less widely accepted, interpretation of these developments in which it is argued that traditionalism has remained the dominant ideology in modern Britain because it is rooted in structural phenomena. From this point of view, traditionalism, not only has a symbolic or legitimating significance, but it also reflects a peculiar capitalist structure which has been able to survive until now (Ingham 1984: 19).

Were it only for chronological reasons, the first contribution of this kind to be cited shall be Perry Anderson's article 'The origins of the present crisis' published in the pages of the *New Left Review* in 1964 (Anderson). For Anderson the 'exceptionalism' of British society is given on the one hand by the dual nature of British capitalism, that is, the existence of a clear dominance of the City of London over the industrial sector which is reflected on the persistence of aristocratic pre-industrial forms in the organization of the civil and political society and ideology. On the other hand, Anderson underlines the existence of a hegemonic position of the capitalist bloc as a whole as opposed to the non-hegemonic though self-conscious bloc of the working class (Anderson 1964). In turn, the explanation of the present class structure in Britain, in Anderson's analysis, is to be found in 'the cumulative constellation of the fundamental moments of modern English history' (Anderson 1964: 28).

In Anderson's conceptualization, the distinctive characteristics of the English class structure, as it has evolved from 1640, can be summarized as follows. After a premature revolution, which transformed the structure but not the superstructure of English society, the landed aristocracy, financially supported by the mercantile, 'moneyed' aristocracy, established itself as the dominant capitalist class in England. Its success was 'economically the floor and sociologically the ceiling of the rise of the industrial bourgeoisie' (Anderson 1964: 39). The industrial revolution, financed by the City of London with the money flowing from the empire, underpinned the birth of the first capitalist industrial *bourgeoisie*. This melded with the aristocracy, which kept its economically and ideologically dominant position, forming a single social bloc. Contextually, the working class developed a separate but subordinate identity, without ever being able to shake the existing economic/social and political establishment (Anderson 1964: 39).

According to Anderson, the contemporary equilibrium in England remains 'a crushingly capitalist one' (Anderson 1964: 50), but within the capitalist class itself one economic and social component is hegemonic: the City, whose origin, as better described by Ingham

(Ingham 1984: 40), dates back to the seventeenth century. Colonized by aristocrats during its long history as no other sectors has been, the City is now both 'the most sociologically revealing and the most sectionally decisive single determinant of the shape of the economy' (Ingham 1984: 40). Moreover, the City, together with its political referents, that is, the Treasury and the Bank of England, triggered British industry decline from the second half of the nineteenth century onwards (Ingham 1984: 40).

Also for Nairn (1977) the origins of British industry decline in the twentieth century have to be identified in the 'exceptional' nature of its capitalist structure, but the question he wants to answer is: 'Why has the old British state lasted so long in the face of such continuous decline and adversity?' (Nairn 1977: 5). For the author the answer is in the historical character of the British state itself (Nairn 1977: 5) and in particular in its two developmental priorities: first, it was the first state to experience the transition from a feudal organization of the state to a modern one with the Civil War of 1640–1688 which signalled the end of absolutism in the British islands; second, it was the first state form of an industrialized nation. At the same time these two priorities represent the basis for the two main paradoxes of the British development: first, what was supposed to be the first modern liberal-constitutional state never itself became modern, instead it maintained its traditional, archaic outlook; second, the first country to experience industrialization never became a genuinely industrialized society (Ingham 1984: 40).

The problem with these interpretations of the development and structure of British civil society is that they fail to identify precisely the economic nature of the success of the City of London throughout history. Moreover, they neglect the role and the interests of the merchant and commercial elites of the City and their alliance with the land-owning elite, even if they clearly identify the importance of the City in explaining industrial bourgeois weakness and the split between the two sectors is seen as a 'basic underpinning of the state structure' (Nairn 1977: 28).

The political relations between the City and industry over the past century are dealt with in much more direct manner in Longstreth's 'The City, the industry and the State' (1979). In particular Longstreth clarifies the relations between the financial sector and the state adopting an 'instrumental' approach, not in the sense that the state is depicted as a neutral instrument in the hands of a cohesive dominant class, but insofar as he sees it as a system penetrated and structured by particular class relations, which may vary from society to society and over periods of time. Moreover, the state can be, and in the case of Britain, has been, dominated by a particular fraction of the dominant class, a *ceta dirigente*, which by no means exercises power consistently in the general interest of the dominant class taken as a whole (Longstreth 1979: 159).

More specifically, as already mentioned by the other scholars discussed above, in the case of Britain, a traditional power bloc, led by the City of London, has predominated over the determination of economic policy since the beginning of the present century. Many of the political struggles over the course of this century can be interpreted as attempts either to over-turn or modify the domination of this 'establishment' in the state system. Yet, despite two world wars, numerous changes of government, the disintegration of the empire, and the institution of social democracy and Keynesian political economy as the dominant force in Parliament, this power bloc has maintained its position, intact, largely thanks to 'pragmatic adaptation' to changing circumstances in the world economy and the national class struggle (Longstreth 1979: 160).

It is not unlikely that such a 'pragmatic adaptation' will represent the key to understand the future of the City of London after the global financial crisis and, most likely, the key to understand its survival as the dominant British sectoral actor, as well as, possibly, its continued success as a global and European financial centre. But on what is this capacity to adapt based? A clearer conceptualization of the City's activities should help to answer this question.

Definition of the City of London

The most important problem concerns the theoretical definition of the City and, consequently, the specification of the precise nature of its relationships with domestic industry. For many authors interested in the subject (Aaronvitch 1961; Overbeek 1980), the City is simply the centre of British finance capital, that is, in the Marxist definition, the fusion of banking capital with large scale productive capital. A number of objections are raised by other scholars against this conceptualization of the City (Ingham 1984; Strange 1971), and an alternative definition has been proposed which puts much more emphasis on a clear identification of the City's economic activities.

At a preliminary stage, it is appropriate to distinguish between the different economic activities of commerce, banking and finance. The term 'commerce' may be taken to refer to the practice of buying and selling, or the promotion of the exchange of commodities, including money and securities. 'Banking' is defined as the acceptance of deposits and the extension of loans at a rate of interest. 'Finance', in its broader meaning, consists in the provision of money capital for other activities such as production, consumption, trade, state expenditure and so on. Whereas, clearly, many of the City's activities are 'financial' in the loosest sense that is, they make money capital available for different uses by means of the markets, they also comprise many commercial practices. Thus, the role of the City's houses as middlemen and brokers in the provision of finance overseas, and domestically for that matter, are best viewed as commercial practices, giving rise to services income. Indeed, net overseas earnings of the City's financial institutions were mainly, if not exclusively, represented until very recently by services income, as Table 7.2 clearly shows (British Invisibles 1996).

Moreover, one of the most distinctive and enduring features of the City's financial role is recognized in the almost complete absence of any direct involvement by its institutions in the means by which surplus value is created (see Figures 7.1 and 7.2). Rather, the City's organizations have acted almost exclusively as intermediaries between investors and borrowers, and have been traditionally characterized by a marked organizational separation from any form of productive enterprise. This has not simply been a matter of an overseas orientation of British 'finance capital' and thus the explanation of British exceptionalism cannot be found only in its imperialist policies. In fact, the City's profits have not been primarily in the form of interest, but rather in the form of brokerage fees or commissions, that is, commercial profit from the trading

Table 7.2   Net Overseas earnings of UK financial institutions.

£million	1984 Total	1994 Total	Services income	Investment income
Banks	3723	8443	7173	1270
Securities dealers	198	2202	1078	1124
Commodity traders, bullion dealers & export houses	499	576	576	–
Money market brokers	49	130	130	–
Baltic exchange	270	262	262	–
Lloyd's register of shipping	27	48	48	–
Finance leasing	72	40	40	–
Fund managers		450	450	–
Insurance institutions	2497	3925	940	2985

Source: British Invisibles, (1996), *Invisibles Facts and Figures*, London: BI.
For more details see British Invisibles, (1996), *The City table 1995*, London: BI.

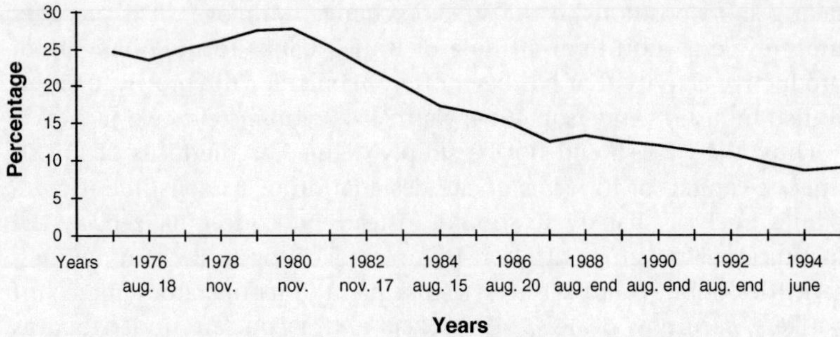

Figure 7.1   Bank lending to manufacturing industry in the UK 1975–1995 (% of bank lending to industry over total banking lending).
Source: Bank of England Quarterly Bulletins, 1975–1995.

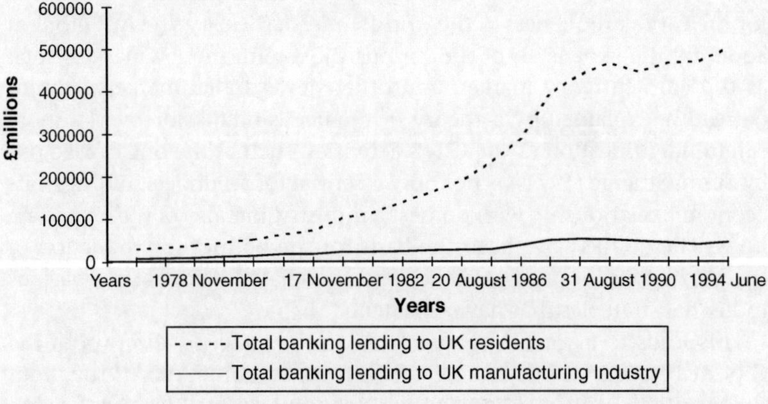

Figure 7.2   Total bank lending to manufacturing in the UK 1975–1995.
Source: Bank of England Quarterly Bulletins, 1975–1995.

in various forms of investment capital. Further, as brokers or interme-diaries in overseas stocks and bonds, as well as domestic ones, the City firms have not necessarily been interested in the successful long-term performance of the particular share issues in which they dealt. Rather, the reverse is true. One of the most frequent criticisms of the British capitalist model is exactly that of 'short-termism', that is, the essentially speculative nature of the activities of the British banking sector, partic-ularly in relation to the buying and selling of corporate shares. This has been very evident in the course of the financial crisis, to the extent that the British authorities have seen it necessary to ban, for the time being, taking short positions in the stock exchange. Moreover, it is precisely the prevalent short-term attitude of British banks to the financing of productive activity that has been often blamed for the present crisis of British industry (Anderson 1964; Nairn 1977; Rubinstein 1977).

Thus, the City should not be simply defined as the locus of British finance capital, or in terms of the designation of its constituent companies such as banks. It should instead be conceptualized as the institutional structure of short-term, or exchanges, in commodities, securities, money and services. Consequently, its operators, merchant bankers, securities dealers, bill brokers and so on, are understood as intermediaries promoting exchanges predominantly within financial and commercial systems, and in this sense they are wholesalers.

This definition allows one, on the one hand, to link the apparently unrelated activities of merchant banking, foreign exchange dealing, bill broking, securities dealing and so on, and, on the other hand, to account for the City's uniqueness in the world. Indeed, the City's revival brought about by the expansion of the various short-term money markets such as the euro-currency market, and other new parallel markets, cannot be readily explained by a theory of finance capital. Moreover, a more careful identification of the City's activities, such as the one carried out by Susan Strange (1971), is not only essential for an understanding of its economic relationship with domestic industry, but also of the City–state links. These links have been the basis for the political reproduction of the City's conditions of existence and the related defeat of the various industrial strategies that have threatened them.

This leads to a second point related to the conceptualization of the City of London, namely, the City's continued dominance throughout the twentieth century despite its own economic difficulties and the consequent growth of industrial opposition. Britain's economic power and, with it, sterling pre-eminence have declined. However, not only has the City survived, but it also prospers as much as it ever did in the late nineteenth and early twentieth centuries.

According to some authors (Ingham 1984; Longstreth 1979), the implementation or maintenance of policies supported by the City, carried out by the state agencies (not necessarily media) of the Treasury and the Bank of England, is owed to the dominance of these institutions within the state system. Their power was not instrumentally related to their penetration by a fraction of bank capital, but was based upon their political role as the real possessors and managers of the state's finances and was the product of a quite autonomous political struggle within the state during the nineteenth century. Moreover, the general coincidence of interests between the City, the Bank and the Treasury in relation to the currency and free trade has not simply been the result of the City's hegemony. During the twentieth century, the Treasury and Bank have also favoured the policies that the City has advocated because of their favourable impact on their own independent practices and institutional power (Longstreth 1979). To support this view, it is worth relying on empirical evidence, which shows how the historical evolution of the City of London, of the Bank of England and of the Treasury was clearly interconnected (Rubinstein 1977).

Thus, more than contrasting an 'instrumental' interpretation of the relation between state agencies and the economy with an 'independent' one, it could be more appropriate to speak about the socio-political dialectic relations between the City and its political referents as historically developed. Similarly, the corollary of the City's persisting hegemony, that is industrial weakness, must also be explained with reference to the specific institutional, mediation and political expression of industrial interests.

Summing up, the main element of British 'exceptionalism' is given not so much by the persistence of a traditional, pre-modern polity, as, of course is the case in Britain, but by the fact that this polity is economically, politically and socially dominated by the City and its social and political allies. Moreover, the City is characterized or, better, defined, not as the core of the 'finance capital', but as the locus of 'short-term' merchant or commercial practices, ranging from insurance to brokerage activities. These activities, while on one side limit to a great extent the expansion of British productive activities, on the other guarantee the prosperity of the City itself as separated from the performance of British economy as a whole. Finally, the explanation of British exceptionalism is not only linked to the establishment, defence and exploitation of the Empire, but is also influenced by the internal dynamics of British social and political development, and, in particular, by the interactions and dialect relations between the City, the Treasury and the Bank of England. There is no hint as yet that the global financial crisis has put under discussion the economic nature of the City of London and can therefore trigger a change in the balance of power between the financial and the industrial capitalist elite, therefore modifying also the British government position towards the EMU. This, as we will see below, has been always informed by the City's macroeconomic interests.

How did a similar configuration of the British financial elite help in previous periods of crisis? This is what will be explored in the next section.

The City's post-war economic revival

The context in which to insert British economic performance between the 1960s and the 1990s is thus that of British 'exceptionalism'. Britain is the only industrialized country hosting a centre with such a large share of the world commercial, banking and financial activities. To the extent that this centre, the City, is unique, also Britain is unique.

The consequences of this enduring economic prosperity for the development of the establishment, the state system and the economy of Britain, can scarcely be overestimated. It is true that after the Second World War the City lived a moment of crisis, as the weakness of the sterling in the world depression and the entrenchment of world economy in protective and nationalist policies undermined both its domestic and international power.[45] However, from 1945 onwards, and particularly during the 1960s, a combination of circumstances led to a return to the City's economic prosperity and political power. From the outset it must be noted that the City's basic practices remained essentially the same and the changes have by no means eliminated the financial separation of the City and industry. Further, they have been actively pursued by the intervention of British authorities, primarily, the Bank of England and the Treasury.

The City's post-war revival has been largely based upon, on the one hand, the growth of new 'parallel' markets, namely, eurocurrency parallel money markets, sterling parallel markets and eurobond parallel markets. Moreover, the revival of some old markets, such as the foreign exchange and London bullion markets, the international section of the London Stock Exchange, Insurance and Baltic Exchange, has also played an important role. The context is that of the decline of the international role of the sterling both as a reserve currency (used primarily by states as an asset in their official reserve) and as a vehicle or transactions currency (used for settlement of international commercial or financial transactions) (Strange 1971).

The definition of the City as the *entrepôt* of merchant and commercial practices more than as the locus of 'finance capital', and the one of the City as composed by a series of quite different international financial market places, help understand how it has been possible for the City to prosper in spite of, on the one hand, the decline in British industrial performances and, on the other, the decline in sterling's international role (Coakley and Harris 1983; Overbeek 1990; Strange 1971).

Therefore, by the 1970s, after a very short period of crisis connected to the change in the international role of sterling and to the development of new financial markets, the City, thanks also to its institutional nexus with the Bank of England and the Treasury, had fully succeeded in re-establishing its leading role in world financial markets and its dominant position in the domestic economic environment.

For many authors (Coakley and Harris 1983; Overbeek 1990; Strange 1971), 1967 is the year in which the City succeeded in overcoming its antagonism with the British productive sector. Moreover, the possibility of open struggle between the two sectors, decreased with the increase in the number of multinationals, always more interested in their overseas operations and, thus, less concerned than small business with the contraction in domestic industrial base. The year 1967 is also when the Labour government agreed, with the International Monetary Fund, on a target for controlling one definition of the money supply, called 'domestic credit expansion' as part of the strings attached to the loan provided by the IMF to support sterling.[46] Thus, 1967 marks the end of orthodox Keynesianism, which had considered the money supply to be unimportant for a macroeconomic policy designed to stabilize the economy near to full employment. From 1967 onwards Keynesianism gave way piece by piece to monetarism until, by the end of 1970s, the government subordinated all its policies to one macroeconomic policy alone: control of the money supply. This much is also clear from both Labour and Tory declarations on the eve of the establishment of the ERM.

In turn, monetarist policies represented the City's preferred set of macroeconomic policies, as public declarations by brokers and banks' officials in the debate over the making of the EMS clearly demonstrate. Exchange rate analysts, operating both in banks and in brokers agencies, expressed their preference for the adoption by the British Government 'of tight monetary policies specifying targets for domestic credit expansion and allowing slightly greater latitude in money supply which would reflect, in addition, any gains or losses in the reserves'.[47] These policies were considered alternative to entering the ERM early in 1979. More explicitly, brokers L. Messel told the sub-committee of the Commons Expenditure Committee that participation in the ERM would involve the abandonment of Britain's monetary sovereignty and of its own independently chosen monetary targets. This would be a step backwards, as the evolution of monetary policy had been towards responsible financial targets focused on domestic economic objectives. The position of stockbrokers Sheppards and Chase was similar. They argued in their 1978 gilt market survey that, if the aim was to stabilize successfully European currencies, the primary step required was not exchange intervention, but harmonization of monetary policy.

These arguments against British entry into the ERM differed to a very large extent from the ones put forward by the other British economic sectors, particularly the CBI and the Trade Unions (Talani 2000), and coincided almost perfectly with the forthcoming Tory government's programme which indeed totally backed the City's position towards the process of European monetary integration.

Let's see below which was the position of the City towards the establishment of the EMU.

The impact of the EMU on the City of London markets and services

The outcome of the analysis so far effected is such that the British financial community generally, and the City of London in particular, emerges as the main domestic counterpart of the government as far as foreign economic policy decisions are concerned. The British stance towards the whole process of European monetary integration has been deeply influenced by the City of London's preferences. It is therefore logical to think that the future British Government's position towards entry into the EMU is also likely to be deeply affected by the City's preferences and interests. It becomes thus necessary to analyse why the UK decided not to join the EMU, which, in turn, is related to the impact that the EMU was perceived to have on the City of London. Indeed, such an impact is also one of the five economic tests to enter that the EMU set the Labour Chancellor of the Exchequer on 27 October 1997. In this section, therefore, the impact of the EMU on each individual market of the City of London, and on the institutions acting in them, will be studied and conclusions drawn on the advantages and disadvantages for London as a leading financial centre from the establishment of a European single currency area.

Well developed money markets, both sterling and foreign currencies' ones, are a key feature of the UK financial system, making a major contribution to, and being partly the result of, London's position as a leading financial centre (Talani 2000).

A market oriented environment, notably the absence of minimum reserve requirements, is a particular strength of these markets. In the wake of the establishment of the EMU the City's position as a participant could have been very adversely affected, if onerous reserve requirements were imposed by the ECB at zero interest rates or at interest rates lower than market ones. London is a leading international, not only European, financial centre, and thus its competitive position towards

New York or Tokyo would be greatly undermined by the imposition of similar restrictions. Moreover, onerous reserve requirements could spur the developments of off-shore euro-money markets, as the EU banks minimize the amount of deposits subject to punitive charges, which, if the UK were inside the EMU area, would necessarily be set outside the City of London, and, possibly in one of its international rival financial centres: this, of course, makes a very strong case against Britain's participation in the EMU altogether. Indeed, if the UK did not participate in EMU, sterling and other London based-money markets would clearly continue in existence, while an ECB regime with reserve requirements set higher than those in the UK, which means any requirement, since in the UK there is none, could help the competitive position of sterling markets or let London become the centre for euro–euro deposit trading, as it would become a natural location for excess liquidity seeking to escape the onerous, or even not so onerous, ECB regime. Moreover, the City's position as an international money market centre, namely, its dominant position in the already established euro-currency and euro-commercial paper markets, would not undergo any threat (Talani 2000).

Moving to the London Foreign Exchange market, when the EMU was established it was already the largest in the world, with a daily turnover of $464 billion in 1995, an increase of some 60 per cent compared to three years earlier and more than the turnover of New York and Tokyo combined (British Invisibles 1996), and with a market share in steady growth of 30 per cent in 1995. The majority of its activity was linked to the US dollar and its dominant role in global trade, focusing, in particular on the dollar/pound, dollar/Deutsch mark and dollar/yen trades with the dollar/Deutsch mark business predominating in the spot market, while in the forward market trades in the three currencies pairs were of the same magnitude (see Table 7.3).

The market was a wholesale one dominated by banks, accounting for over 70 per cent of trading, and its truly international nature was made clear by the fact that non-UK owned banks were responsible for almost 80 per cent of market turnover, while sterling was involved in less than 20 per cent of all transactions (BBA 1996: 31). Given its evident global character, if the UK remained outside the EMU area, the competitive threats for London as a centre for foreign exchange trading activity were judged to be fairly low while, on the contrary, it was anticipated that the City would still remain a major location for euro-trading. The loss of revenues consequent on the disappearance of former currencies would clearly be directly proportionate to the number of currencies

Table 7.3 Relative shares of total turnover in London by currencies traded (1995).

	Spot	Forward	Total
	%		
£/US$	3.1	8.3	11.5
US$/DM	**11.8**	9.7	**21.5**
US$/Yen	5.7	**11.3**	17.0
US$/Swiss Franc	1.7	3.7	5.5
US$/ French Franc	0.9	4.5	5.5
US$/Canadian$	0.5	1.9	2.4
US$/Australian$	0.4	1.2	1.6
US$/lira	0.4	2.9	3.4
US$/Peseta	0.2	1.8	2.1
US$/Other EMS	0.8	5.1	5.9
US$/Other	1.2	2.9	4.2
£/DM	2.8	0.4	3.2
£/Other	0.4	1.0	1.3
DM/Yen	1.9	0.3	2.2
DM/other EMS	4.8	0.9	5.7
ECU denominated	1.1	3.0	4.1
Other Cross Currencies	2.3	0.8	3.1

Source: Bank of England Quarterly Bulletin, November 1995.

participating in the EMU, as well as dependent on the turnover of euro-trading. However, it would certainly be lower if sterling did not take part in the single currency area, since trading in sterling would not disappear.

On the other hand, if the UK entered the single currency area, the disappearance of trades between former national currencies in the EMU area would account for less than 20 per cent of turnover on the London market, a lower proportion than that estimated for the other European Foreign Exchange, and, again, this loss could be overcome by trading in euros (Levitt 1996a).

Overall, the London Foreign Exchange would remain neutral to the EMU whether sterling entered or whether it did not enter, the only likely implications being legal ones, namely the need for agreement on relevant market conventions and of legal preservation of contracts continuity in conversion from previous currencies to euros.

Finally, as far as the infrastructure is concerned, the fact that most of the foreign exchange trades are settled on a bilateral basis means that there will not be the same need for centralized infrastructural preparation that will be required in the money whole markets.

As far as capital markets are concerned, the transition to a single currency would have an immediate impact on the City-based government and corporate debt markets, including the euro-markets, even if the UK did not participate. Regarding the corporate bond market, if the UK participated from the outset, UK corporations would have the option, but not the obligation to issue bonds denominated in euros in the transition phase from 1 January 1999 until 1 January 2002, but after the latter date, all new issues would have to be in euro. This raised two major issues, the first one concerning the resolution of legal problems relating to continuity of contracts (BBA 1996: 14), and the other one relating to the ability, if not need, for companies to re-denominate in euros existing debt even before the start of phase 3, with all that it implied in terms of costs and of the decision over the legal framework in which to effect these operations. However, corporations could of course continue to issue debt in other non-EMU area currencies, and also via the euro-bond market, allowing for the development and establishment of a euro–euro bond market, that is, an off-shore market in bonds denominated in euros, which, were the UK inside the EMU, would obviously be outside London, thus certainly undermining London's share of primary and secondary international bonds trading. If the UK did not participate in the EMU, then UK corporations could still issue euro-denominated debt, either as foreign bonds within an EMU-area state, or as euro-bonds in the euro–euro-bond market which, with the UK outside the EMU, would certainly be located in London.

With respect to the British government's bond market, if the UK participated in the EMU from the outset, new gilt issues after 1 January 1999 would be denominated in euros, as would new central government debt issues in all EMU area states. However, as the credit risk posed by each central government issuer would still differ, pricing of all such debt would also show differences. Regardless of the EMU, primary market activity would remain national oriented, at least as long as restriction on cross-border primary dealing were not withdrawn, while secondary market activity would concentrate in London as it did already. This scenario would be unchanged even if the UK did not enter the EMU, but a potential threat would arise if EMU area states lifted the local presence requirements for the primary market for central government bonds only for each other, and not for non-participants: UK based firms would then miss an opportunity to compete for this business. Some concerns were also expressed over the ability for the City to maintain its share in non-sterling business, including that of the new euro-market. We have seen above how unfounded similar concerns were (Talani 2000).

At the time, it was felt that the impact of the EMU on the London share markets would be gradual. If the British Government decided to enter, the London market could benefit from the ending of currency restrictions on the investment of institutional investors in the EMU area, but at the same time the advent of the single currency might reduce the number of individual stock exchanges in which the investors seek listing, thus intensifying the competition with the City (Talani 2000).

In the event that the UK did not participate in the EMU, equity markets would continue in sterling. However, it was possible that issuers from within the EMU area would wish to trade in euros on the SEAQ. Overall, the City seemed confident that, if preparations were carried out in due time, and British markets had adequate access to euro-liquidity and payments mechanisms, and, generally, if the EMU countries did not adopt discriminatory measures, then the UK, even outside the EMU, could live with its competitive pressures (Talani 2000).

Regarding the derivative markets, if the UK participated in the EMU then all exchange listed contracts related to sterling interest rates, along with other EMU area interest rate contracts and the ECU contract, would cease to exist and be replaced by a euro-rate contract. As well over 90 per cent of trading volume in interest rate and bond products was at that time composed by assets in currencies which could potentially be replaced by the euro, it would be of critical importance for LIFFE to win high market share of the new markets (see Table 7.4).

If the UK did not take part in the EMU, then sterling rate and gilt contracts would continue to be traded, so that the proportion of trading

Table 7.4 Overall EMU impact activity on Turnover in Financial Futures and Options – Principal Exchanges.

Rank	Exchange	1994 Turnover (mn contracts)	% Potential EMU impact* (in percentage)
1	Chicago Mercantile Exchange	156.31	10.65
2	LIFFE	148.73	92.27
3	Chicago Board of Trade	139.48	0
4	Marche' a Terme international de France	93.1	91.65
5	Deutsche Terminborse	49.32	41.84

*Percentage of volume of trade in any potential EMU currency interest rate or bond instrument in relation to the total volume of financial contracts.
Source: BBA 1996.

volume that would be replaced by euro-denominated contracts would be around 70 per cent. As seen above, the LIFFE did not have any problems in keeping its dominant position after the establishment of the EMU despite the UK remaining outside it. Also in the OTC markets there was no scope for competitive threats in the event of the UK remaining outside the EMU (Talani 2000).

Moving to the impact of the EMU on some key City services, as far as fund management was concerned, according to the Institutional Fund Managers' Association, the direct impact of the EMU on the industry was likely to be fairly limited (BBA 1996). Although the extension to the whole EMU area of currency matching rules, requiring up to 80 per cent of assets to be denominated in the currency in which the liabilities arise, would increase the scope of asset diversification in the common currency area, thereby also increasing the opportunities for banks with fund management capabilities (Levitt 1996a), UK fund managers could benefit from the impact on currency matching rules even in the case of non-participation in the EMU.

The City of London was also extremely competitive in corporate banking thanks to its undisputed expertise and professionalism. However, competitive pressures from within the single currency area were expected to increase a lot with the entry of the UK into the EMU, since corporations would be likely to rationalize treasury operations and existing banking relationships in the EMU area. Also competitive pressures from outside might have increased as a consequence of the imposition within the EMU of a relatively onerous regime, for example reserve requirements, on the banking industry. The impact on corporate banking would clearly be less if the UK did not participate in the EMU (BBA 1996).

Finally, as UK insurers were much more involved in the US market than their European counterparts and the majority of the London market business was conducted in dollars, EMU impact on this business was judged to be fairly limited.[48]

Conclusion

In conclusion, as the Thatcher Government «wait and see» attitude towards the Exchange Rate Mechanism of the European Monetary System perfectly matched the British financial sector preferences for a set of monetarist practices inconsistent with the pegging of the exchange rates, also the British Government's «wait and see» attitude towards the Maastricht way to the EMU concealed a balance between the pros and the cons of EMU for the City of London which is still pending on the cons side.

That the preferences of the British financial community might change after the global financial crisis is, of course, a possibility that cannot be discarded *a priori*. However, it is possible to claim, on the basis of the analysis of the impact of the EMU on the City's markets and institutions, that, *rebus sic stantibus*, the City of London would still prefer the British Government to avoid committing the UK to EMU.

Indeed, as the success of the City of London has always been determined by its ability to adapt to the changing environment, its markets and institutions will certainly be able to react to the global financial crisis. However, it is precisely this capacity to change quickly to react to the changing global environment that can be put under discussion by entry of the UK into the EMU. In turn this 'pragmatic adaptation' has been recognized by the scholars interested in the development of the British capitalist elite as an almost 'ontological feature' of the British financial sector. Certainly it is one of the main elements of the definition of the City of London adopted in this chapter.

In 1998, as today, British participation in EMU would certainly undermine this capacity of the City of London by first of all imposing restrictions on the working of its markets and institutions. More generally the City would lose by being submitted to external controls, whereas, even in the new British regulatory environment, following the events of October 2008, controls for the wholesale money markets are only represented by a discretionary supervisory role of the Bank of England while capital markets after the Big Bang are self-regulated through the endogenous organizations of the Securities Investment Board (SIB) and of the SROs. Moreover, entry into the EMU will affect the City's international primacy by eliminating the possibility for London to keep its role as the main off-shore market in euro or in euro-denominated assets,[49] a role that, were the UK to join the EMU, would certainly be developed by one of its major world competitors.

Finally, it is also necessary to take into consideration the domestic economic consequences of joining a monetary union. These are usually included in the all-embracing expression of «loss of sovereignty» and, in the case of the City of London, this would mean losing the possibility to influence domestic monetary and exchange rate policies, through, for example, the linkage between the Bank of England, the Discount Houses and the commercial banks in the traditional money market, with all that it implies in terms of loss of domestic political power (Levitt 1996b).

Given all this, it should not be particularly surprising that the debate over the entry of the UK into the euro-area has not yet been officially re-opened by the British Government, and, in the opinion of the author it is unlikely to be re-opened despite the global financial crisis.

Notes

1. See *The Guardian* on-line, www.guardian.co.uk
2. Ibid.
3. Ibid.
4. Ibid.
5. Ibid.
6. Ibid.
7. Ibid.
8. Ibid.
9. Ibid.
10. Ibid.
11. See *Dispatches*, Channel 4, 25 August 2008 and 18 May 2009, http://www.channel4.com/programmes/dispatches/ as accessed on 18 May 2009. See also *The Financial Times*, October/November 2009 various issues.
12. See UK Trade and Investment Department on line: https://www.uktradeinvest.gov.uk/ukti/appmanager/ukti/sectors?_nfls=false&_nfpb=true&_pageLabel=SectorType1&navigationPageId=/financial_service, as accessed on 22 May 2009.
13. Ibid.
14. Ibid.
15. Ibid.
    AIM is the London Stock Exchange's international market for smaller growing companies. On AIM you will find a wide range of businesses ranging from young, venture capital-backed start-ups to well-established, mature organizations looking to expand. For data see http://www.londonstockexchange.com/en-gb/products/companyservices/ourmarkets/aim_new/About+AIM/ as accessed on 21 May 2009.
16. The London International Financial Futures and Options Exchange (LIFFE), a futures exchange based in London. LIFFE is now part of NYSE Euronext following its takeover by Euronext in January 2002 and Euronext's merger with New York Stock Exchange in April 2007. See http://www.euronext.com/landing/indexMarket-18812-EN.html as accessed on 19 May 2009.
17. See UK Trade and Investment Department on line: https://www.uktradeinvest.gov.uk/ukti/appmanager/ukti/sectors?_nfls=false &_nfpb=true&_ pageLabel=SectorType1&navigationPageId=/financial_ service, as accessed on 22 May 2009.
18. The five economic tests were:

    1. Are business cycles and economic structures compatible so that we and others could live comfortably with euro interest rates on a permanent basis?
    2. If problems emerge is there sufficient flexibility to deal with them?

3. Would joining EMU create better conditions for firms making long-term decisions to invest in Britain?

4. What impact would entry into EMU have on the competitive position of the UK's financial services industry, particularly the City's wholesale markets?

5. In summary, will joining EMU promote higher growth, stability and a lasting increase in jobs?

19. See *The Times*, http://www.timesonline.co.uk/tol/money/property_and_mortgages/article4004332.ece as accessed on 19 May 2009. See also *The New York Times*, http://www.nytimes.com/2009/02/01/realestate/01mort.html?ref=todayspaper as accessed on 19 May 2009.

20. See http://www.computerweekly.com/Articles/2008/12/05/233751/50000-it-jobs-could-go-in-global-bankingsector.htm as accessed on 19 May 2009.

21. See http://www.bankingtimes.co.uk/03112008-formation-of-lloyds-banking-group-puts-30000-jobs-at-risk/ as accessed on 19 May 2009.

22. See http://www.smh.com.au/news/opinion/bad-signs-as-the-cbd-empties/2008/12/09/1228584832867.html as accessed on 19 May 2009.

23. See http://news.efinancialcareers.com.au/newsandviews_item/newsItemId-17093 as accessed on 19 May 2009.

24. See http://www.reuters.com/article/domesticNews/idUSTRE50L12T20090122 as accessed on 19 May 2009.

25. Ibid.

26. See *The Financial Times*, various issues October/November 2009.

27. Michael Artis is currently the Welsh Assembly Government Visiting Research Professor in the University of Swansea. He is a Fellow of the British Academy and Research Fellow of the Centre for Economic Policy Research.

28. Iain Begg is Professor at the European Institute, LSE. See Begg, I., (2009), 'Time to Look Beyond the Five Tests?', in Bishop, G. et al. (eds), (2009), p. 20.

29. Willem H. Buiter is Professor of European Political Economy European Institute, London School of Economics and Political Science, CEPR and NBER.

30. For the past two decades, Graham Bishop has specialized in the deregulation of Europe's financial markets due to the Single Market programme and monetary union. He has been an adviser to both the House of Commons and House of Lords on EU financial issues, has been a member of several key European Commission committees and represented the European Parliament in monitoring the integration of EU capital markets.

31. David Lea – (Lord Lea of Crondall) AGS TUC 1977–1999, Vice President ETUC 1994–1999; Treasury Advisory Group on the Euro 1998–1999.

32. John Palmer is a leading writer and commentator on European Union affairs. From 1975 to 2006 he was the Brussels-based European Editor of *The Guardian*. From 1996 to 2006 he was the Founding Political Director of the European Policy Centre in Brussels. He is an experienced radio and television broadcaster. Current positions: *Member of the Advisory Council of the European Policy Centre, Brussels; *Member of the EU Advisory Board of the European Foundation for Management Development, Brussels; *Member of the Advisory Council of TASC (Think Tank for Action on Social Change), Dublin; *Member of the Advisory Board of the Federal Trust,

London; *Visiting (Practitioner) Fellow with the European Institute, the University of Sussex, UK; *Member of the Advisory Group of the Governance of Globalization Network, Globus et Locus, Milan.

33. Stefan Collignon was Professor at the London School of Economics, Harvard University and now teaches at S. Anna School of Advanced Studies, Pisa. www.stefancollignon.eu

34. Nick Crosby is an independent management consultant specialising in EU affairs, corporate strategy and political advocacy. He runs a cross party European ideas and discussion network, the Jean Monnet Circle which is dedicated to the promotion of pro-European thinking and action. Nick has a broad business foundation having worked as an investment manager, a financial services consultant for PwC and also an internet entrepreneur. Nick's European experience includes work as an adviser to the Britain in Europe in Campaign and Director of the European Movement. Nick's philosophy on European integration is to focus on the practical and human part of the project. In the words of Jean Monnet, 'Nous ne coalisons pas des Etats, nous unissons des hommes' – We are not bringing together states, we are uniting people.

35. Brendan Donnelly was a Member of the European Parliament from 1994 to 1999 and a founder of the Pro-Euro Conservative Party (1999–2004.) Before he had worked for the Foreign and Commonwealth Office, the European Parliament and the European Commission.

36. Nicolas Stevenson is Head of European Equity Strategy at Mirabaud Securities in London. He has worked in European economic and financial analysis for over 30 years. He writes in his personal capacity.

37. Emeritus Professor of Economics, University of Copenhagen, Member of the Delors Committee on EMU 1988–1989.

38. See *The Financial Times*, various issues.

39. The first European General Counsel and Compliance Director of Daiwa Securities, Dirk Hazell was an arbitrator at the SFA and ran IPMA before becoming the CEO of the Environmental Services Association in 1999. With an MA from the University of Cambridge, where he was an Exhibitioner, he is a barrister.

40. Will Hutton is executive vice chair of The Work Foundation, professorial fellow at the LSE and regular columnist for *The Observer*. He has written a number of books including *The State We're In*, *The Writing on the Wall* and *The World We're In*. Will Hutton writes in a personal capacity.

41. Richard Laming is Director of Federal Union and secretary of the European Movement.

42. Peter Sutherland is a former EU Commissioner. He writes in his personal capacity.

43. Wolfgang Münchau is associate editor and columnist of *The Financial Times*, with a special focus on European economics and politics, and global finance. Together with his wife, the economist Susanne Mundschenk, he has founded eurointelligence.com, an internet service that provides daily comment and analysis of the euro-area, targeted at investors, academics and policymakers. Wolfgang was one of the founding members of *Financial Times Deutschland*, the German language business daily, where he served as deputy editor from

1999 until 2001, and as editor-in-chief from 2001 until 2003. *FT Deutschland* is now firmly established.

44. See Anderson, Perry, (1964), 'Origins of the present crisis', in *New Left Review*, No. 23, January–February 1964, pp. 26–53; Nairn, Tom, (1977), 'The twilight of the British state', in *New Left Review*, No. 101–102, February–April 1977, pp. 3–61; Rubinstein, W.D., (1977), 'Wealth, èlites and the class structure of modern Britain', in *Past and Present*, No. 76, August 1977, pp. 99–126; Longstreth, Frank, (1979), 'The City, Industry and the State', in Crouch, Colin (1979), *State and economy in contemporary capitalism*, London: Croom Helm, pp. 157–191; Ingham, Geoffrey, (1984).

45. For a thorough account of the inter-war developments in British capitalism, see Overbeek, H., (1990), Global capitalism and national decline: the Thatcher decade in perspective, London: Unwin Hyman, Chapter 3.

46. For a thorough analysis of the credit and monetary controls introduced in the UK during the 1960s and 1970s, see Artis, M.J. and Lewis, M.K., (1981), *Monetary Controls in the United Kingdom*, Oxford: Philip Allan.

47. See City Comment, 'Euro Snake may cure rather than kill', *The Daily Telegraph*, 12 October 1978. See also Clift, B. and Tomlison, J., (2008), 'Negotiating Credibility: Britain and the International Monetary Fund, 1956–1976', in *Contemporary European History* (2008), 17: 545–566; Cambridge University Press Web site http://journals.cambridge.org/action/displayAbstract; jsessionid=ACE3D58908358E36A2923E5365CF5E10.tomcat1?fromPage= online&aid=2359744 as accessed on 1 May 2009.

48. In fact, in these cases premiums are usually kept down by reliance on high investment returns.

49. In its December 1997 report on the euro, the Bank of England clearly claims: 'The introduction of the Euro represents an opportunity for London rather than a threat. There will be a vigorous Euro-euro market in London, just as there is a vigorous Euro-DM, Euro-franc, Euro-$ and Euro-yen now.' See Bank of England (1997), Practical issues arising from the introduction of the Euro, Issue No. 6, 10 December 1997, p. 12.

References

Aaronvitch, S. (1961), *The Ruling Class*, London: Lawrence & Wishart.

Anderson, P. (1964), 'The origins of the present crisis', *The New Left Review*, 1(23), January–February 1964, 26–55.

Artis, M. (2009), 'British Membership of the Euro: Time to Think Again?', In Bishop, G. et al. (eds), *10 years of the Euro: New Perspectives for Britain*, Published by John Stevens, Sarum Colourview, London Office Web site: http://www2.lse.ac.uk/intranet/LSEServices/divisionsAndDepartments/ERD/pressAnd InformationOffice/PDF/10yearsoftheEuro.pdf as accessed on 28 January 2010.

Artis, M.J. and Lewis, M.K. (1981), *Monetary Controls in the United Kingdom*, Oxford: Philip Allan.

Bank of England (1997), Practical issues arising from the introduction of the Euro, No. 6, 10 December 1997.

Basset, R. (2009), 'Winning Hearts and Minds: The Battle for British Public Opinion', in Bishop, G. et al. (eds), *10 years of the Euro: New Perspectives for*

Britain, Published by John Stevens, Sarum Colourview, London Office Web site: http://www2.lse.ac.uk/intranet/LSEServices/divisionsAndDepartments/ ERD/pressAndInformationOffice/PDF/10yearsoftheEuro.pdf as accessed on 28 January 2010.

Begg, I. (2009), 'Time to Look Beyond the Five Tests?', in Bishop, G. et al. (eds).

Bishop, G. (2009), 'Britain's Eternal Vulnerability: Sterling', in Bishop, G. et al. (eds).

Bishop, G., Buiter, W., Donnelly, B and Hutton, W. (2009), *10 years of the Euro: New Perspectives for Britain*, Published by John Stevens, Sarum Colourview, London Office Web site: http://www2.lse.ac.uk/intranet/LSEServices/divisions AndDepartments/ERD/pressAndInformationOffice/PDF/10yearsoftheEuro.pdf as accessed on 28 January 2010.

BBA, British Banking Association, Association for Payment Clearing Services, London Investment Banking Association, (1996), Preparing for EMU: the implication of European Monetary Union for the banking and financial markets in the United Kingdom. Report of the EMU City Working Group, London: BBA, APACS, LIBA, September 1996, Background Papers, Money Markets.

British Invisibles (1996), *Invisibles Facts and Figures*, London: BI.

Buiter, W. (2009), 'The Overwhelming Economic Case for the United Kingdom Adopting the Euro', in Bishop, G. et al. (eds).

Clift, B. and Tomlison, J. (2008), 'Negotiating Credibility: Britain and the International Monetary Fund, 1956–1976', *Contemporary European History*, 17: 545–566, Cambridge University Press Web site http://journals.cambridge.org/ action/displayAbstract;jsessionid=ACE3D58908358E36A2923E5365CF5E10. tomcat1?fromPage=online&aid=2359744 as accessed on 1 May 2009.

Coakley, J. and Harris, L. (1983), *The City of Capital: London's Role as a Financial Centre*, Oxford: Basil Blackwell.

Collignon, S. (2009), 'Sovereignty, Democracy and the Euro', in Bishop, G. et al. (eds).

Crosby, N. (2009), 'The European Consequences of David Cameron', in Bishop, G. et al. (2009)

Donnelly, B. (2009), 'The Silence of the Lambs', in Bishop, G. et al. (eds).

Green, D. (2009), 'The Euro and European Supervision – Does the UK being "out" matter?', in Bishop, G. et al. (eds)

Hazell, D. (2009), 'Securing Sustainable Capital Markets', in Bishop, G. et al. (eds).

Hutton, W. (2009), 'Time to be Brave...', in Bishop, G. et al. (eds).

Ingham, G. (1984), *Capitalism Divided*, Houndmills, Basingstoke Hampshire: Macmillan Education LTD.

ILO, International Labour Organization (2009), 'Impact of the Financial Crisis on Finance Sector Workers', Issues paper for discussion at the Global Dialogue Forum on the Impact of the Financial Crisis on Finance Sector Workers, Geneva, 24–25 February 2009, International Labour Office: Geneva http://www.ilo.org/wcmsp5/groups/public/---dgreports/---dcomm/ documents/meetingdocument/wcms_103263.pdf as accessed on 18 May 2009.

Laming, R. (2009), 'Should Britain Join the Euro? A lesson from history', in Bishop, G. et al. (eds).

Lea, D. (2009), 'Let's Save the Pound – Make it the Euro-Pound', Bishop, G. et al. (eds).

Levitt, M. (1996a), European Monetary Union-The impact on banking, Royal Institute of International Affairs Conference, 13–14 March 1996, London.

Levitt, M. (1996b), 'EMU: a view from the banking sector', *Journal of European Public Policy*, 3(3), 499–514.

Longstreth, F. (1979), 'The City, Industry and the State', in Crouch, Colin, (ed.), *State and Economy in Contemporary Capitalism*, London: Croom Helm, pp. 157–191.

Munchau, W. (2009), 'The benefits of Euro area membership from a purely economic perspective', in Bishop, G. et al., (ed.).

Nairn, T. (1977), 'The twilight of the British state', New Left Review, 101–102, February–April 1977, 3–61.

Orlowski, L.T. (2008). Stages of the 2007/2008 Global Financial Crisis: Is There a Wandering Asset-Price Bubble? Economics Discussion Papers, No 2008-43. http://www.economics-ejournal.org/economics/discussionpapers/2008-43   as accessed on 18 May 2009.

Overbeek, H. (1980), 'Finance capital and the crisis in Britain', Capital and Class, 11, Summer 1980.

Overbeek, H. (1990), *Global Capitalism and National Decline: The Thatcher Decade in Perspective*, London: Unwin Hyman.

Palmer, J. (2009), 'Joining the Euro – By Rational Decision or Through Crisis?', in Bishop, G. et al.

Perkin, H. (1969), *The Origins of Modern English Society, 1780–1880*, London: Routledge and Kegan Paul.

Rubinstein, W.D. (1977), 'Wealth, èlites and the class structure of modern Britain', in Past and Present, 76, August 1977, 99–126.

Seymour, D. (2009), 'A Fight We Can Win', in Bishop, G. et al., (eds).

Stanworth, P. and Giddens, A. (1974), *Elites and Power in British Society*, Cambridge: Cambridge University Press.

Stevenson, N. (2009), 'Sterling and the Myth of UK Economic Performance', in Bishop, G. et al., (eds).

Strange, S. (1971), *Sterling and British Policy: A Political Study of an International Currency in Decline*, London: Oxford University Press.

Sutherland, P. (2009), 'Facing Reality', in Bishop, G. et al., (eds).

Talani, L.S. (2000), *Betting for and against EMU*, London: Ashgate.

Thygesen, N., (2009), 'The UK Framework for Macroeconomic Policy', in Bishop, G. et al., (eds), p. 198.

Conclusion: Towards a New Global Financial Regime?

Leila Simona Talani

Who is in charge of controlling the international banking system? Who should decide what represents an irresponsible behaviour by financial institutions? Is there anything like an international regulatory regime for the financial sector? Do we need one? Is it feasible to establish one? Similar concerns inform all the contributions to the present publication and the answer to these questions will define the future of the international financial structure. Of course, similar questions may be posed also at a national or at a regional level but, in any case, addressing these issues is precisely what is required to be able to evaluate the global crash in an appropriate way.

The need for global economic governance of the banking and financial sector has been underlined in a number of international forums and, in theory, it enjoys the support of leading world politicians. At the European level, however, it must be noted that to date there is nothing like a pan-European regulatory regime for the euro-area banking and financial systems. Indeed even after the global financial crisis, in the euro-area banking and financial supervision remains in the hands of the national central banks. There is an idle clause in the Maastricht Treaty that gives the ECB a formal role in banking supervisory policy. However, this has not yet been activated and it does not look like it will be activated soon (Talani, Chapter 7).

Indeed, Cafruny notes (Chapter 6) that the European Union does not seem to have been particularly equipped to cope with the financial crisis nor it seems to have the political will and capacity to establish an effective regulatory regime for financial services at the regional level.

The European Commission was taken completely by surprise by the global financial crisis and the subsequent recession. Moreover, the European responses to the financial crisis have been pretty scattered and erratic, and the EU authorities have not been capable of initiating coordinated responses to the crisis. The ECB did little to curb the expansion of the financial sector and to stop growing speculation in the Central and Eastern European Countries by powerful Western European banks, which as a result became heavily exposed. The Commission seemed to be more interested in liberalizing the labour and product markets and in allowing for a widespread deregulation of the financial sector, UK style. The EU member states still regulate their own banking and financial sectors and the idea of having a single EU bank regulation is a highly controversial and divisive topic. Equally, macroeconomic responses to the crisis have not been co-ordinated at the EU level. Stimulus programmes were decided at the level of the nation state, had a national scope and produced a number of controversies regarding 'financial protectionism' as relating to the support of national industry or national economic players *vis-a-vis* their European competitors. This might even have a disruptive impact on the EU single market programme. Finally, external support for Europe's periphery has been largely delegated to the IMF (Cafruny, Chapter 6).

Moreover, Plashcke (Chapter 4) successfully demonstrates that there is a limited potential of the euro as an international reserve currency. Although the international role of the euro has increased somehow in the ten years following its introduction, there are a number of limits to its further expansion. The improvement in the international role of the euro took place mainly in its first years of existence (up to 2002–2003). Subsequent developments are essentially due to the appreciation of the European currency with respect to the US dollar or are limited to the euro-zone's neighbouring countries. Furthermore, there does not seem to be sufficient scope to furthering the development of the euro as an international currency in the political, institutional and ideological framework of economic policy making in the EU. As a consequence, the idea of the euro rivalling the dollar as an international reserve currency remains largely a dream.

These institutional constraints may be removed in the future. The current global financial and economic crisis could indeed have stimulated further reflection on the role of the EU and the euro in the international monetary system and in the global economic governance.

However, although at the onset of the global crash the weaknesses of the US economy were pretty evident, this did not lead to a run on the US dollar or to a strengthening of the international role of the Euro. On the contrary, the crisis, rather than exposing the limits of global dollar dominance, has highlighted the lack both of credible alternatives to US power (monetary and other) and of the incapacity of the EU to take the lead of the global economy. The reasons why the EU is not equipped to face these challenges are identified by Plashcke (Chapter 4), among other things, in its weak institutional and political mechanisms: lack of proper coordination mechanisms for economic-policy making in a broad sense, lack of adequate mechanisms for financial regulation, a lack of a proper international strategy for the euro and a general lack of an offensive economic-policy strategy.

Furthermore, there does not seem to be much hope for the future. The Lisbon Treaty does not seem to be the answer to the institutional weaknesses of the EU with respect to global economic governance. Indeed, it does not introduce any major reform in the present political and institutional framework of economic policy making of the EU, a framework which did not allow the EU to challenge the US as an international economic point of reference before, during and after the global financial crisis (Plaschke, Chapter 4).

There is, finally, very little evidence of growing European solidarity in the face of recession. Central and Eastern European countries are in a very dire situation as they are experiencing a serious decline in their industrial production as well as the bursting of the housing bubble with all that means in terms of capital shortage. This is further aggravated by the almost complete dominance of the CEECs' banking system by Western banks, especially Austrian, German, Italian and Swedish (Cafruny, Chapter 6). Indeed, the depth of the recession in the East is a consequence of the failure of the post-1989 growth model embedded in the EU accession programme and based on the dominance of foreign finance, the integration of Eastern economies into the Western financial model, and regulatory convergence with the EU (Cafruny, Chapter 6). The risk is that the CEECs will collapse both economically and socially as a consequence of the outflows of foreign capital. At present the situation is kept under control not so much by the intervention of the EU Commission, as by the loans provided by the IMF, which says a lot about the degree of solidarity in the EU. Since November 2008 the IMF has agreed to intervene to support financially 11 countries in the region, starting with Latvia, Hungary and Ukraine. Amongst them, only Poland has received a special treatment by virtue of its positive track-record in financial stability. The other countries will have to implement pro-cyclical structural adjustment programmes that will certainly have serious repercussions on the standard of living and the employment level of their populations. All of this takes place under the wings of the IMF as if entry into the EU had never happened.

One of the explanations for the lack of regulation of the European financial markets (and for the little hope that this will change in the future) is traced by Talani (Chapter 7) in the role played both at the regional (EU level) and at the national level by the City of London.

The first issue that needs addressing with respect to this topic is the theoretical definition of the City. What do we mean by 'City of London'? How is it possible to identify its role in both the national and European arenas of policymaking? The definition proposed in this contribution puts much emphasis on a clear identification of the City's economic activities.

Starting from the distinction between different economic activities of commerce, banking and finance, Talani concludes that although, clearly, many of the City's activities are 'financial' in the loosest sense, that is, they make money capital available for different uses by means of the markets, they also comprise many commercial practices. Thus, the role of the City's houses as middlemen and brokers in the provision of finance overseas, and domestically for that matter, are best viewed as commercial practices, giving rise to services income (Talani, Chapter 7). Indeed, the City's profits have not been primarily in the form of interest, but rather in the form of brokerage fees or commissions, that is, commercial profit from the trading in various forms of investment capital. Further, as brokers or intermediaries in overseas stocks and bonds, as well as domestic ones, the City firms have not necessarily been interested in the successful long-term performance of the particular share issues in which they dealt. Rather, the reverse is true. One of the most frequent criticisms to the British capitalist model is exactly that of 'short-termism', that is, the essentially speculative nature of the activities of the British banking sector, particularly in relation to the buying and selling of corporate shares. This has been very evident in the course of the financial crisis, to the extent that the British authorities had to ban, for the time being, taking short positions in the stock exchange. Moreover, it is precisely the prevalent short-term attitude of British banks to the financing of productive activity that has been often blamed for the present crisis of British industry.

Thus, the City should not be simply defined as the locus of British finance capital, or in terms of the designation of its constituent companies such as banks. It should instead be conceptualized as the institutional structure of short-term, or exchanges, in commodities, securities, money and services. Consequently, its operators are understood as intermediaries promoting exchanges predominantly within financial and commercial systems, and in this sense they are wholesalers.

This definition allows one, on the one hand, to link the apparently unrelated activities of merchant banking, foreign exchange dealing, bill broking, securities dealing and so on, and, on the other hand, to account for the City's uniqueness in the world. A major consequence of this definition of the British financial sector is that it needs to escape regulation to be able to thrive.

Talani shows (Chapter 7) that the success of the City of London has always been determined by its ability to adapt to the changing environment. Therefore, in the lack of regulatory constraints, its markets and institutions will certainly be able to react to the global financial crisis (and they have already started to do so!). However, it is precisely this capacity to change quickly to react to the changing global environment that can be put under discussion by adopting strict financial markets and banking sector regulation, including the minimal regulatory requirements connected to entry of the UK into EMU. In turn this 'pragmatic adaptation' has been recognized by the scholars interested in the development of the British capitalist elite as an almost 'ontological feature' of the British financial sector. Certainly it is one of the main elements of the definition of the City of London adopted in this chapter.

More generally the City would lose by being submitted to external controls, whereas, even in the new British regulatory environment, following the events of October 2008, controls for the wholesale money markets are only represented by a discretionary supervisory role of the Bank of England while capital markets after the Big Bang are self-regulated through the endogenous organizations of the Securities Investment Board (SIB) and of the SROs (Self Regulatory Organizations).

Given all this, it should not be particularly surprising that the UK and the City of London have always been opposed to the introduction of regulation in the EU as far as the working of the financial and banking sectors are concerned. But is this enough to prevent regulation from being introduced at the global level after the global crash? And what kind of regulation would be needed to prevent any similar crisis to ever occur in the future?

Much of the answer to the above questions depends on where we identify the sources of the present crisis.

Fazio (Chapter 5) recalls two main views of the origins of the global crash. In the first perspective, which is the most widespread, domestic failures in industrial countries, especially the US, are to be blamed. These include: a relaxed monetary policy, regulation failure in the subprime market and the inadequacy of financial institutions and rating agencies.

Within this interpretation, Jones (Chapter 3) underlines that the causes of the financial crisis are generally traced back to a combination of three factors.

The first factor was the securitization of the sub-prime and alt-A mortgages in the United States.

The second factor was that these mortgage backed securities were easily sold thanks to inappropriate risk rating and the growing availability of over-the-counter quasi-insurance cover against default risk in the form of credit default swaps.

The third factor was a perverse system of incentives for all the operators involved in the financial sector that allowed them to downplay the risk and thereby increase the likelihood of collapse.

From an alternative point of view, the origins of the crisis have to be traced in global imbalances as related to the excess of savings in emerging markets and the lack of assets in which to invest them (Fazio, Chapter 5; Plaschke, Chapter 4). This produced asset bubbles in industrial countries, via a reduction in the long-term interest rates. The international role of the dollar allowed for global imbalances to consolidate as the US would not be able to finance the large private deficits without the accumulation of foreign reserves by foreign central banks, especially the Chinese one. In practice, stockpiling US assets by emerging central banks in particular prevented US interest rates from increasing, which would have allowed the reduction of both private debt and the public external deficits. If this were the case, both emerging and industrial countries' governments are to be blamed for the crisis and the measures that will have to be taken to avoid similar situations in the future need to account for both sides of the problem. Ironically, notes Fazio (Chapter 5), the same policy prescriptions for strengthening developing countries' resistance to crises (that is, strong currencies, strict monetary policies, surplus of trade balances) may have contributed to the development of global imbalances leading to the global crisis.

De Grauwe (Chapter 1) proposes two sets of solutions, one short term and another long term. In the short term there is no alternative to a return of Keynesian economics. Governments will have to use budget expenditure and thus incur fiscal deficits to support aggregate demand. The idea of balancing government budgets would not work. Private savings increases would indeed be prevented by the decline in national income and the only antidote to this so-called 'Keynes' savings paradox' is for governments to spend.

Moreover, public governments do have to fund the process of bank recapitalization as when agents distrust private debt they turn to government debt, deemed safer. Governments will have to accommodate for this desire.

Finally, governments and central banks will also have to support asset prices, in particular stock prices, even by intervening directly in stock markets to buy shares.

In the long term, however, the only solution is to change the global regulatory environment.

There are two possibilities to achieve this aim; the first one is termed by De Grauwe the Basle approach and the other the Glass-Steagall approach (Chapter 1).

In the Basle approach the fact that banks will go on performing both traditional and investment bank activities is not put under discussion and regulation is concerned only with governing the risks that these banks can take. According to De Grauwe this approach has completely failed both in the Basle 1 accord and in Basle 2. The reason why this approach does not work and will never do is because it assumes efficiency of financial markets. This assumption has proved totally wrong. Therefore, Basle must be abandoned.

The only workable solution is to revert to the Glass-Steagall Act approach, or put differently, to return to narrow banking in which banks are precluded from investing in equities, derivatives and complex structured products. Only financial institutions, like investment banks, which are forbidden from funding these investments by deposits (either obtained from the public of from other commercial banks) could invest in risky products.

Thus, the world would return to a system in which retail and deposit banking activities are tightly regulated and separated from investment banking activities.

Needless to say, a similar return to narrow banking would require an international cooperation to be put in place and implemented.

Would it be possible? Maybe the answer is what Collignon (Chapter 2) terms 'the moral economy of capitalism'. Maybe, to achieve an international regulatory regime that would work to contain crises, capitalism would need to be moral. But whether we believe that there is any morality in capitalism or not, maybe crises are simply embedded in the capitalist system and there is no way to avoid them.

Index